Business Network Transformation

Business Network Transformation

Strategies to Reconfigure Your Business Relationships for Competitive Advantage

Jeffrey Word

JOSSEY-BASS
A Wiley Imprint
www.josseybass.com

Published by Jossey-Bass
A Wiley Imprint
989 Market Street, San Francisco, CA 94103-1741—www.josseybass.com

Readers should be aware that Internet Web sites offered as citations and/or sources for further information may have changed or disappeared between the time this was written and when it is read.

Limit of Liability/Disclaimer of Warranty: While the publisher and author have used their best efforts in preparing this book, they make no representations or warranties with respect to the accuracy or completeness of the contents of this book and specifically disclaim any implied warranties of merchantability or fitness for a particular purpose. No warranty may be created or extended by sales representatives or written sales materials. The advice and strategies contained herein may not be suitable for your situation. You should consult with a professional where appropriate. Neither the publisher nor author shall be liable for any loss of profit or any other commercial damages, including but not limited to special, incidental, consequential, or other damages.

Jossey-Bass books and products are available through most bookstores. To contact Jossey-Bass directly call our Customer Care Department within the U.S. at 800-956-7739, outside the U.S. at 317-572-3986, or fax 317-572-4002.

Jossey-Bass also publishes its books in a variety of electronic formats. Some content that appears in print may not be available in electronic books.

Library of Congress cataloging-in-publication data has been applied for.
ISBN 978-0-470-49414-1 (cloth)

Printed in the United States of America
FIRST EDITION
HB Printing   10 9 8 7 6 5 4 3 2 1

CONTENTS

Acknowledgments

Every book begins with a story (or in this case, hundreds of stories), so to understand how this book got into your hands, I'd like to start its story from the beginning.

The genesis of this book can be traced back to hundreds of conversations that have occurred between SAP and the customers and partners in its business network over the past several years. SAP has a very unique vantage point into the strategy-making process at over 80,000 companies around the world. Even more importantly, SAP has customers in every link of the value chain, in every industry, everywhere in the world, which provides them with a rare perspective on the types of things that are happening *between* companies. This position gives SAP a unique vantage point to spot emerging trends in business dynamics and allows them to work with their customers to design process-centric software to enable these new ways of doing business.

It is from this perspective that SAP's co-CEOs, Henning Kagermann and Léo Apotheker, started to formulate a concept that could explain the proliferation of collaborative processes and the disintegration of traditional value chains that they were seeing in SAP's customer base. It was also at this time that SAP began its own BNT journey and was prescient enough to apply its experiences to the development of the core BNT theory—after all, SAP is a very large, global corporation that operates in a highly competitive marketplace. So, in the truest spirit of BNT, Henning and Léo funded a team to coordinate a group of the most brilliant minds in business to help investigate and explain these new processes and strategies that SAP was seeing in its customers.

The end goal of the BNT project was always to "give away" the knowledge that was uncovered through the course of the project in order to make it available to the widest audience possible. It wasn't until later in the project that the idea for this book emerged as the best way to convey the overall concept to a large audience. In this way, SAP could help all of its customers by advancing the level of understanding of BNT and making it easily accessible to everyone. On behalf of the contributors to this book and the companies who benefit from the knowledge produced by these efforts, I would like to sincerely thank Henning and Léo for their support and guidance in making BNT an approachable, actionable, and valuable concept for businesspeople around the world.

In a sense, the production of this book on business network transformation was a test bed for all of the best practices and learnings from our research into BNT about how to orchestrate a collaborative team of customers and partners to generate a new kind of value. This book exemplifies all of the best qualities and outcomes that can be achieved from building a collaborative network of aligned resources to achieve a goal. Therefore, there is a large and varied network of individuals who helped make this book a reality. A small team at SAP coordinated hundreds of people, from the thought leaders who did the research and wrote the chapters, to the companies who shared their stories, to the publisher who got this book into your hands. It would be difficult to thank them all individually, but I'd like to extend my deepest gratitude to the following people.

First, to the team at SAP who has worked tirelessly over the past several years to orchestrate such a unique and groundbreaking approach to advancing thought leadership for the benefit of their customers: Peter Graf, Barbara Holzapfel, Amit Sinha, Kijoon Lee, Don Bulmer, Peter Auditore, Carly Cooper, Stacy Comes, Holly Sharp, and Kevin Cox.

This work could never have been completed without the cooperation of companies who were willing to talk with us about their groundbreaking new strategies for BNT. Their stories form the fabric of BNT and are the key element in the book to making BNT "real." Again, there are too many to mention, but I would especially like to thank the following companies for their cooperation and openness with the BNT book team: Nokia, DHL, Disney, TSMC, NVIDIA, Novartis, Hugo Boss, Harley Davidson, Procter & Gamble, Coca-Cola Enterprises, Asian Paints, Tesco, Nike, Lionsgate, Colgate, Intel, RIM, Deutsche Bahn, Ogilvy & Mather, Sports Chalet, and many others.

The contributors have been phenomenal collaborators and have shown me how all of the best qualities of a researcher, teacher, and businessman manifest themselves into a "thought leader." I owe a great debt of gratitude to all the contributors individually and as a group, and it has been a great personal and professional pleasure to work with them on this project. I owe a special thanks to Geoff and Philip—you've both been wise and thoughtful palmers guiding me on this journey. I would also like to commend the contributors for their instant agreement to donate all of the royalties from this work to the United Nations World Food Programme. Hopefully, we'll feed some hungry stomachs as well as hungry minds.

I'd also like to express my gratitude to John Wiley & Sons. I've been extremely fortunate to work with great professionals in my book-writing adventures. The team from Wiley (Jossey-Bass) has shown me again that given the right set of circumstances, even a 200-year-old company can act like a startup.

Finally, no book is written purely during "work hours" and family is often the unintended "collateral damage" when deadlines are looming. This book came together at a very fast pace and involved a lot of extra hours of time away from family. So I'd like to especially thank my wife and children for their understanding and empathy during the compilation of this book.

Introduction

Jeffrey Word, Editor

Director, Center for Business Network Transformation &
Vice President of Product Strategy, SAP AG
Manchester Business School

This book is about the evolving nature of global business and the ways that a company's network of relationships (with suppliers, customers, and other partners) is being reconfigured to derive competitive advantage and increased profitability.

Business network transformation (BNT) is a true market movement and isn't something that can be ignored. As the pace of business change accelerates and businesses become increasingly connected, business networks provide the new source of competitive advantage for companies. We are now witnessing a global transformation into dynamic and orchestrated business networks in which each entity is focused on its key differentiation while collaborating with others in its network to deliver higher shared customer value, speed of innovation, and cost benefits.

As companies specialize, they become better at what they do best and focus on achieving higher returns on capital. Companies rely on partners not only to take on non-core activities so that resources can be funneled into innovative activities, but also to collaborate with them for new product development and new ways to enter attractive markets. This requires companies to build new competencies in managing collaborative relationships, with well-understood process handoffs, information access, and service-level agreements; appropriate checks and balances on product quality and brand promises made to customers; and visibility into risk and performance across the business network.

Nowadays, companies don't innovate, manufacture, market, or sell alone. We all work in concert with other players in our business network of design partners, suppliers, channel partners, outsourced vendors, co-innovators, customers—and even competitors. It isn't hard to see that companies have become more and more dependent on their partner networks over the past several years. In some industries these networks are quite apparent; in others, they are rather shady. The most obvious evidence of the influence of these globally interconnected networks can be seen by the instantaneous spread of the financial crisis in late 2008. The spider's web of credit-swaps, loan guarantees, and hedge funds unraveled at lightning speed in a globally distributed network of banks, pension funds, mortgage companies, and governments, impacting nearly every financial institution on the planet instantly.

Globalization and deregulation are empowering companies to discover innovation and talent from all corners of the world to enter emerging high-growth markets that require new partnerships. The rising power of customers is driving companies to look outside their own four walls for new ways to serve the end customer. Companies in the value chain must act as one entity to serve the end customer who is armed with more information and has more choices than ever before.

Competitive pressures are squeezing margins and commoditizing new innovations more rapidly, requiring companies to collaborate with each other for faster innovation and out-tasking to specialists in the value chain for lower cost structures. And last, advances and proliferation in IT are enabling work to be rapidly transferred between geographically separated companies in a connected world.

Advances in communication and collaboration technologies have enabled companies to leverage larger business networks more effectively. The Internet has opened up the storefront of every business to global commerce. BNT cannot be contemplated without the support of a robust IT infrastructure that enables rapid change at low costs, process-wide visibility, and secure information-sharing for all network participants.

But this global dispersion of work, enabled by technology, has a high price as well. These newer, unstructured collaboration technologies must work seamlessly with the earlier, structured IT investments in operational efficiency, such as ERP systems. The cost of integration and rapid change is quite high for a company living in the twenty-first century, but relying on a twentieth-century IT platform makes the task of transforming their business network quite difficult.

There are also several macroeconomic trends that have emerged as a result of the globalization and outsourcing movements of the past several years that require companies to manage their partner relationships more effectively. But, despite the advances in technology and trends in globalization, very few companies have truly mastered how to succeed in a networked world, not just survive.

This book is the product of the collaborative efforts of some of the most recognized thought leaders in business today to explore and analyze BNT. Over the past several years, the emerging concepts around business network transformation have been studied from various angles by the contributors to this book with a clear focus on understanding *what* is happening to traditional value chains, *how* companies are impacted by the transformation, *who* is successfully adapting and thriving in the new environment, and *where* this evolution is headed.

Through a bit of luck and circumstance, in 2008, we were able to gather a diverse group of business experts and coalesce around the overall concept of BNT. Although the different contributors may have started out with what seemed to be unrelated perspectives on emerging phenomena in the business world, it quickly became evident that they were actually looking at the same megatrend, only from slightly different angles.

We learned very early in our research that it is extremely difficult, if not impossible, to categorize BNT as one specific "thing." Rather, the concept of business network transformation is better described as an umbrella framework to help understand how the underlying themes interact and what areas of your business are affected. To help you grasp both the macro and micro concepts of BNT, we have structured the book so that we begin with the strategic "big picture" of BNT and provide some concrete examples of BNT in action, and then we dive into more function-oriented chapters to explore BNT from several different angles. Finally, we close with some horizontal concepts that focus on the critical resources and road map for a successful BNT strategy.

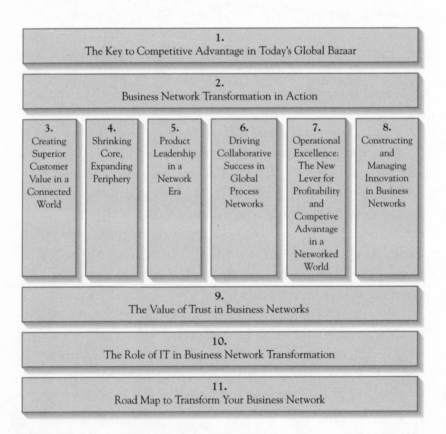

1.
The Key to Competitive Advantage in Today's Global Bazaar

2.
Business Network Transformation in Action

| **3.** Creating Superior Customer Value in a Connected World | **4.** Shrinking Core, Expanding Periphery | **5.** Product Leadership in a Network Era | **6.** Driving Collaborative Success in Global Process Networks | **7.** Operational Excellence: The New Lever for Profitability and Competitive Advantage in a Networked World | **8.** Constructing and Managing Innovation in Business Networks |

9.
The Value of Trust in Business Networks

10.
The Role of IT in Business Network Transformation

11.
Road Map to Transform Your Business Network

We hope that this book helps you understand not only how business network transformation manifests itself in your industry, but also how to gain some very pragmatic insights into using BNT as a strategic lever to improve your company's competitive advantage and profitability. It's not a question of *if* BNT is going to happen to you; the real questions are *when* it is going to change the competitive dynamics in your industry and *how powerful* the impact on your company will be. Hopefully, through the insights gained from this book, you'll be able to answer those important questions and develop a strategy to take advantage of the opportunities that BNT presents to your company.

Business Network Transformation

Chapter 1

The Key to Competitive Advantage in Today's Global Bazaar

Transforming Your Business Network

Philip Lay and Geoffrey Moore

Managing Directors, TCG Advisors

Recently, we have been conducting research into an emerging business phenomenon that we are referring to as *business network transformation* (BNT). We believe that BNT is a descriptive framework that can help executives to focus on the dynamics of business networks in their markets. At minimum, these dynamics constitute environmental forces that must be taken into account by every company, regardless of size or industry position. For more powerful companies, they also represent a source of leverage that can be used for competitive advantage. Finally, for leading companies that are willing to pursue high-risk, high-reward strategies for growth, they represent untapped sources of innovation and competitive performance that can shift the balance of power in an industry under change.

Setting the Context

Three major trends in business dynamics today are setting the context for a new focus on business network transformation.

1. The dominant thread of the BNT concept is driven by globalization. This leads immediately to commoditization, providing

better prices for consumers in developed economies, and laying the foundation for selling back into developing economies once their level of affluence rises. Commoditization, however, threatens established business models and profit margins and thus creates a Darwinian forcing-function for differentiation in order to escape from the lowering price trend of the marketplace. Differentiation, in turn, implies specialization, which involves leaving certain tasks to other companies while focusing resources on tasks which lead to differentiation. Hence the rising relevance of business networks under the relentless pressure on each participant to differentiate in a global economy.

2. Networks serve to help both on the context and the core[1] sides of the equation. On the *context* side, they enable outsourcing of work that brings no differentiation. However, much of this work is mission-critical, and the need to insure the outsourcer against quality or performance failures is paramount. Unfortunately, in the past few decades since service-level agreements (SLAs) were first implemented, they have not always kept pace with the demands of the client company's business. Sometimes this has been because the client company commissioned mission-critical services from the lowest bidder, or because they simply handed off a broken process for someone else to fix without an agreed set of expectations regarding what the process or service levels would need to look like, or because the SLAs have been insufficiently thought-out or automated. Hence the need today for SLAs based on meaningful performance criteria, and the real-time systems that can monitor, alert, and escalate failures to enable both sides of the relationship to respond as needed before things have worsened beyond repair.

3. Networks also serve to enable and amplify *core*, or differentiating, processes. Here innovation is achieved in collaboration with others in the network, putting new stresses on communication systems to cut through the cycle time of developing next-generation offerings. Networks must transform in order to enable a new level of intimacy, sharing data that previously was kept private.

We shall describe the different types of networks and the corresponding strategies for leveraging the resources of each company's business network.

Given the speed with which these distributed processes need to operate and the visibility into partners' operations that is needed, BNT cannot be successfully managed without robust IT capabilities throughout the network. On the IT side we see a companion set of new dynamics. The era of building out the great systems of record to enable global commerce is largely over. We can now do business at a global scale, but somewhat stiffly and awkwardly. The goal now is to become more nimble and adaptive.

Inter-enterprise processes are the new focus. Internal productivity is still a concern, but the real opaque zones where productivity can be sacrificed is *between* companies rather than inside them. Hence the need for a suitable response from IT with suitable platforms, composite applications, real-time operational analytics, and the like.

This is leading to a new systems design paradigm. Instead of beginning by designing the database, and then the transaction flows in and out, and then the reporting requirements, these systems begin with "reporting in real time"—the on-demand information and transaction processing requirements of the key person at the moment of truth (with a customer, in a design dialog, on a manufacturing line, about to approve or deny credit). And instead of asking that person to jump through hoops for the system, we are asking the system to jump through hoops for that person. In IT terms, this can only be done in a modern systems environment where SOA-enabled facilities can be readily reassembled to meet an increasing diversity of immediate needs. (See Chapter 10 for Andrew McAfee's discussion of IT enablement of BNT.)

Now let's take a look at the transformational impacts we are seeing. First, we'll look at how business networks are transforming us, then we'll assess how we are able to transform business networks to our advantage by playing a game we call *strategy chess*.

Business Network Dynamics

We have found that there are two types of networks corresponding with the two types of business architectures that have evolved as truly scalable: the complex systems model, whose sweet spot is large-ticket items sold to businesses and governments, and the volume operations model, whose sweet spot is goods and services sold to consumers (see Figure 1.1).

Whereas the complex systems enterprise is designed around serving the needs of the target customer, since they are the scarce ingredient in the system, the volume operations enterprise does not focus on its customers, because they are not the scarce ingredient in this system. Instead it focuses on the enablers of scalability, the levers that allow it to serve high-volume markets.

Of the two models, the complex systems approach is optimal for getting a new market or a new category of offer off the ground. Typically targeting deep-pocketed corporate and public sector customers first, it leverages a collaborative network to develop next-generation offerings that address expensive, hard-to-solve problems. As these solutions begin to standardize, the complex systems model incorporates more and more volume operations components to reduce costs, lower prices, and open up the market to

Figure 1.1 Two Types of Business Enterprises: Complex Systems vs. Volume Operations

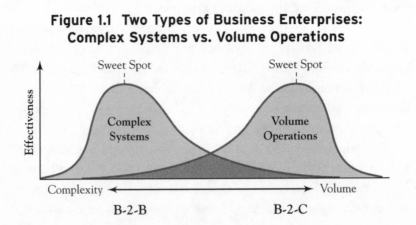

more and more customers. There is a period where the two models operate in harmony, with enough complexity still in the system to pay the complex systems price and enough repeatability to enable a volume operations player to sell in volume.

Eventually, however, the solution becomes so standardized that it commoditizes, and the market will no longer pay the complex systems overhead. Instead "good enough" becomes good enough, and the volume operations model takes over. The complex systems players can delay the transition, but at some point they must capitulate and move on to create the "next next" generation of offering, starting the cycle all over again.

The biggest challenge that collaborative networks made up of complex systems players have is actually letting go of businesses that have been workhorses for them for years, and in the process abandoning or at least reframing the relationships that enabled them. By contrast, the biggest challenge the coordinated networks made up of volume operations players have is stepping up to the next generation of "not quite ready for prime time" offerings where the demands of service and support are at their highest but the volumes are not there yet.

Strategy and the Stronger Hand

Large corporations often field businesses from both sides of this model. Consider HP, with its consumer PC and printer businesses, and its enterprise server and outsourcing offers. Consider Motorola with both network infrastructure and handsets. Or consider pharmaceutical and semiconductor companies that use complex systems for sales and marketing to win prescriptions or a design-in, but then fulfill orders through a volume operations backend that distributes pills or chips through distributors. And both models can "cheat" into the other's space. Thus high–net worth private banking and custom designed homes are complex systems businesses sold to consumers, and component manufacturing and call centers are volume operations businesses sold to businesses.

But all that said, for the most part, complex systems businesses succeed by selling million-dollar deals to thousands of corporations whereas volume operations businesses succeed by selling sub-$100 offers to tens of millions of consumers; the two are run under very different guidelines with very different best practices. Over time most corporations gravitate toward one or the other of these two models, and that in turn influences the type of business network it teams up with.

The Two Types of Business Network: Collaborative and Coordinated

Business networks evolve into two distinct models, each optimized for a different end goal, as shown in Figure 1.2.

The *collaborative network* has a peer-to-peer structure in which each member of the network has direct access to every other member. It is optimized for tackling high complexity problems through highly interactive relationships, operating essentially as a virtual project team. The making of a contemporary movie provides a good case in point, as does the management of a merger or acquisition, the development of a new drug, a new computer system, or a next-generation aircraft. Often in these networks a single company will take the lead in orchestrating the network to achieve the particular end goal in view; this role is not permanent, the company's power being circumstantial due to a privileged relationship with a customer, a key resource, or a critical body of domain expertise.

The *coordinated network* has a back-to-front structure that it inherits from an earlier instantiation of this model as a value chain[2]. The difference between the two is that a value chain is truly linear, one's "customer" being the company to the right in the chain, whereas in a coordinated network all companies focus on

Figure 1.2 Two Types of Business Networks

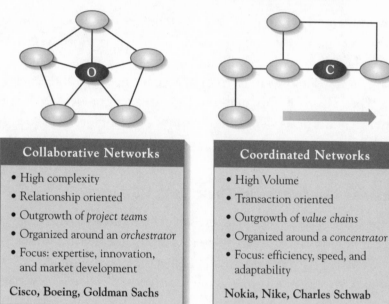

Collaborative Networks	Coordinated Networks
• High complexity	• High Volume
• Relationship oriented	• Transaction oriented
• Outgrowth of *project teams*	• Outgrowth of *value chains*
• Organized around an *orchestrator*	• Organized around a *concentrator*
• Focus: expertise, innovation, and market development	• Focus: efficiency, speed, and adaptability
Cisco, Boeing, Goldman Sachs	**Nokia, Nike, Charles Schwab**

the end customer, and the network supports multiple routes, jumps, and leaps as an offering moves from raw materials to fully delivered offer.

Coordinated networks specialize in high-volume transactional offers where economies of scale provide competitive advantage. The retail demand and supply chain provides a familiar example, as do online media sites, airlines, discount brokerages, mobile digital services, casinos and theme parks, and consumer electronics contract manufacturing. Often in these networks a single company gains sufficient power over the rest of the chain to dictate terms, whether as a key brand provider or a large retail customer owner. In these situations the rest of the network is driven to achieve increasing efficiency, speed, and adaptability, but gains an asymmetrically low share of the returns for so doing.

Networks and Your Stronger Hand

The net of all this is that complex systems enterprises feel more at home in collaborative networks while volume operations enterprises align more with coordinated networks. Conversely, they are challenged when they must interface with a network of the opposite type. This is highly material because each model needs the other to perform services that it cannot perform for itself, as Figure 1.3 illustrates.

Business Networks in Their Sweet Spots

In the past two years, we conducted over 40 interviews with C-level executives in companies in a dozen or more different industries.

Collaborative networks tend to have their biggest impact when complex systems companies come together to develop a new market and/or solve a high-value problem. Their peer-to-peer structure brings together the best thinking available, typically including participation from early adopting customers who help co-design the offer. Architecture is a critical concern because the problems are so complex each firm only solves a piece of the whole and must have a clear line of sight into how their piece integrates into the overall system. (See Chapter 5 for N. Venkatraman's discussion of architecture in product leadership.) Downstream, a well-designed stable architecture means that modules can be reused even when other parts of the system are being reengineered and can plug in provided they conform to the established interface standards. Over time, such architectures allow collaborative networks to stabilize around vertical markets where they can repurpose past work, spending more time customizing existing systems than inventing whole new custom systems from scratch. Consider, for example, the ongoing relationships among the companies that make up corporate computing, enterprise software, enterprise hardware, and systems integrators—or the investment bankers, buy-side fund managers, and sell-side fund managers that make up the capital markets.

Figure 1.3 Business Networks in Their Sweet Spots: What We Learned from 40+ Interviews

Collaborative Networks	Coordinated Networks
• Target next-generation green-field market opportunities to: • Develop new markets • Exploit high-value umbrellas • Drive standards and interfaces to: • Enable modular development in parallel with downstream systems integration • Increase reuse for productivity • Pursue market-specific solutions to: • Increase customer value, reduce market risk • Decrease complexity, reduce integration risk • Struggle to: • Accept commoditization and move on • Entrust to partners non-core processes that are mission-critical	• Target low end of mature complex systems markets to: • Enter new markets • Exploit high-price umbrellas • Drive commoditization to: • Lower base prices to drive down overall cost of offer • Grow volume operations to scale • Pursue mass customization to: • Recapture margin • Retain low-cost efficiencies • Struggle to: • Collaborate to enter new markets • Get downstream visibility in existing networks

Collaborative networks struggle to accept commoditization and move on. This is where we often see the "creative destruction" described by Joseph Schumpeter[3] in the early part of the last century, where volume operations companies take over the bulk of the market, and complex systems consolidate in a slow growth huddle at the very top of the pyramid. These networks also struggle with the challenge of outsourcing mission-critical processes that are no longer core to their competitive differentiation. This requires a level of volume operations discipline and standardization that goes against their customizing ways, and they often use their buying power to demand custom services that in the end do not serve either their or their customers' real interests.

Coordinated networks leverage the "ice-breaker" function of the complex systems model to enter new markets and exploit the high-price "umbrellas" in place. They drive commoditization to achieve price elasticity effects that expand the market and lower costs per unit. This in turn drives up the volume, which enables the model to repeat the cycle, driving more and more growth as the market moves "down the pyramid." This same commoditization, however, erodes even their own margins eventually, forcing these networks to specialize (hence the rise of the network model to replace the vertically integrated corporation) and also to mass-customize (creating segment-specific value without abandoning the mass production cost benefits).

Coordinated networks struggle mightily when they must collaborate to develop a new market. The problem here is that the *concentrator*, who has been driving the market to achieve the efficiencies and scale of the past, lacks the goodwill to get the other players in the network to work together with them. All the "win/win" models needed to reward such collaboration have been designed out of the system, the concentrator having beaten down everyone to feed its coffers. (See Chapter 9 for Jeffrey Dyer's discussion on building trust in networks.) Even getting sell-through information from a retailer can become a real challenge as partners fear that any profit opportunity will be snatched away as soon as it is revealed.

Business Network Transformation

So much for the dynamics of business networks. They are hardly new. What we should take away from the previous discussion is that there is plenty of opportunity for miscommunication between the two types of networks, as in a "men are from Mars, women are from Venus" scenario, as well as strategy mistakes that grow out of trying to apply the principles of one type of network to the operations of the other.

Now let us turn to what happens when these networks transform, either under the influence of technology change, deregulation, globalization, or, as is sometimes the case, through the strategic intervention of a single, well-placed enterprise.

When we talk about business network transformation, there are two senses in which we can use the verb *transform*. One focuses more on business network transformation as an evolution in the economic landscape, a change we did not initiate (passively) but must factor into our strategic thinking going forward. The other focuses on the strategic opportunities that may arise out of proactively transforming (actively) the business network of which we are a part. This latter is heady stuff indeed, particularly when combined with platform innovation to create a highly differentiated, highly sustainable form of competitive advantage.

For some time now business networks have been transforming in multiple sectors of the economy. Examples of collaborative networks undergoing structural change include:

- **Pharmaceuticals:** Under the impact of new science, higher drug development costs, and political backlash against the high price of drugs.

- **Financial Services:** Under the impact of disintermediating electronic exchanges, commoditizing trading margins, complex financial instruments, and globalization.

- **Software:** Under the impact of cloud computing, open source development, services-oriented architectures, and new business models.

- **Consulting Services:** Under the impact of globalization; the rise of India; low-cost, high-speed communications networks; and collaboration-enabling technologies.

- **Electronic Equipment:** Under the impact of the same forces, organizing around the rise of China.

Examples of coordinated networks undergoing transformation include:

- **Advertising:** Under the impact of digital media, Internet-enabled ad networks, personal video recorders, and the Web.
- **Consumer Electronics:** Under the impact of technology convergence, wireless networks, digital media, and disruptive changes in distribution.
- **Media and Entertainment:** Under the impact of digital content, digital rights management, mobile video, MP3 music players, and user-created content.
- **Telecommunications:** Under the impact of wireless Internet, broadband convergence, quadruple-play business models, and ad-supported services.
- **Airlines:** Under the impact of discount business models, self-service travel booking, and rising fuel costs.

When business networks in your sector are transforming, you must adjust your strategy accordingly. To do so, you must first take stock of the changes under way. A "Who-What-Where-When-Why-How" model works just fine for this (see Figure 1.4). The key is to detach yourself from your parochial interests while you are building the model so that you can see clearly both the threats and the opportunities before you.

The Example of Digital Media and Consumer Advertising

In Figure 1.5 you can get a sense of the dynamics currently impacting a number of different participants in the digital media and consumer advertising industries.

Figure 1.4 Mapping Networks in Transformation: Understanding Threats and Opportunities

Who	Map the network and the major players in it
What	Identify material changes and their impact on negotiations
Where	Locate the epicenter of the transformation
When	Gauge progress by new business process adoption
Why	Deconstruct the new economics in comparison to yours
How	Analyze the new processes and assess your capabilities

Use these inputs to drive an executive-level strategy discussion

Figure 1.5 Mapping Networks: An Example, Digital Media and Consumer Advertising

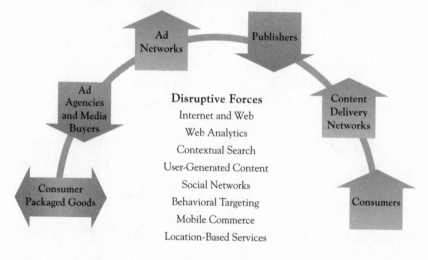

The digital media revolution is impacting not only non-digital media but also advertising in ways that are truly transformative. The Consumer Packaged Goods (CPG) companies that buy access to consumers have not changed that much, nor have the consumers themselves relative to the goods that CPG companies sell. But everything in between has changed dramatically.

This map shows the arc that takes a CPG marketing dollar and acquires a consumer impression or response from it. In the new arc, ad agencies and media buyers are being marginalized by Search Engine Marketing and Optimization, and by Ad Networks, both of which extract their power from commoditizing the media buying function. Publishers, on the other hand, are being marginalized by the sheer volume of content on the Web. Even premium titles have trouble holding their audiences in this exploding medium. This, in turn, has caused power to shift to the content delivery networks, for only they can know what content—and thus what marketing—the consumer actually viewed or engaged with. This "metadata" (i.e., data about data, in this case consumer preference data) is becoming the hottest property on the Web. Finally, consumers as a bloc have gained enormous power as all these constituencies are vying for their attention and willing to trade off something in order to gain it.

A map like this is needed by every member in this value chain so that they understand how the business network transformation under way impacts their strategic position in the industry. Standing pat with a red down arrow seems very dangerous indeed, but it is equally concerning to be blessed with a green arrow and then realize you are not doing much to leverage it.

Conclusion and Exercises for Management Teams

Seven Early Warning Signs that BNT May Be upon You

On many occasions we have been asked by executives what the warning signs are that business network transformation "is happening". To assist CEOs and their management teams in confirming whether or not their organization and/or their business network is showing signs of significant disruption, we have produced a list of Seven Early Warning Signs, as described in Figure 1.6.

Any two or three of the above symptoms can indicate that your company is in imminent danger—or that you are already being commoditized at a pace faster than you can respond.

Here are some suggestions for what executives should do in order to avoid "being transformed" on someone else's terms. We suggest that management teams consider these steps:

1. Map your network.

    If it leads you to the usual suspects, you need go no further.

    If it leads to power shifts under way, put on your running shoes.

Figure 1.6 Seven Early Warning Signs

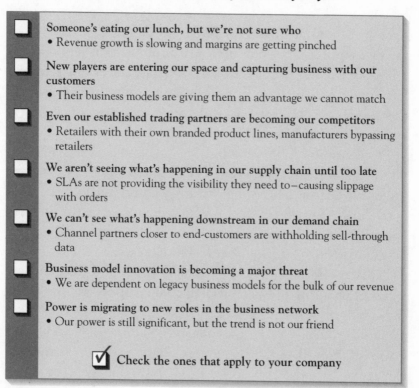

Someone's eating our lunch, but we're not sure who
• Revenue growth is slowing and margins are getting pinched

New players are entering our space and capturing business with our customers
• Their business models are giving them an advantage we cannot match

Even our established trading partners are becoming our competitors
• Retailers with their own branded product lines, manufacturers bypassing retailers

We aren't seeing what's happening in our supply chain until too late
• SLAs are not providing the visibility they need to–causing slippage with orders

We can't see what's happening downstream in our demand chain
• Channel partners closer to end-customers are withholding sell-through data

Business model innovation is becoming a major threat
• We are dependent on legacy business models for the bulk of our revenue

Power is migrating to new roles in the business network
• Our power is still significant, but the trend is not our friend

☑ Check the ones that apply to your company

2. Create your company's BNT strategy.

   Network power comes in stages.

   IT strategy should be aligned with network strategy.

3. Identify enabling IT systems for BNT.

   Standards-based systems of record are the point of entry.

   Communications and collaboration are the advanced investments.

By now, it should be obvious that business network transformation is not another passing fad, but rather a tectonic shift in the rules that business will be played by in the twenty-first century. In some industries, the shift in dynamics might be occurring so slowly it isn't noticeable yet. In others, the massive quake occurred a few years ago and the survivors are still digging out of the rubble.

Whether your company is competing in a coordinated network for volume operations, a collaborative network for complex systems, or both at the same time, BNT forces are in play all around you.

By adopting a "business network transformation" mindset and following the steps above, executive teams and boards can play "strategy chess" by gaming out the relationships in your network, the disruptive or transformational dynamics that are impacting it, and how your company's role needs to adjust going forward.

At this point, we will pause the strategic discussion of BNT to allow you to explore the various angles of BNT in the remaining chapters of the book. You will see how BNT manifests itself in the different operational areas of your company, how leading firms have successfully used BNT to leverage the capabilities of their partners, suppliers, and customers, and how IT enables BNT. In Chapter 11, we will pick up again on BNT's strategic implications as firms travel through the evolutionary journey towards a fully mature BNT strategy. Once you have seen how companies execute BNT in its various forms throughout the remaining chapters of this book, the final chapter will show you how companies evolve through a certain set of phases as they embrace BNT into more areas of their business.

Chapter 2

Business Network Transformation in Action

Marco Iansiti

David Sarnoff Professor of Business Administration,
Harvard Business School
Director, Keystone Strategy

Ross Sullivan

Director, Keystone Strategy

By now, you've probably realized that business network transformation (BNT) is happening to all sizes of companies in all types of industries and in every geography. However, what might not be so clear is *how* BNT is transforming those companies' strategies and how BNT is being used by companies to gain competitive advantage, improve profitability, and get closer to customers. In this chapter, we will try to provide several examples of BNT "in action" to illustrate the ways that companies are successfully transforming their business networks to achieve new levels of collaboration and manage intra-company business processes more efficiently.

BNT helps companies achieve competitive advantage by developing and automating business processes that extend across their network of partners, suppliers, and customers. The process of collaboration and specialization enabled by BNT drives greater return on investment by delivering increased value from fewer internal resources. Through BNT, a leading company assures that each member of its business network contributes the benefits of its unique capabilities to produce customer solutions that none of the network participants could have produced alone.

While business networks are not new, BNT is a new and different way to manage and extract value from those networks. Traditional "value chain" networks are formed incrementally, through a series of individual business relationships. BNT optimizes the business network in a holistic fashion, reaching across multiple entities, integrating diverse assets, and leveraging global capabilities to maximize the value created and captured by end customers and each network participant along the way.

At its core, BNT is therefore a fundamental change in the business processes employed by a firm. BNT is the process of combining a company's unique value-creating capabilities with those of its network to create a customer offering no single firm could have produced independently. This necessarily requires a shift in the way the firm leading the transformation manages itself and collaborates with its partners. In turn, this virtual integration relies on the support of systems for gathering, analyzing, and sharing information both internally and externally.

Connecting and coordinating the flow of information between companies in a business network is *the* critical factor to a network's success. Until recently, this has been challenging to achieve. For many complex products and services such as microprocessors or pharmaceuticals, the information required in product development and production processes is particularly costly to transfer between entities. Large vertically integrated firms have traditionally dominated these industries because the transaction costs for information transfer between smaller, more specialized entities were often prohibitive.

In recent years, we have witnessed technological breakthroughs and environmental forces that facilitate greater information exchange between organizations, removing barriers and shifting the competitive balance towards companies that fully engage their business networks. Business networks are beginning to reach real critical mass and have an important impact on a company's competitive advantage across industries, even in the most complex business environments. These breakthroughs can be seen through three primary "BNT enablers": 1) wide deployment of ERP systems, providing the foundation for cross-company deployments; 2) SOA, Web-based, and other open architectures, enabling low-cost, flexible process design across companies; 3) globalization and deregulation of markets, providing the incentive to reduce costs and optimize production and distribution.

As these BNT enablers have taken hold, a company can more readily make use of the unique and highly developed capabilities of its partners, freeing internal resources to further differentiate its own capabilities. Companies are recognizing that the benefits of partnering for some of these core assets outweigh the benefits of vertical integration and no longer strive to retain all critical skills in-house. Efficiently deploying assets and capabilities, both those controlled by the company and those throughout the network, is a win for *everyone*. Yet, gone are the days when blanket statements about "core" capabilities will suffice. Those companies that embrace BNT are carefully *designing* their operating infrastructure both internally and externally to ensure the highest competitive advantage and full utilization of their business network.

To realize the benefits BNT enables, a roadmap for identifying and exploiting relevant opportunities is required. Successful BNT implementation begins with analysis of industry trends and the design of an overarching strategy to address industry challenges through BNT principles, and is followed by the execution of this strategy through targeted activities.

BNT Implementation Principles

A viable BNT strategy leverages the advantages BNT offers to address challenges and exploit opportunities within an industry. Through extensive research of the operation and impact of business networks over the last decade, we have identified a set of five guiding principles common to successful BNT initiatives, as shown in Figure 2.1. We have found the guiding principles to apply across business network transformation initiatives, regardless of function or industry.

The following paragraphs summarize and provide examples of each of these BNT principles:

1. **Create Superior Customer Value:** Value creation is a prerequisite to BNT adoption. Organizations hoping to build business networks must therefore carefully consider the value proposition not only to their own customers, but to all prospective members of the network and their customers. BNT holds the potential to create value throughout the network by integrating the unique capabilities of participants to create products and solutions that go beyond the capabilities of any single company. This distribution of competencies allows each company to focus on honing its own unique capabilities that bring competitive advantage to the network. To be effective, the network must be structured to realize the exceptional competencies of participants to create new value at every connection point within the network. (See Chapter 3 for Mohanbir Sawhney and Ranjay Gulati's discussion on building superior customer value.)

Figure 2.1 Five Guiding Principles Common to Successful BNT Initiatives

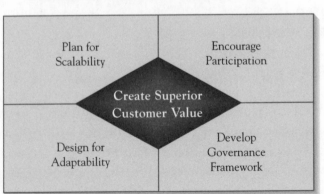

2. **Design for Adaptability:** The robust but rigid systems and processes that have been the standard for large vertically integrated companies are impediments to growth for business networks. Successful business networks are designed to anticipate and respond to changes in the environment and the network itself. The result is a network that adapts to meet new challenges more readily than a single company ever could. Systems and process semantics need to be designed with open, extensible interfaces that make their use and integration straightforward. This loosely coupled design should include clearly defined and scalable frameworks for integration and coordination between business processes and back-end IT systems. The most successful networks also develop low-cost, low-risk methods of experimenting with changes in the network and its processes. Andrew McAfee explores the technical aspects of this concept in greater detail in Chapter 10.

3. **Plan for Scalability:** To be scalable, the value created by the network must increase more rapidly than the costs of participating as the network grows. Poorly architected systems and processes have often failed to meet this test, with costs outstripping the value created by the network, leading to rapid collapse. Early in their development, business networks should invest in processes and tools that enable scalability at every level, and from a technology and business process perspective. The ability of companies to easily enter and exit the network and minimal transaction costs are two significant factors that can enhance scalability. (See Chapter 6 for John Hagel III, John Seely Brown, and Gautam Kasthurirangan's discussion on global process networks.)

4. **Encourage Participation:** Gaining critical mass in usage is often the network's greatest challenge. Business networks must achieve minimum viable scale and scope in order to survive, let alone to prosper. A company will need to design incentives and processes to encourage value-generating firms to join and to encourage the firm's employees to be active participants. To be effective, these incentives must offer clear and compelling value to each participant.

5. **Develop Governance Framework:** Effective business networks establish a governance framework. In Chapter 1, Geoffrey Moore and Philip Lay laid out the concept of "orchestrators" in "collaborative" networks. In collaborative networks, the orchestrator is ideally positioned to oversee the structuring and management of the network as it evolves, effectively establishing the "rules of the road" that all participants should observe. This added responsibility carries with it the benefit of increased control over value distribution and the potential to obtain greater competitive advantage than would be available to a follower. An effective governance framework serves to help clarify roles, coordinate incentives, and manage externalities that can affect the business network. The framework should also drive the sustainability of the network by defining expectations, setting standards, and verifying performance. For example, business networks should *secure* sensitive information flows by establishing clear processes and systems to isolate sensitive data from the participants' upstream and downstream competitors. By securing data, networks encourage information flow between network participants. Networks should also monitor and react to the health and performance of the network's participating firms to ensure the overall network remains healthy. Weakness in any domain can undermine the performance of the entire network.

Businesses that do not apply these BNT principles are less likely to effectively leverage their business networks, and risk becoming a BNT follower rather than a leader. Furthermore, the same BNT enablers that have made it much easier to rapidly form and extend business networks have also enabled rapid growth of uncompetitive business networks. An example is the rapid rise and fall of business-to-business marketplaces in the late 1990s. While these networks experienced rapid growth, their design ultimately proved uncompetitive as the network increased in scale. Ariba, for instance, saw its market capitalization decline from a high of $32B in mid-2000 to $1B a year later.

BNT Implementation Framework

Execution of BNT strategy requires a clear roadmap for creating or transitioning to a business network that will provide benefits and bolster competitive advantage for the BNT orchestrator. Tangible initiatives and projects must be launched that support the over-arching BNT strategy, while dovetailing with existing structures and operations.

In BNT, functional processes traditionally managed within an enterprise expand across multiple companies. This expansion impacts multiple functions, but all can benefit from a holistic approach to change management that bridges traditional functions to change policies and procedures that enable BNT. In this new environment, leadership must focus on driving network-wide strategic initiatives from these BNT trends and then translating those initiatives into implementation approaches and specific processes.

While the specifics of BNT execution are highly situational, there is a consistent framework underlying successful implementations. Within this framework, the BNT principles serve as goals and guideposts. This implementation framework helps to apply the principles and can guide a business's decisions at each stage of the BNT process. The framework brings together disparate functions and external partners to extend business processes beyond the enterprise. The process begins with an assessment of the BNT trends bearing most directly on the business and ends with a set of specific actions leading to business network transformation (see Figure 2.2).

Phase I: Understand Industry Trends

While industry analysis is an ongoing activity within any strategy setting process, the realization that BNT offers solutions to many of today's industry challenges presents an opportunity to create a competitive advantage for firms that systematically develop a BNT

Figure 2.2 BNT Implementation Framework

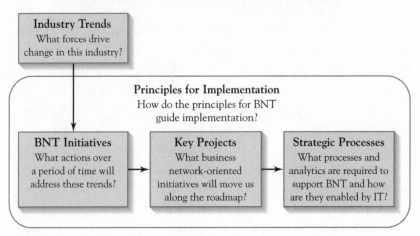

strategy. Industry-specific trends often form the impetus for BNT action. Trends that cause concern, such as increasing costs or decreasing revenues, can often be addressed through expansion and restructuring of the business network.

In the pharmaceutical industry, a marked drop in R&D productivity has forced firms to rethink their innovation processes. Successful firms have been those that have approached the problem holistically and effectively leveraged their business networks to meet the challenges of the industry. While flexible information systems have made R&D efforts that extend beyond the company possible, it is the industry trend towards decreasing profitability that has driven change.

Phase II: Develop BNT Initiatives

Once BNT is accepted as a viable means of addressing industry trends and challenges, initiatives must be crafted to set a comprehensive BNT strategy. These initiatives move the firm and its business network from their current state to that envisioned as creating greater competitive advantage for the orchestrator and the network. BNT initiatives identify those activities that, over a period of time, create this advantage throughout the network. Initiatives that fully integrate the BNT implementation principles are more likely to provide sustainable value creation throughout the network, and sustainable advantage for the orchestrator.

In response to negative R&D productivity trends, leading pharmaceuticals changed their vertically integrated strategies to open their innovation process and include outside entities. Successful pharmaceuticals companies have used the BNT principles to guide their open innovation strategy. For example, Novartis has established hundreds of R&D relationships to leverage the unique capabilities of specific academic, government, and startup entities. Novartis designed the network to enable companies to easily enter and exit the network, making it both more *scalable* and *adaptable* to industry changes. (See Chapter 7 for Randall Russell's discussion on strategic themes for BNT, analogous to BNT initiatives.)

Phase III: Identify Key Projects

While the BNT initiatives set the strategy, the key projects execute the strategy. The BNT principles serve both to guide design of the BNT initiatives and to translate those initiatives into action through targeted projects. Projects can include the creation of new processes to enable efficient interaction among network constituents, developing new capabilities for conducting the firm's core operations within the network, or recruiting and encouraging the participation of entities with unique capabilities to bring value to the network's customers.

In the Novartis example, it was important to *encourage participation* from a broad cross section of entities that had unique competencies that add value to the network but may not have the resources to effectively participate. They enticed participants by making a carefully optimized 50,000-compound library freely available to network participants. This compound set allows academic institutions to focus on their unique competencies in "therapeutic areas" and provides Novartis with a much larger, virtual, compound-screening workforce than would be available to them in-house.

Phase IV: Strategic IT Support

Investments in underlying IT infrastructure enable and reinforce the objectives set out in a firm's key projects. In fact, it is impossible to effectively coordinate today's sophisticated business networks without the mobility of information and analytics woven into the fabric of the networks business processes. Investment needs to focus on those information capabilities required to build and maintain the desired network structure.

In the Novartis compound project, the company *planned for scalability* by investing in an IT initiative to automatically translate resulting data from their partners' systems to an in-house database, enabling Novartis to rapidly extend the network of partners. (See Chapter 10 for Andrew McAfee's discussion on IT-enabled business network transformation.)

Each of the implementation framework phases is ongoing and iterative—while Phase I must initially proceed Phase II, etc., thereafter each phase must be routinely reevaluated and made current to address changes in the industry and network environments.

The design and execution of a BNT strategy can unlock competitive advantages available only to a well-designed network of firms, each of which contributes unique customer value. While the implementation process varies by company and network, there is a systematic approach that is characteristic of successful transformations. The framework covered here provides a guide to companies that have identified BNT as a solution to the challenges facing their industries. The process begins with a deeper look at the trends within the industry, and progresses to the development of initiatives, projects, and the strategic support to address industry trends by leveraging existing or created business networks.

It should be noted that while execution of a BNT strategy has some similarities with traditional supply-chain improvement, the approaches are fundamentally different. Improvements within a supply chain typically focus on improving individual relationships, almost universally with the aim of reducing costs for both parties. BNT is different: BNT is a holistic approach to addressing challenges inherent within an industry through a combination of internal and external capabilities. BNT seeks to realize this advantage by creating and structuring business networks that are mutually beneficial to all participants. BNT focuses on maximizing the utilization of the unique capabilities of each participant while reducing duplicative or inefficient effort. The essence of this approach is captured in the BNT principles, and must be borne in mind at each stage of BNT implementation.

BNT Case Studies

A vast array of companies operating in a wide range of industries have employed BNT principles to create competitive advantage for themselves and their networks. While the details of each implementation differ, the underlying BNT principles and concepts are common. Three case studies are presented here as illustrative examples of the processes by which companies transform their operations to take advantage of business networks. In each of these cases, the orchestrator followed the BNT implementation framework to create networks that embodied the principles of successful BNT implementations.

Novartis, Hugo Boss, and NVIDIA are firms that secured competitive advantage through BNT processes in their respective industries. Novartis dramatically strengthened its research pipeline by creating a collaborative network for early-stage compound screening and encouraging participation in the network through resource and value sharing with members. Hugo Boss became a leader in releasing up-to-the-minute fashions by reducing its time to market and increasing customer feedback to manage a coordinated network of suppliers and retailers. NVIDIA carved a niche for itself as the premier GPU designer by investing in unique design capabilities and creating a comprehensive business network to undertake supply-chain management, manufacturing and assembly, and distribution functions.

Novartis

The convergence of a number of critical industry trends over the past two decades has placed pharmaceutical companies under intense pressure to improve R&D productivity. The decline of blockbuster drugs, increased competition from generics, and downward pricing pressure due to regulation have all constrained industry revenues. Simultaneously, development costs have steadily increased, with a single drug requiring an average of $1B and ten years to bring to market. The imperative has therefore been to increase the number of drugs developed while concurrently decreasing the R&D costs to bring each of these products to market.

Prior to 2002, Novartis had conducted its new-drug discovery process almost exclusively through an internal network of distributed research facilities. This process resulted in under-utilization of information, as research performed at one site was not readily available to researchers at other sites. Further, Novartis was solely responsible for performing all stages of the new-drug R&D process, as partnerships were not a prominent aspect of Novartis's research strategy. In this situation, establishing a more expansive business network offered several benefits. Through specialization and collaboration, Novartis could improve the cost-efficiency of its research process by reducing duplicated effort and inviting the participation of academic researchers. Simultaneously, Novartis could increase the range of compounds explored by tapping the specialized expertise of researchers outside of the company.

In 2002, Novartis established the Novartis Institute of Bio-Medical Research (NIBR) in Cambridge, Massachusetts. The objectives of the NIBR were to integrate the scientific knowledge of the diffuse Novartis research centers—located in Basel, Switzerland; La Jolla, California; and Singapore—and to expand collaboration with external organizations. The network of internal and external groups overseen by the NIBR was structured to encourage participation by offering unique value to each member. Furthermore, participation was made straightforward through the use of open interfaces that facilitate information transfer between members and a clear governance structure that makes participation transparent and secure. The strategy was designed to *create unique value* for each party in the NIBR network.

For Novartis, the benefits of collaboration are exploration of a greater number of compounds than could be achieved internally and reduced research costs per compound. These benefits derive from the contributions of a greater number of expert researchers than Novartis commands in-house, and the inclusion of academic researchers who are not compensated financially.

These academic partners, in turn, gain access to a library of 50,000 compounds made available only to academic collaborators. This library was chosen from an internal library of 1.5 million compounds, and offered a manageable yet representative sampling of the complete compound landscape. Academic collaborators screen this compound library in search of drugs with long-term therapeutic value. Results are shared publicly on the NIH PubChem database and Web site, creating notoriety for academic researchers that publish screening results.

Novartis *encouraged participation* in the network by making collaboration straightforward through a number of streamlining initiatives. A Novartis IT system automatically translates and stores the results of partners' research on an in-house database. This interface allows for efficient information sharing within the network and minimizes the costs required to compile standardized data. Furthermore, the legal documents required to join the network were structured to be clear and quick to complete, reducing the administrative burden on collaborators.

The burden on collaborators is further reduced through a clear *governance framework* provided by NIBR to guide and structure the collective effort of the network. The collaboration process is secure and transparent, with clear NIBR terms and guidelines for partici-pation. The focus of the network is chosen by the selection of the compounds made available to collaborators. For promising projects, the Novartis Venture Fund, one of the largest corporate biotech venture funds, is accessible to NIBR to provide necessary resources.

The focus on streamlined participation and clear governance also serves to reduce transaction costs, thereby *planning for scala-bility*. The costs of participation are held at a low level for both collaborators and Novartis, thereby allowing the incremental value created by each additional collaborator to be captured by the network.

The NIBR network has produced significant results for Novar-tis since its inception. Innovation alliances have been established with almost 300 academic institutions and over 100 external com-panies. Under the program, Novartis has increased its pipeline of development from 81 projects at the end of 2001 to 150 highly regarded projects in 2007.

Hugo Boss

At the turn of the century, the fashion industry was in the midst of a secular shift in consumer purchasing behavior. Demand for high-end fashion products was becoming increasingly unpredictable, with consumer tastes changing rapidly, and the more responsive brands most successfully capitalizing on fluctuations in preferences. The majority of the industry, however, retained a push model whereby designers would create collections in isolation; those col-lections would then be released item by item as allowed for by the manufacturing and distribution systems in place. Typically, collec-tions would arrive unpredictably throughout a three-month season. This structure meant that designs were based on last year's demand data and were not supplied in a way that allowed for coordinated marketing and retail of product lines.

Recognizing these trends, in 2004 Hugo Boss launched a strate-gic initiative to transform its business to become a more flexible and responsive designer, manufacturer, and distributor. To more readily serve specific customer segments with targeted offerings, the Hugo Boss brand was divided into multiple smaller organizations tasked with managing specific brand identities ("Boss," "Boss Orange," "Boss Black," "Boss Woman," "Hugo"). Each of these smaller organizations was then transformed from the supply-driven model historically employed to a demand-driven model that allowed for rapid response to customer purchasing behavior. The initiative was executed on a brand-by-brand basis over a three-year period, allowing the improvements to be made incrementally and manageably.

The network *created unique value* for both Hugo Boss and its partners. For Hugo Boss, the benefits were increased sales and profitability. Sales were driven through offerings that more closely aligned with consumer demand, increasing both units sold and price per unit. Profitability was further enhanced through reduced inventory carrying costs and tighter control over excess inventory at the end of a season. For partners, Hugo Boss *encouraged participation* by offering information on customer demand and a closer relationship with Hugo Boss. The POS information and analysis provided by Hugo Boss to its channel partners could be used to drive marketing and purchasing decisions, improving partner profitability. For suppliers, a closer relationship with Hugo Boss would mean more steady and predictable orders from the company.

To put the initiative into action, several projects were chosen that would bring Hugo Boss closer to its customers through greater transparency throughout the channel. Improved systems for collecting and analyzing POS data allowed for rapid feedback on trends in design preference and marketing effectiveness. Simultaneously, the business network was *designed for adaptability*, with improved responsiveness to demand feedback provided through close relationships with suppliers and channel partners. These relationships were supported with rapid and open information sharing to reduce logistics costs and lead times. These benefits were distributed throughout the network, providing tangible benefits for companies partnering with Hugo Boss, and thereby encouraging further participation. Hugo Boss itself was able to bring to market more timely designs at a lower cost.

IT investment was required to enable the success of the strategic projects, and ultimately the overarching initiative. An SOA-based business process platform was used to manage information both within Hugo Boss and across the network. Hugo Boss has *planned for scalability* by creating an information infrastructure that keeps participation costs low, while offering significant benefits to partners in the form of information and analysis. This information system is designed to accommodate each sub-brand and efficiently supports future growth and acquisitions. Furthermore, the ability to operate the new system in parallel with existing systems allowed continuity of operations as each brand was transformed to the new model.

Hugo Boss manages its business network through a *governance framework* that positions the company as the coordinator of suppliers, distributors, and retailers. Information is securely transferred up and down the supply chain by Hugo Boss using its business process platform. Decisions regarding how the brands should react to changing customer preferences are made solely by Hugo Boss, and rapidly relayed to the relevant partners.

The results of Hugo Boss's BNT initiative have been dramatic. Clothing lines are now designed based on rapid demand feedback and delivered within a one-week target window. This has allowed Hugo Boss to bring to market up-to-the-minute designs, producing a competitive advantage over suppliers with longer lead times and reduced demand visibility. As a result, the gap between costs and willingness-to-pay has remained wide. Average fashion industry profits were 4 percent in 2006, while Hugo Boss achieved 14 percent for the year.

Looking to the future, Hugo Boss plans to continue to expand its BNT initiative. The creation of a Web storefront will create an additional channel for both sales and rapid consumer purchasing information. Expansion of the SOA-based business platform further back into the supply chain would allow Hugo Boss to manage its suppliers' operations as closely as it does its own.

NVIDIA

Extremely short product life cycles in the semiconductor industry necessitate nimble and responsive supply chains. Simultaneously, exceedingly investment-intensive manufacturing processes create pressure to maximize asset utilization. Together, these trends drive the industry towards specialization, with significant advantages to be had by firms that successfully carve out a niche for themselves while coordinating with partners to complete the supply chain.

To capture this advantage, NVIDIA has developed best-of-breed graphics processing unit (GPU) design capabilities while simultaneously constructing a far-reaching business network to manufacture its designs and bring its products to market. NVIDIA's chips are integrated into a wide range of third-party and OEM products. NVIDIA's business network is designed to allow the company to continue to invest solely in improving its GPU design capabilities, thereby maintaining the company's leadership position. This strategy *creates unique value* for NVIDIA's customers, as they receive products based on cutting-edge GPU designs and produced through incredibly cost-effective manufacturing processes.

NVIDIA's business network is inherently *designed for adaptability*, as the unique capabilities of the company's partners can be added and removed from the network as dictated by demand. The network includes semiconductor foundries, assembly and test companies, and channel partners. The multi-tiered distribution channel includes thousands of card manufacturers, OEMs, channel partners, and retailers.

To effectively manage its disaggregated supply chain, NVIDIA generates a real-time, comprehensive view of work-in-process and finished goods throughout the supply-chain and channel-partner networks. This information is used to determine end demand and to guide product design to meet user preferences, thereby driving sales and profitability. NVIDIA has *planned for scalability*, as extensible interfaces keep the costs of participation low for partners, thereby creating greater value throughout the network.

NVIDIA *encourages participation* by publishing demand data and analysis for use by its channel partners, thereby allowing network participants to optimize their own businesses. This information includes visibility into the purchasing behavior of end users, board manufacturers, and OEMs. Additionally, NVIDIA provides forecasts of future sales by SKU, allowing supply chain partners to plan their production cycles accordingly.

To optimize its supply chain and distribution channels, NVIDIA provides a *governance framework* that provides clear instruction to each of its partners. To carry out this task, NVIDIA has developed systems for securely collecting information at every step along its supply and distribution networks. Orders are then communicated to partners along with supporting analysis.

To govern its supply chain, the company began by negotiating shop-floor level access with all of its manufacturing partners. It then developed a front-end application to be used by each of these partners to actively monitor the flow of inventory throughout the manufacturing process. Data is collected twice daily, allowing for a product-by-product view into WIP inventory across the network.

For its distribution network NVIDIA gathers sell-in, sell-through, and sell-out data for each of its products. Due to the difficulty of this task in the fragmented semiconductor industry, NVIDIA has enlisted the help of InfoNow, a third-party channel data-management company. InfoNow collects data from channel partners, including board and distribution partners, and aggregates and scrubs the data to provide NVIDIA with a complete view of its chips in the channel. This data is uploaded three times per week, directly to NVIDIA's business platform.

NVIDIA has achieved a prominent place in the personal computer ecosystem by taking a central position in a business network that is focused on creating value for network participants and customers. Silicon fabs, assembly, and test partners all benefit from

NVIDIA's predictable consumption of their respective production capacities, while NVIDIA is able to create a steady supply of its core product without owning manufacturing assets. Channel partners provide broad distribution for NVIDIA, and in return are afforded great visibility into the demand trends of the overall market.

Conclusion

Leading firms are increasingly finding that the solutions to their business challenges lay in combining their unique best-of-breed capabilities with those of their business partners. This transformation from a company-centric model to a network-centric one is enabled largely by technology that reduces barriers to information transfer between firms. This same technology, however, also makes the rapid creation and growth of uncompetitive networks possible. It has therefore been our intent to outline the requisite principles and implementation framework that guide competitive networks and are absent in uncompetitive ones.

The vision and drive for improvement must come from within an individual company and are highly specific to the firm's business environment. Our research has shown, however, that there are commonalities across successful BNT initiatives. The five principles of BNT implementation have been observed to be embodied within successful BNT strategies. While all five principles are required to exploit the advantages BNT offers, specific principles may be of greater relevance in addressing the specific challenges facing a firm and may therefore form the core of a particular BNT strategy.

The overarching principle that must permeate every facet of any BNT initiative is that the business network must create value for customers. In turn, this requires that each firm within the network create unique value, collectively leading to an offering no single firm could have matched. To provide sustainable competitive advantage in the face of ever-changing industry trends, business networks must also be designed for adaptability. Rigid, built-to-last systems cannot rise to new challenges and opportunistically exploit ever-changing market conditions in the way that flexible networks can. Beyond adaptability, scalability is also critical to sustained advantage. As the network grows, costs of participation must not increase more rapidly than value is created.

Once designed, a network must be populated by firms that offer unique value-creating capabilities. Encouraging participation of these firms requires structuring the network and offering incentives such that firms see clear and compelling value in participation. Finally, the network must be governed to ensure the health and security of its participants and to retain the advantages sought by the leading company.

These principles provide the structure for BNT strategy, while execution requires thoughtful development and implementation of this strategy. Here, our research shows that BNT leaders that approach the process in a systematic and holistic manner are the most likely to succeed. The implementation framework presented consolidates our findings into four phases of BNT strategy design and execution:

1. The first step towards BNT implementation is to analyze industry trends with the aim of discerning challenges and opportunities addressable through BNT.

2. The second step is to create a BNT strategy supported by initiatives that identify those activities that, over a period of time, will create competitive advantage for the leading company through the network.

3. The third step is to identify projects that support these initiatives and tangibly transform the network from its current state to that envisioned by the BNT leader.

4. The fourth step is to develop the underlying IT infrastructure and capabilities required to support the chosen projects and to facilitate the information gathering and dissemination that forms the core of successful business networks.

BNT provides a fundamentally new model for coordinating a company's operations by looking beyond internal capabilities to determine the combination of firms and institutions that will create the greatest value for customers. Across virtually all industries, a range of firms have employed BNT principles to address trends and challenges facing their industries. Leading companies can capture a greater share of this value than followers and are better positioned to ensure continued competitive advantage through management of the network. Firms that carefully design their networks as solutions to industry challenges are most likely to become leaders of competitive networks.

Chapter 3

Creating Superior Customer Value in a Connected World

Mohanbir Sawhney

McCormick Tribune Professor of Technology
Kellogg School of Management
Northwestern University

Ranjay Gulati

Jaime and Josefina Chua Tiampo
Professor of Business Administration
Harvard Business School
Harvard University

In the early twenty-first century customers are more demanding than ever, and difficult economic times make them all the more so. As customers tighten their wallets and increase their demands, firms face greater pressure to provide superior customer value. Reducing costs, improving efficiency, and even creating more compelling goods may not be enough to satisfy customers anymore, not if what the customers ultimately want is to design the firm's offerings themselves. What is a firm to do when customers will not be satisfied easily? The answer is, in a word, collaboration—with suppliers, partners, and customers in creating and delivering value—on a scale not seen before in the annals of business. Nearly every aspect of business—from product design to the idea of value itself—stands to be transformed by twenty-first-century collaboration, made possible by twenty-first-century information technologies.

Collaboration requires connectivity—you must connect in order to collaborate. We believe that advances in connectivity are fueling a revolution in collaboration, and enhanced collaboration is opening up new opportunities to create superior customer value. In a connected world, the processes by which value is created, delivered, shared, and communicated are being transformed. We are witnessing the emergence of *collaborative value exchanges*, where customers become active participants in designing, delivering, and communicating value (Sawhney and Kotler, 1999). We are seeing the evolution of *collaborative business processes*, where firms work closely with partners and suppliers to design, make, and sell their offerings (Gulati and Kletter, 2005). And we are seeing the rise of *collaborative business networks*, where traditional value chains are being dismantled and reassembled as business networks where firms leverage the capabilities and resources of a network of partners to reduce costs and to create innovative value propositions (Gulati, 2007). The emergence of collaborative value exchanges, collaborative business processes, and collaborative business networks is a defining theme in the evolution of business enterprises in the new century. Enterprises of the future will need to collaborate in all three ways in order to compete and win customers.

We begin this chapter by highlighting the new possibilities that digital networks create for firms as they seek to collaborate with customers. Next, we focus on the role that digital media play in transforming the way customers and firms collaborate to create value. We show how these collaborative value exchanges can also extend to the firm's partners. By taking the collaboration concept to the ecosystem level, we suggest that firms can greatly enhance their business processes and value propositions by creating collaborative business networks. We then highlight the important role of enterprise technologies as enablers of collaborative business processes and collaborative business networks. We conclude by identifying key strategy implications for firms as they seek to evolve their offerings, business processes, and ecosystems in a connected world.

Digital Networks and Customer Collaboration

Digital networks offer several new capabilities that allow customers to engage actively in the firm's value creation activities. Networks make it easier and cheaper to engage large numbers of customers in an interactive dialog (Sawhney and Prandelli, 2000; Nambisan, 2002). Networks also allow firms to tap into the social dimension of customer knowledge by listening in to spontaneous conversations among customers in virtual communities. And networks improve the firm's "peripheral vision" by using independent third parties to access customer knowledge that lies beyond their immediate grasp. Let's consider each of these capabilities individually:

- **Reach—Allowing firms to reach beyond current customers, markets, and geography**. The Internet is a global medium with unprecedented reach. It provides people, regardless of their location or time zone, with a vast amount of information, thereby lowering the search costs for finding exactly what or whom they want. In this way, the Internet facilitates extended connectivity that is crucial for tapping into distributed customer expertise.

- **Scalability—Extending reach without compromising richness**. Virtual environments break the age-old trade-off between richness and reach (Evans and Wurster, 1999). Firms can not only engage with more customers in collaboration, but they can do so without compromising the richness of the collaboration. In the physical world, communicating rich information requires physical proximity and expensive face-to-face interactions. However, in virtual environments, firms can have rich interactions with a large numbers of customers on an ongoing basis.

- **Persistence—Persistent ongoing engagement instead of episodic interactions**. Advances in information and communications technologies have made industries more global and have blurred the boundaries between industries (Prahalad and Ramaswamy, 2004). The joint effect of geographical and industry convergence is that firms are much less likely to find all the competencies needed to support innovation within their four walls and hence interact more frequently. Digital networks can be used to coordinate activities and information sharing between otherwise disconnected pools of knowledge and competencies on a systematic and global basis, at a lower cost than in traditional, offline environments.

- **Speed—Reduced latency in the "sense-and-respond" cycle.** Real-time interfaces allow companies and customers to effectively deal with important information that changes suddenly and unpredictably (Andal-Ancion, Cartwright, and Yip, 2003). The Internet has a powerful effect in increasing the flexibility of the firm's external network, allowing the firm to involve different partners at different times, and also allowing it to transform weak relations into strong relations and vice versa, depending on the complexity of the knowledge that needs to be transferred. Real-time, two-way, and low-cost communication makes it easy to consolidate specific customer relationships on a contingent basis through ad-hoc virtual communities and online.

- **Peer-to-Peer—Allowing access to customer-generated social knowledge.** The Internet also vastly augments the firm's capacity to tap into the social dimension of customer knowledge by enabling the creation of virtual communities to collect and analyze knowledge that develops through spontaneous conversations among customers. Customers self-select themselves on the basis of the focused interests promoted by specific customer communities. This self-selection means that customers are highly involved and motivated to share knowledge with other customers and community managers, making their contribution both richer and less expensive than in the offline world (Reichheld and Shefter, 2000).

- **Indirect Ties—Allowing access to the partners' partner knowledge.** While direct ties play a key role in determining the network access, indirect ties are also useful because firms learn not only from the knowledge of their partners but also from the knowledge of their partners' partners (Gulati, 1995; Gulati and Gargiulo, 1999). The Internet also serves as an important tool for generating indirect ties. It is a low-cost open platform; anyone anywhere can connect to it and contribute to the public discussion. Therefore, it is easy to access the knowledge of partners once removed from direct partners (Afuah, 2003), as well as the knowledge of customers' customers. The Internet positively impacts on the number of indirect ties that firms can develop because it allows them to access electronic archives and virtual communities of partners' partners, absorb this already codified and digitized knowledge, and recombine it in new ways.

These customer-centric capabilities of digital networks are transforming the nature of interactions between customers and firms, and this in turn is creating a profound shift in the way that customer value is created.

Transformation of Customer Interactions and Implications for Value Exchange

The ultimate purpose of commerce is to exchange value in interactions between two or more parties. A value exchange occurs when a marketer offers something of value to a customer in return for the customer's money and effort. In fact, marketing scholars have long viewed marketing as an exchange of value (Bagozzi, 1975). While the concept of a value exchange is enduring, the nature of these exchanges is being transformed because the interactions that firms can have with customers in digital environments are fundamentally different in three important ways.

First, digital interactions are inherently *interactive*. Interactivity permits personalization of value exchanges because marketers can iteratively learn about customer preferences and behaviors, and they can use this learning to customize offers and messages. For instance, the online DVD rental company Netflix uses a collaborative filtering algorithm called Cinematch to learn about the movie preferences of its customers, and then uses this learning to make personalized movie recommendations that customers would like. The more interactions that Netflix has with its customers, the more precise the personal recommendations become. Personalization of media and value exchanges is evident in personalized Internet services (e.g., MyYahoo), personalized e-commerce (e.g., Amazon.com's personalized store), personalized ownership web sites (e.g., "My Account" on the BMW USA web site), and personalized media (e.g., In2TV, a personalized TV service on the Internet offered by AOL and Time Warner).

Second, digital interactions are increasingly becoming *social*. Customers are themselves becoming creators of media, and customer-generated media (CGM) is playing an increasingly vital role in customer decision-making (Blackshaw, 2008). Through blogs, reviews, and discussion forums, customers share expertise and get product feedback and information from each other. And this user-generated content is invaluable in the customer decision making process as it is considered to be unbiased and credible. In fact, social media are getting embedded into commerce to create "social commerce"—where customers connect to one another in ways that drive commerce transactions. For instance, BazaarVoice.com provides online commerce vendors with services that enable customers to rate and review products, ask and answer questions, and share personal experiences. Adding user-generated content helps increase customer confidence and builds brand loyalty. Social media are becoming an integral component of the marketing communication mix, as companies harness the creativity of their customers and customer communities to create better offerings and more relevant marketing communications.

Third, digital interactions are becoming *rich*, with the availability of video and multimedia on desktops as well as on mobile devices. Audio and video capabilities allow marketers to tell their brand stories with a level of engagement and depth that was impossible to achieve with text-based online advertising or even with television advertising. Consider how Motorola's Government and Public Safety Solutions unit is using rich media to engage customers. Motorola created a campaign called "Technology That's Second Nature,"[1] aimed at showcasing Motorola's complex technology solutions for emergency responders like firefighters and police officers. The campaign features a fictional city called Cityscape. Within this city, users can interact with several video vignettes that showcase Motorola's communication products in action. For instance, in the evacuation scenario, users are taken to an area of the city where a stadium has to be evacuated because of a power outage. The scene features a police commander using a Motorola digital radio and ruggedized notebook computer to act on evacuation plans; an emergency medical technician using a Motorola handheld computer to communicate with the hospital; and power company personnel using Motorola's customer service request system to manage traffic and work-flow requests. The immersive environment creates a very high level of customer engagement and involvement.

These shifts in the nature of interactions have profound consequences for how value gets created in exchanges. Customers are becoming *empowered* as they have full access to information in value exchanges. It is no longer possible to profit from customer ignorance. And it is imperative for marketers to do what they say and say what they do, as their marketing claims can be verified very quickly by skeptical customers. Customers are also becoming *engaged* in the co-creation of value (Seybold, 2006). In the words of A. G. Lafley, the CEO of P&G, customers no longer want to "lean back" and passively receive marketing offerings and messages. Instead, they want to "lean forward" and become active participants in value exchanges.

Collaborative Value Exchanges with Customers

As customers become active participants in value exchanges, it changes the very concept of a market and how value gets created in the marketplace. The market is no longer viewed as a place where value is *transferred* from marketers to customers—instead, it is a forum where value is *co-created* with customers (Prahalad and Ramaswamy, 2004; Sawhney, 2002). Value exchanges are evolving from a "Command and Control" mindset that has characterized marketing in the mass-market era to a "Connect and Collaborate" mindset that is more in tune with the times. We are moving towards the age of *collaborative value exchange* (CVE)—an approach to value creation that leverages the expertise, creativity, and efforts of customers in defining, delivering, and sharing value. The CVE recognizes the fact that customers have tremendous expertise, experience, and insight that can be harnessed to create superior customer value. The CVE spans inbound development of offerings as well as outbound marketing communication (see Figure 3.1) in six steps.

CVE begins with *collaborative ideation*—inviting customers to contribute their ideas and suggestions for creating new products or for improving existing products and services. One such example is Dell's IdeaStorm initiative, where customers are asked for their suggestions to improve Dell's products and customer experience. IdeaStorm, launched in February 2007, is an online community where customers can post their ideas on Dell products, technologies, services, and operations. The community votes on the best ideas and community members discuss ideas with each other. Dell commits to acting upon the ideas, and it posts a weekly update on the site to keep the community informed about the ideas that it is implementing or plans to implement. As of December 15, 2008, over 10,800 ideas had been posted and over 83,000 comments had been received on the ideas. Most of Dell's new products since the launch of the site have benefitted from these ideas.

Figure 3.1 Collaborative Value Exchange: An End-to-End View

Beyond the idea stage, *collaborative concept development* involves soliciting new product concepts or working with customers to refine new product concepts. At this stage, highly skilled and creative customers are solicited for their inputs, and there is usually some economic reward or recognition involved. For instance, Nokia, the world's largest mobile device manufacturer, has created the Nokia Concept Lounge, an online space where designers can share ideas and thoughts on future concepts related to personal communications. Concepts are voted on by a community, and contributors of winning concepts can earn cash awards, travel to Helsinki to interact with Nokia designers, and see their concepts turned into virtual new product concepts by Nokia. By creating this platform for collaboration, Nokia is able to tap into worldwide design talent in an extremely cost-effective manner. Some of the best ideas in the world now pour into Nokia just for the price of running and staffing a web site.

Collaborative design engages customers in the design process for new products. Consider National Semiconductor's WEBENCH online toolkit for power supply, wireless, and microcontroller design. Engineers need only one to two hours using WEBENCH to specify a design; analyze it; customize it until it is optimal; and order chips, boards, software, or completed custom prototype boards for delivery. Three hundred thousand registered engineers use WEBENCH to create more than 1,000 designs per week. National Semiconductors estimates that design engineers save 80 to 90 man-hours per design, representing customer productivity savings of $75–$100 million.

Collaborative pricing involves customers becoming active participants in defining the prices that they want to pay and adapting prices to their changing needs. For instance, Hewlett-Packard, the world's largest computer company, has introduced a program called "partition pricing" for its high-end servers. The partition pricing program lets customers pay for only the capacity they use instead of paying upfront for server capacity that they might not use. Through this on-demand capacity and flexible pricing program, customers can pay as they go and pay as they grow. And customers can better align their costs with their changing demands and needs.

Collaborative positioning and messaging involves customers in the creation of marketing communications campaigns. An interesting example of the use of social networking sites for promoting products is the Stunning Nikon site that Nikon created to promote its D80 Digital SLR camera in collaboration with the social networking photo site Flickr. Nikon gave away cameras to talented photographers they identified on Flickr and asked them to share their best images with Nikon. The collage of images was then posted on the Stunning Nikon web site. The site showcases the images, features interviews with photographers, and provides links to the photographers' Flickr pages.

Finally, the CVE can extend to *collaborative support,* where firms can offer customers technical support and they can also invite customers to support each other with support issues. For instance, Cisco's NetPro forum is an online community where networking professionals come together to ask questions, share suggestions, and get information about networking products, technologies, and solutions. NetPro members are rated for the quality of their contributions to the community, and Cisco experts mingle with customers in a rich dialog.

To create collaborative value exchanges, firms need to address several questions. Which customers should they collaborate with? At the ideation or design stage, firms should collaborate with customers who are highly creative and technically skilled. However, at the stage where products or marketing campaigns are being tested, firms may choose to engage with a broader set of customers who are more representative of the broader market. Firms also need to consider the *return on collaboration* for customers—what's in it for them? In some instances, when customers offer serious creative input and intellectual property, they need to be offered economic rewards for their contributions. In other cases, when customers contribute advice or expertise in a more informal manner, social rewards such as recognition and ratings may suffice. Finally, firms need to consider how they can create trust with customers to initiate and sustain the collaborative exchange. Transparency related to intellectual property, responsiveness to customer suggestions and feedback, and personal participation of senior executives in the collaboration process are ways to build trust in collaborative exchanges. (See Chapter 9 for Jeffrey Dyer's discussion on building trust in business networks.)

Extending Collaborative Value Exchanges: From Customers to Partners

Collaborative value exchanges are not limited to customers. Firms are also creating new forms of collaborative exchanges with their partners, suppliers, and other entities in their business networks in the pursuit of a common goal to create superior customer value. (See Chapter 8 for Henry Chesbrough's discussion of open innovation in business networks.) The traditional paradigm of innovation as a closed, firm-level activity is giving way to a more open and externally focused approach to innovation that harnesses the creativity and resources of partners to accelerate innovation and to create superior innovation outcomes (Gulati and Kletter, 2005; Gulati, 2007; Nambisan and Sawhney, 2007).

Consider Proctor & Gamble's Connect+Develop Initiative, in which P&G reaches out to a diverse set of external constituencies for ideas, new products, and technologies (Lafley and Charan, 2008). According to their CEO A. G. Lafley, P&G wants to be known as the best company in the world at external collaboration. Almost 50 percent of P&G's new products now involve some external collaboration. In some cases, P&G even collaborates with competitors in its quest for superior customer value. For instance, P&G entered into a collaborative venture with Clorox, who owned the Glad brand for bin liners, to create a new line of plastic film products using the Press-n-Seal and Force-Flex technologies that it had developed, complemented with the brand equity and distribution reach that Clorox brought to the table. The new products created by the joint venture have dramatically increased sales for Clorox, and have made Glad into a billion-dollar brand. Both companies benefitted from the venture, and so did consumers because of the innovative products that resulted from the venture.

The Rise of Collaborative Business Networks: From Customers to Partners to Networks

As firms embark on a virtual tango with customers and partners to co-create value, they quickly discover the limits of their own internal capabilities to deliver on all the elements of the offerings that customers may desire. While customer pressures push firms towards quickly delivering end-to-end solutions, resource and internal capability constraints restrict their ability to do so. Even if their internal capabilities and resources are not a constraint, firms may find that the cost of going it alone is too high, or the time that it would take them to go to market by themselves is too long.

One way forward is to leverage a network of partners. A collaborative business network can provide valuable inputs that the firm uses (freeing up its resources to focus on downstream activities) as well as complementary products or services that can be part of its broader offering. By moving in this direction, firms begin to shrink their core by outsourcing greater portions of their own production processes while at the same time expanding their periphery of offerings to customers (Gulati and Kletter, 2005; Gulati, 2007). (See Chapter 4 for Ranjay Gulati and David Kletter's discussion on core and periphery.)

Apple offers a compelling illustration of this simultaneous shift whereby it has progressively reduced what it produces and even designs and has shrunk and redefined what it considers to be its core competencies. At the same time, it has partnered with a broad array of firms who produce a whole host of i-accessories that are sold through its Apple stores. Consider Apple's ultra-thin iPod Nano. Apple worked with Cypress Semiconductor (click-wheel control chip), PortalPlayer (audio chips), and Samsung (flash memory) to create a high-quality, best-selling product that achieves an estimated gross margin of about 50 percent.[2] (See Chapter 6 for John Hagel, John Seeley-Brown, and Gautam Kasthurirangan's discussion of PortalPlayer's role in Global Process Networks.) While it is difficult to make a precise cost analysis, we can reasonably assume that Apple's suppliers provide the firm with key inputs more cost-effectively than Apple itself could, given the deep specialization and huge economies of scale the supplier firms enjoy. The same seems to be true with its development of the iPhone. At the same time that Apple has shrunk its core down, it has sought to expand the footprint of value available to its customers by entering into a diverse set of partnerships through which its partners create accessories as well as software applications that are available to Apple customers through its stores, both online and offline. Leveraging this array of ties allows Apple to focus on connecting and understanding its customers while at the same time directing its partnerships to ensure that it can deliver what its customers value. And it can do all this in a much more cost-effective and timely manner than if it had tried to do so itself.

We believe that the partner-centric strategy that Apple follows is part of a systemic trend for creating superior customer value in a connected world. With the rising complexity of technologies and growing customer needs, it is likely that a move towards disintegration of the value chain may be more than just a fad embraced by some firms. Firms increasingly recognize that the benefits of vertical integration are not only outweighed by their costs (speed, cost, and bureaucratic costs), but also that the disadvantages of outsourcing are not as great as they used to be. Of course, this partner-centric approach only works if firms are adept at connecting with their customers to recognize unmet needs, as well as at times identifying partners and collaborating with them to deliver customer value. The capabilities required thus shift from design and develop, to connect and develop. As a firm's innovative capacity becomes defined more and more by what its partners can deliver, its ability to connect and co-create value with them becomes ever more important.

Making Collaboration Happen—
The Role of Enterprise Technologies

As collaboration in business networks becomes a source of competitive advantage, the success of firms increasingly depends on their ability to effectively connect and collaborate with customers and partners. Firms need to be able to "consume" business process inputs from partners as well as to "produce" business process outputs for partners. By connecting information that is distributed across different departments in a firm as well as among various partners in a business network, firms can better sense customer needs, buying patterns, and preferences. And they can respond more speedily and effectively by coordinating their actions with their partners. Consider the health care industry as an example. Managing a patient's end-to-end lifecycle of a disease can help in taking preventive measures that may reduce the need for expensive acute care. However, in order to predict which patients are more likely to require such early intervention, it is important for the patient's entire medical record to be available to health care providers as well as payers. This requires the business processes of all the participants in the network to be connected. It also requires an integrated data warehouse to track patients across all their interactions with the health care system. Enterprise technologies play a vital role in making collaboration a reality.

Consider how P&G has leveraged enterprise technologies by partnering with SAP, the world's largest enterprise software company, to enhance the scale, flexibility, and agility of its business network. SAP's Business Suite powers all the key operational systems at P&G, ranging across financial systems, manufacturing, order processing, and HR systems. P&G uses a combination of processes from the Business Suite as well as components of SAP's Industry Solution to track consumer and export business processes in its network. By integrating and standardizing its business processes, P&G is able to derive superior economies of scale and to reduce operating costs. Process standardization has also greatly enhanced P&G's agility. When P&G acquired Gillette, it was able to integrate Gillette's business processes with its backbone within 15 months, which is a phenomenal achievement given the massive size of the acquisition. And most importantly, from a customer value standpoint, P&G's emphasis on thinking externally about innovation would not be possible without the agility and speed that derive from its use of standardized and integrated enterprise technologies.

P&G's example points to the three key benefits that collaborative enterprise technologies offer. The first benefit is excellence in execution. By enabling the creation of collaborative business processes that span the entire business network, the processes become simultaneous, hand-offs between processes are minimized, and customers get a superior and more seamless experience. The second benefit is innovation. By being able to connect diverse capabilities of specialized partners, firms can create innovative value propositions and offerings that no individual participant in the network could create on their own. The third benefit is the ability to generate and use insights and business intelligence across the network. For instance, a sales promotion created by P&G may lead to a spike in demand for a P&G customer like Walmart. Enterprise technologies allow firms in a business network to proactively sense and speedily respond to opportunities and threats, and to be more responsive to customers. What's more, they can effectively orchestrate activities across their business networks and "own" the customer experience without having to actually perform the myriad activities or own the assets that are required to deliver on the customer experience.

Strategic Implications for Firms

This reconfiguration of the value chain has profound implications for firms. It forces a reassessment of where they want to focus their internal efforts while at the same time requiring them to build relational capabilities related to building and managing an entire ecosystem of partnerships. Whether it is the hub of an ecosystem or simply a member of someone else's ecosystem, every firm has to confront tough questions pertaining to the creation and governance of such constellations of firms. At the same time, competitive dynamics within industries can shift away from firm-to-firm contests and toward constellation-to-constellation contests.

First and foremost, it is important for firms embarking on this path of externalization of activities to remember that it all begins with the customer. Such partnering efforts can be narrowly construed as ways to cut costs, but such a mindset can be very limiting. While many such ties can be opportunity-driven based on the availability of a partner or a pre-emptive move against a rival, it is important to keep the bigger picture of customer value in view. The deep connections to customers should be the ultimate goal, while building an ecosystem is a means to achieving that goal.

Second, it is important to remember that there are no sacred cows when firms begin to shrink and expand at the same time. Activities that may once have been viewed as untouchable elements of the core may be candidates for outsourcing to partners. Take the case of clinical trials as well as research and development in the pharmaceuticals industry. Both were once viewed as central to the pharmaceutical enterprise and both are now being aggressively outsourced by many of these firms.

Third, firms must recognize that as they rely upon suppliers for key inputs and upon partners for key elements of the value they deliver to their customers, they need to be much more discriminating in their choice of members in their ecosystem. Not only must they share similar goals but also similar values when it comes to their emphasis on connecting and delivering value to their customers. In the case of suppliers and partners, firms will increasingly rely upon them to co-create what they believe customers value, and this may at times necessitate connecting those firms to their own customers. If they don't share the same passion for connecting and collaborating with customers, the partnership and the virtuous cycle between the firm and its customers is likely to break.

Fourth, in the same way that firms invest resources in developing internal capabilities in activities such as innovation, talent management, and manufacturing, they also need to find ways to enhance their relational capabilities. Most studies of inter-firm partnerships report an extremely high rate of failure of such ties but also a disparity of failure rates across firms (e.g., Gulati and Wang, 2003; Gulati, Lavie, and Singh, 2008), suggesting that there may be some inherent capabilities that differentiate failure and success. We also know that those firms that create some centralized unit to focus on its partnerships and clearly delineate a role for them do better as well (Kale, Dyer, and Singh, 2002). Hence, it is important for firms embarking on this journey to ensure that they fully comprehend how to build and manage such ties and ensure their success.

Finally, an important internal factor that can interfere with the success of partnerships and their ability to deliver customer value relates to the dilemma of how to share the spoils among the partners. Clearly the hope for most firms building an ecosystem is that they can create a larger pie for all to share. However, it is still difficult to decide how to apportion the value that customers perceive from the entire offering among the partners who contribute to the offering. Absent clear guidelines and some norms of fairness in the sharing of the pie, firms may find that internal squabbling can lead to a rapidly shrinking pie.

Conclusion

As customers become active participants in value exchanges, *it changes the very concept of a market and how value gets created in the marketplace*. The market is no longer viewed as a place where value is *transferred* from marketers to customers—instead, it is a forum where value is *co-created* with customers. In the increasingly connected world we live in, interactions between firms and customers are being transformed. Digital networks allow interactions to become more interactive, more social, and richer. Firms can engage customers at a scale and with a level of engagement that was impossible to imagine until recently. This revolution in interaction in turn is leading to a transformation of value exchanges from one-way "command-and-control" exchange to two-way "connect-and-collaborate" exchanges. Collaboration extends across the entire spectrum of value-creation activities, from the generation of ideas to the delivery of offerings.

Collaboration also extends beyond the boundaries of the firm to embrace a broad array of partnerships that deliver value to their customers. Increasingly, firms are unable or unwilling to extend themselves and own or build all the disparate pieces that may go into the value bundle that customers desire. In an era of cost-cutting and a relentless credit-crunch, firms conserve their own resources and increasingly shrink their core while relying on a network of suppliers who design, develop, and build key elements of the inputs they need. Supplementing this rich array of supplier ties, is a broad panoply of partnership with firms who produce complementary offerings that firms can provide to their customers along with their own product or service. This expansion of the value footprint is thus accomplished with limited investments by the firm itself. At the same time, firms must also confront their own internal silos and foster greater collaboration among them. In embarking on this journey, it is important to note that the aggressive will quickly build their own ecosystems of partnerships where they themselves are the primary keepers of the customer connection, while the timid will choose to be part of someone else's ecosystem. The choice is yours to make!

Chapter 4

Shrinking Core, Expanding Periphery

The Relational Architecture of High-Performing Organizations*

Ranjay Gulati

David Kletter

Vice President at Booz Allen Hamilton

If you were to build a company today from the ground up, what kind of organizational strategy and structure would you design to ensure its long-term success? What behaviors would you seek to encourage? What conflicts would you try to circumvent? What culture and values would you attempt to instill? If you were to create an ideal in terms of an operating model for success, what would it look like?

One thing is certain: whatever organization you might construct, whatever the industry, whatever the competitive playing field, the organization would be built on *relationships*. According to our research, winning organizations are discovering that capital takes many forms, not just financial, and that effectively exploiting and leveraging relational capital is an important route to long-term success. Defined as the value of a firm's network of relationships with its customers, suppliers, alliance partners, and internal subunits, *relational capital* is fast becoming one of the major currencies of modern commerce.[1]

---

*This chapter is reprinted from "Shrinking Core, Expanding Periphery: The Relational Architecture of High Performing Organizations" by Ranjay Gulati and David Kletter, published in *California Management Review*, 2005, (47/3): 77–104, by The Regents of the University of California. By permission of the Regents.

Historically, companies focused their expertise and business processes on managing physical assets (e.g., manufacturing facilities, products, retail locations) and more recently on intellectual assets (e.g., R&D, patenting). Now, however, companies are increasingly applying a disciplined approach to managing their network of relationships, effectively treating these relationships as assets—increasingly precious assets.

Winning companies define relationships in a very consistent, specific, and multifaceted manner. While competitors may close business deals and dub them "relationships," top-performing companies take a more expansive and long-term view. They focus extraordinary enterprise-wide energy on moving beyond a transactional mindset as they develop trust-based, mutually beneficial, and enduring relationships with key constituencies both inside and outside of their organization.

Ironically, as top performers extend their organizational borders, reach out to external partners, and render their borders more porous, they are simultaneously contracting their organizational centers and outsourcing increasing portions of their activities. They are shrinking their core by increasing focus on fewer activities while outsourcing the remainder to strategic partners. This has led to an explosion of partnerships on the vertical dimension that includes ties up and down the value chain. At the same time that they are shrinking their core, top performing firms are expanding their horizons by trying to provide customers with greater sets of products and services, many of which may come through partnerships with other firms and are bundled together into what are loosely called customer solutions. This has led to an expansion of partnerships on the horizontal dimension with firms that may provide complementary offerings to their own. This "shrinking core, expanding periphery" phenomenon is evident across an array of industries and is one of the hallmarks of a new operating model—what we call the "relationship-centered organization." The relational architecture that such firms create provides them with a pathway to profitable growth by allowing them to simultaneously focus on their top and bottom lines. They manage their costs through shrinking the core and enhance revenue streams through expanding their periphery. This sounds easier than it is to execute and therein lies the ultimate differentiator of successful firms.

Methodology

In order to explore the ways in which relationship-centered organizations are developing in today's business world and to discover the lessons that we can learn from these developments, we conducted a survey of *Fortune 1000* companies. One hundred twelve CEOs and other senior executives from these companies across a range of industries responded to a questionnaire comprising 115 questions on the organizational challenges and imperatives companies perceived in their markets. Of these firms, one hundred that were on the *Fortune 1000* list in both 2000 and 2002 were retained for analyses. We then stratified the performance of these firms into quartiles based on their total returns to shareholders for the five years from 1995–2000 and 1997–2002 in order to isolate those distinguishing attributes that differentiated top-quartile respondents from the others as well as to control for the market bubble in the late 1990s.[2] Needless to say, the gap in the valuations assigned top- and fourth-quartile respondents in 2000 is dramatic, with a less dramatic gap in 2002 driven by the overall market decline. The core of our analysis is to elucidate the attributes of the firms that were sustained performers—that is, in the top quartile in both 2000 and 2002.

In addition to the survey, we conducted interviews with leaders at top-quartile firms who were willing to discuss their responses in more detail. We also conducted a workshop on best practices in which we invited all participating firms to send a representative.[3] Our research was specially designed to uncover not only the "what" of successful organizational relationships but also the "how." It is one thing to recognize that winning organizations sell solutions or share information and collaborate with their internal and external partners, but it is another thing entirely to be able to describe exactly *how* they execute these behaviors to assure superior results and what the journey looks like as they embark on this endeavor.

One of the companies we studied that exemplifies this focus on relational capital is Starbucks. Starbucks has long understood the importance of relationship building, not only with its customers, but also with its suppliers, alliance partners, and internal business units. Indeed, the "Starbucks experience" is predicated on the creation of enduring, multifaceted relationships. While brewed from high-end Arabica beans, Starbucks coffee is ultimately a high-priced commodity in a reasonably competitive space. To retain its market leadership, the company needs a tie that binds consumers to its brand on a very personal level, and that tie should not be just the coffee, but also the relationship the local Starbucks barista enjoys with his or her daily customers. Starbucks focuses the bulk of its energies on solidifying that relationship. It creates a comfortable coffeehouse environment in which a "My Starbucks" relationship can easily develop. It staffs its stores with well-trained, highly motivated baristas who enjoy one of the best compensation and benefits packages in the retail industry. Its line organization is closely aligned with internal staff units that support them. It searches the world for the highest quality coffee beans and builds a long relationship with the subsistence farmers who produce it. It allies with or acquires partners who can supplement its brand experience with music or ice cream or a night to Chicago. In short, it develops a multidimensional relationship with its customers, which in turn rests on the multiple relationships it cultivates as a company between its internal subunits, suppliers, and alliance partners.[4]

Leveraging Relational Capital

As companies refocus around their core businesses and build a simultaneously expanding-shrinking firm, they have become increasingly reliant on their ties to four sets of critical stakeholders that span both vertical and horizontal axes and include customers, suppliers, alliance partners, and intra-organizational business units. As they involve customers in product/solution development, share more and more information with vendors, and build wider and longer bridges with existing alliance partners (sometimes forging new ones), they are also developing more collaborative relationships among organizational subunits at every level. Figure 4.1 depicts how successful companies move outwards from the center on one or more of the four dimensions. On each of these relationship dimensions, successful firms work their way up a ladder in which they intensify their collaborative efforts with that particular constituent.

Along each of these four dimensions, the relationship progresses from transactions to collaboration until, in an ideal world, a company and its key stakeholders all have a vested interest in the continued health and productivity of their relationship. What may start as an arrangement entailing minimal coordination and cooperation quickly expands into one that encompasses synchronous coordination and active cooperation. Suppliers are strategic partners, internal subunits are mutually aligned collaborators, alliance partners are part of a mutually reinforcing set of business relationships, and satisfied customers are collaborating on co-developing and receiving solutions.

The relationship-centered organization with its relational architecture depicted in Figure 4.1 is a networked, agile, and highly adaptive entity that transcends traditional boundaries as it develops deep and collaborative relationships with internal subunits, customers, suppliers, and alliance partners. Such organizations appreciate that their competitiveness in today's marketplace and the lure of achieving profitable growth hinges on their ability to leverage their "relational capital" by extracting full value from their various partners—both internal and external, spanning both vertical and horizontal boundaries—and they are creative and consistent in this endeavor. As markets globalize and as keeping pace with innovation becomes increasingly challenging, the complexities involved in running a business multiply. The majority of our

Figure 4.1 The Multi-Faceted Nature of the Relationship-Centered Organization

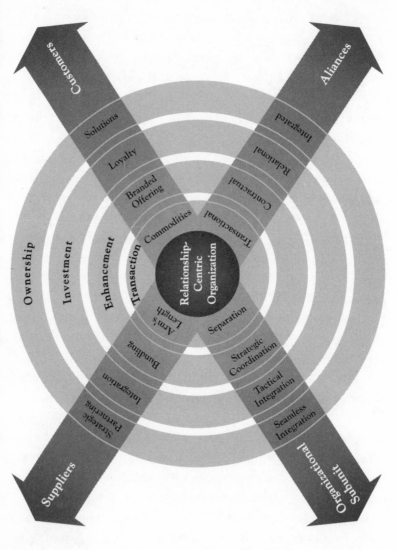

survey respondents agreed that product/service attributes, information systems, and organizational structures are, in general, becoming more complex. As a result, the successful firms are reaching out more and more to access appropriate expertise, adopting a multidimensional approach as they expand their universe of critical relationships.

First Dimension of Relational Capital: Customers

While customers have long been hailed as the "boss" in bumper sticker slogans and corporate values statements, their central role in sustaining the economic fortunes of the modern enterprise is being freshly acknowledged. No longer is the customer merely the "someone" who buys your product or service; rather, he or she is the "someone" whose problem your organization exists to solve.[5]

Furthermore, the expectations of these "someones" are on the rise. While 59 percent of our survey respondents found meeting customer expectations to be a significant challenge in the past, 84 percent now consider it to be a significant challenge moving forward. Sixty-eight percent of the companies we surveyed project that it will be increasingly difficult to access new customers, and 52 percent believe it will be difficult to access new geographical markets. Underlying this drive to cement high-value customer connections is the recognition that while retaining customers remains far easier than acquiring them, ultimately both are important. Relationship-centered organizations joined their poorly performing peers in acknowledging the difficulties associated with attracting new customers and entering new markets in the current environment in our survey. An important element underlying the challenges in serving customers profitably is the growing pressures of commoditization that plague a wide range of industries today as a result of which firms are forced to compete on price. Through the confluence of an array of factors ranging from growing international competition and maturing technologies to open standards and customers' reduced willingness to pay for premium products, many industries face emerging pressures of commoditization. These can be particularly deadly in technology-intensive industries where firms must still generate enough of a surplus to invest in innovation and development.[6]

What distinguishes relationship-centered organizations is their reaction to these mounting challenges and expectations. More than two-thirds of the top-quartile firms we surveyed devote primary strategic focus to meeting customer expectations and building long-term customer relationships, a much higher percentage than the bottom-quartile companies who are far more focused on cutting costs and shedding underperforming assets. Relationship development, as one might expect, thus seems to take a back seat when the question of corporate survival is at stake.

At the same time that winning companies are building new relationships, they are also strengthening the ones they have already formed by climbing a ladder of increasing mutual responsibility and mutual commitment within these customer relationships. This becomes particularly important for those firms seeking ways to differentiate themselves by extending their product/services to encompass a broader array of offerings that solve customer problems. As companies climb these ladders together with customers, they each share more of the burden of sustained collaboration and realize more of the mutual benefit (see Figure 4.2).

On the lowest rung of the customer relationship ladder, no significant relationship exists between buyer and seller, as products are only commodities—bought and sold transactionally—and are not differentiated from each other in the marketplace. In order to move one rung up from this state, companies must strengthen the relationship between their customers and their products. This is achieved by forming a set of expectations about a product in the customer's mind and creating a brand that represents the company's implicit promise to deliver against those expectations in the future. The relationship here is between the customer and the product, not between the customer and the seller; the relationship would thus be expected to move with the product if, for example, the brand were

Figure 4.2 Customer Relationship Ladder

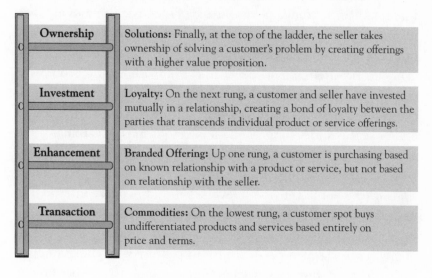

Ownership	**Solutions:** Finally, at the top of the ladder, the seller takes ownership of solving a customer's problem by creating offerings with a higher value proposition.
Investment	**Loyalty:** On the next rung, a customer and seller have invested mutually in a relationship, creating a bond of loyalty between the parties that transcends individual product or service offerings.
Enhancement	**Branded Offering:** Up one rung, a customer is purchasing based on known relationship with a product or service, but not based on relationship with the seller.
Transaction	**Commodities:** On the lowest rung, a customer spot buys undifferentiated products and services based entirely on price and terms.

sold to another company. At the third tier of the ladder, the two parties invest in one another's success—in economic terms, by creating a "switching cost" that creates a bond of loyalty between the two companies. This could take many forms, including physical (e.g., co-location or establishing facilities in near proximity to one another), intellectual (e.g., sharing and/or licensing intellectual property), personnel (e.g., dedicating staff to work the interface across the companies), and monetary (e.g., "gain sharing" or other financial rewards for mutual success). At the highest rung of the ladder, the customer-seller relationship is strongest, transcending and redefining the traditional boundaries of the two companies. Here the seller takes ownership for success of a portion of the customer's business, offering a solution to a problem that the customer faces, and receives compensation not based on the volume of products or services but on a successful outcome from the buyer's standpoint. Of course, a given company may operate at multiple points on the ladder simultaneously. Many leading companies have effectively segmented their customer base and created offerings tailored to different customer segments, with differing depths of relationships.

Our survey and our field interviews supported our contention that top-quartile companies are ahead of their peers in moving their relationships with customers up this ladder. Winning companies are more engaged in key collaborative behaviors with customers. These firms are experiencing deeper connection with their customers in very major ways: information sharing with customers; linkages to customers via computer networks; shifting from selling products and/or services to selling "value-added solutions"; customer input into the development of products and services; and the longevity of customer relationships (see Figure 4.3). Across these very dimensions, we saw uniformly high levels of intent to share information with customers and link to them via computer networks among top- and bottom-quartile performers (responding at a level of five or greater on a seven-point scale). In fact, in 2002 the difference between the sustained performers and bottom-quartile performers was only 5 percent for information sharing (with 100 percent of sustained performers reporting to us that they planned to increase the

Figure 4.3 Trends in Customer Relationships, All Respondents

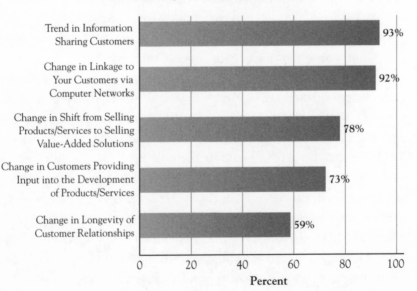

amount of information they shared with customers), and 95 percent of bottom-quartile performers reporting to us that they planned to do the same. Furthermore, computer networks seem to be the medium of choice, with 100 percent of sustained performers reporting the plan to increase sharing using the Internet, and 95 percent of bottom-quartile performers reporting plans for the same.

The differences in practices between sustained performers and the other companies in the survey were most pronounced in the shift from selling products and services to providing integrated solutions, the amount that customers provide input into the development of new products/services, and the focus on the longevity of customer relationships.

From Selling Products to Providing Customer Solutions. An important consequence of the move by top performing firms to pay greater attention to their customers has been the shift from selling products to selling what has loosely been described as customer solutions. In an increasingly competitive and transparent global environment where customer expectations are on the rise, it has become harder for many established companies to maintain their profit margins while selling traditional products and services. Established industry players are confronting the reality that product-based differentiation is more costly and difficult to maintain than ever before, and product differences are increasingly less meaningful. Value has, in effect, migrated downstream from suppliers toward customers. Rather than continue to accept the inevitable, companies of all descriptions in diverse industries are looking for opportunities to differentiate by developing higher-margin "solutions" businesses.[7]

Our survey indicated that most companies are trying to climb the rungs of the customer relationship ladder as they move from a singular product/service orientation to a more blended solutions-driven approach (see Figure 4.4). A solution is not—despite what many believe—an extension of an existing product line or the mere bundling of services with products. It is instead a fundamentally

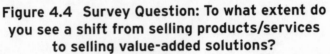

Figure 4.4 Survey Question: To what extent do you see a shift from selling products/services to selling value-added solutions?

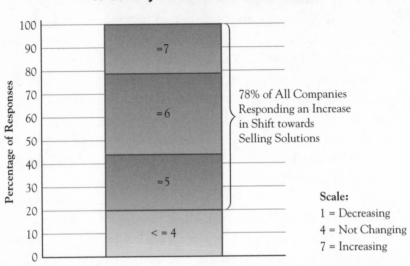

new approach to *creating* incremental value in the system for the customer and, by extension, for the solution provider. A solution is typically developed as a combination of products, services, and knowledge (e.g., risk management, performance guarantees, and customer consulting), and is a supplier's customized response to a customer's pressing business need. It is the logical next step in the customer value proposition, one that promises increased profits, stronger customer relationships, and greater competitive differentiation to those providers who get it right (see Figure 4.5 for some examples across a range of settings). For example, rather than selling simply lubricants, which may be tough to differentiate and may typically be purchased as commodities at the lowest available price, a solution value proposition could combine the products with deep expertise in the application of lubricants to a particular situation. This would make a shift from a pure "product" sell to selling a combined set of products and services that together enhance machine performance and guarantee the maintenance of the enhanced level of performance over time.

Figure 4.5 Evolution of Solution Value Proposition

Industry	Traditional Product	Value-Added Services	Traditional Value Proposition	Solution Value Proposition
Truck Manufacturing	• Trucks	• Financing • Service	"We sell and service trucks"	"We can help you reduce your lifecycle transportation costs"
Chemicals	• Lubricants	• Product support • Application design • Materials analysis	"We sell a wide range of lubricants"	"We can increase your machine performance and uptime" • Maintenance analysis • Performance guarantees
Pharmaceuticals	• Drugs	• Product support • Outcomes-driven information database	"We sell pharmaceuticals"	"We can help you better manage your patient base"
Telecom	• Phones	• Billing	"We can serve multiple needs (e.g. voice, data)"	"We can be your single-point connection to the world"
Pharmacy Benefit Management	• Benefit plan management • Mail order prescription delivery	• Administration • Breaking bulk	"We can lower your healthcare costs"	"We can be your single source for all benefits management, including long-term care and disease management"

As companies transition from transacting in products and services to developing value-added solutions *in partnership with* their customers, the risks they naturally assume increase. A common lament we hear among fledgling solutions providers is, "Our customers are thrilled, but we're not making any money." One of the critical distinguishing features of a true solutions relationship is that value is *not* reapportioned but rather new value is created and *shared*. Hence in structuring solutions, winning companies and their customers focus on the creation of value and on the establishment of performance monitoring metrics that will both measure gains and distribute them equitably.

Moreover, top-quartile companies make sure they build solutions with the "right" customers. They rigorously segment their customer base according to relative cost-to-serve and profitability. Clearly, successful companies want to focus their greatest efforts on enhancing the value proposition they offer to their most productive relationships. Not every customer is interested in buying solutions. One of the companies we interviewed as part of our survey categorized customers as gold, silver, bronze, and lead, reserving special resources and attention for its gold and silver clientele—while encouraging the "lead weight" to shop elsewhere. Examples abound of companies trying to advance their customer base up this value ladder. At the same time that they focus their attention on select customers, successful firms are also attentive to extending the duration of those relationships. One attribute on which top-quartile survey respondents differed was on the degree of emphasis they placed on improving the longevity of customer relationships: while 67 percent of sustained performer respondents thought it was critical, 50 percent of bottom-quartile firms thought it was critical (as indicated by a response of five or greater on a seven-point scale on the survey questions).[8]

At the same time that successful firms focus their efforts on crafting solutions for select customers, they also see the value in engaging customers in crafting those solutions. As a result, another observed attribute that sets sustained performers apart from their peers is the willingness to incorporate customer input into product and service designs. Our survey showed that fully 92 percent of sustained performers planned to increase the amount of collaboration with customers during product development, as compared to 73 percent for the overall survey respondents (as indicated by a response of five or greater on a seven-point scale on the survey questions).[9]

The move towards selling solutions appears in different shades in different industries. In many traditional business-to-consumer markets, this takes the form of a shift from offering products to endeavors to offer experiences or lifestyles as Starbucks has tried to do. In many business-to-business markets where manufactured products are bought and sold, this manifests itself in the form of trying to combine a broader array of products with complementary services to create a more comprehensive offering for the customer. Many pure services firms have also embraced these ideas as well and offer solutions that encompass a broader array of services that are provided to customers in a more accessible manner. In all these instances, the solution provider tries to use a solutions approach to get closer to the customer and create some meaningful differentiation between their offerings and those of others. Perhaps since so many firms are now embracing this concept, the next logical question is—are solutions going to become table-stakes and a commodity as well in the years to come?

One example of a consumer-centric company that has tried to broaden its offering in this way is Harley Davidson. Through its Riders' Edge program, Harley Davidson tries to deepen its connection and build closer relationships with its customers. It provides its network of independent dealers with all the tools and resources they need to get potential customers over the biggest hurdle to owning a Harley: securing a license to drive it. Harley Davidson, in partnership with state DMVs, has created an educational safety course to teach people how to drive a motorcycle. After teaching customers to drive the bike, Harley dealers then schedule you for a road test and ferry you there; they even lend customers the bike to take the test—all of this for $250, which is credited to your purchase of a Harley Davidson motorcycle when you pass.

Harley Davidson's devotion to helping customers fulfill their dreams does not end there. It actively cultivates a network of Harley Owners Groups (or H.O.G.s) across the country, with a dues-paying chapter in 1,200 dealer communities. In fact, one of the conditions of being a Harley Davidson dealer is that they foster a local H.O.G.

by organizing rallies, rides, and other Harley-centric activities in their service area. Now 800,000 owners strong, H.O.G.s do a lot to spread the Harley Davidson mystique. An active rental program also acts as a great feeder system for new purchases. Credit services, branded parts and accessories, and a full line of Harley Davidson attire and merchandise complete the portfolio of customer products and services. Harley Davidson does not pitch price or specs, it pitches a "lifestyle."

Teradata, a Division of NCR, is another example of a technology company that has transformed itself from a traditional product- or service-centric organization into an organization focused on solutions that are targeted to major corporations in key industries around the world. In the mid-1990s, NCR began the process of consolidating a portfolio of hardware, database software, and services into a combined offering focused on customers, and soon began complementing its core database offering with complementary applications and services. Today, Teradata has consolidated and coordinated its entire company around providing such solutions, which are combinations of Teradata's portfolio of hardware, software, and services aimed at specific business problems in specific industries—such as Yield Management for Airlines, Contract Compliance in the transportation industry, Customer Retention for retail banks, and Network Optimization for communications companies. The typical solution sale at Teradata is on average about one-third hardware, one-third software, and one-third professional services. The goal is to make a solution that is greater than the individual parts, which occurs when Teradata develops a full understanding of the customer problems and creates an offering that can solve those problems.

A key component of Teradata's solution orientation arises from its close partnerships with customers that can be seen in how it develops software. Rather than build its own isolated applications around its own internal expertise, Teradata partners with its key customers to build integrated solutions to industry-specific problems, infusing key insights from select customers to create applications that fully leverage Teradata's key strengths. An example of this approach is National Australia Bank, who partnered with Teradata to develop Relationship Optimizer, an analytical CRM solution that enables customer-oriented and personalized dialogs with hundreds of thousands or even millions of customers of major B2C businesses, such as retail banks. This application has allowed the bank to not only create an effective communication channel with its large number of customers, but it also allows them to identify discrete individual customer "events" every day and react to them in a timely manner (events are such things as unusual deposits or a discontinuance of an automatic paycheck deposit). Such events in turn allow the bank to identify potential opportunities for the bank to contact the customer and provide a product or service to those customers in a proactive and timely manner. This joint project between Teradata and the National Australia Bank has resulted in a reliable and successful application that is now in its fourth generation (Teradata CRM) and is now being leveraged by other industries worldwide.

In addition to partnering directly with select customers, Teradata also provides multiple venues to easily connect customers with each other and share knowledge and best practices. Along with its annual users conference where best practice customers share their insights and experiences with others, Teradata regularly schedules webinars throughout the year and invites customers and other experts to engage in interactive dialog with a business or technical user of a specific solution. The customer usually leads the dialog, not Teradata.

Quest Diagnostics is another company that has helped extend the longevity of its customer relationships by developing a comprehensive "wellness" solution designed to help large employers contain costs and reduce employee absenteeism. Based on an evaluation of employees' blood tests, lifestyle, habits, hereditary factors, and modifiable risks, Quest's Blueprint for Wellness™ program red flags looming health risks to the employees of client customers and helps companies manage existing ones through robust disease management programs. Individual employees receive a confidential and fully customized report, while employers receive the data in aggregate with meaningful comparisons (e.g., with industry norms, prior year results) and return-on-investment data. Detailed health reports, interventions, and hotlines provided by Quest allow clients to better manage their workforce and health care expenditures on a continual basis. Moreover, they help Quest develop a direct relationship with individual employees, who are playing a greater role in health care decision making as they assume more and more of the associated costs.

Second Dimension of Relational Capital: Suppliers

Relationship-centered organizations recognize the importance of maintaining strong and enduring ties with key suppliers as markets become more dynamic and demanding. They see the importance of building partnerships in this critical vertical dimension of the value chain as crucial to their success.[10] As firms realize the importance of cost containment in increasingly competitive markets, they see the logic of "shrinking their core" and begin to shift activities previously viewed to be core to their business to external suppliers. In doing so, they hope to reap benefits from economies of scale or depth of specialization. The globalization of the manufacturing and services industries has made it advantageous for firms to tap into local expertise on very economical terms. In doing so, they recognize that suppliers are an integral part of the value they offer their own customers, especially as complete solutions—which require more pieces from suppliers—constitute a greater part of their "product" mix. Consequently, relationship-centered organizations are climbing a relationship ladder with suppliers (see Figure 4.6).

The most basic form of relationship that a company can have with its suppliers is one in which the company purchases each product or service as an isolated transaction. Interaction with the supplier occurs only to place the order, take delivery of product, and arrange for payment; in an increasingly electronic world, this "inter-

Figure 4.6 Supplier Relationship Ladder

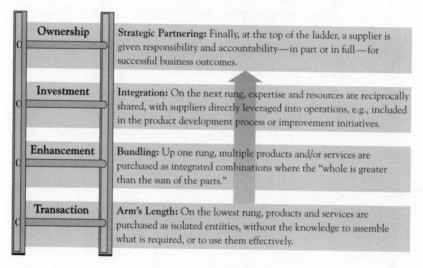

Ownership — **Strategic Partnering:** Finally, at the top of the ladder, a supplier is given responsibility and accountability—in part or in full—for successful business outcomes.

Investment — **Integration:** On the next rung, expertise and resources are reciprocally shared, with suppliers directly leveraged into operations, e.g., included in the product development process or improvement initiatives.

Enhancement — **Bundling:** Up one rung, multiple products and/or services are purchased as integrated combinations where the "whole is greater than the sum of the parts."

Transaction — **Arm's Length:** On the lowest rung, products and services are purchased as isolated entiities, without the knowledge to assemble what is required, or to use them effectively.

action" may occur entirely between machines. Moving one rung up from this "transaction" level, companies work with their suppliers to leverage their knowledge and expertise. On this "enhancement" rung, a richer and broader dialog occurs, including discussion of the company's objectives for the products and services, exploration of alternatives, and often a contractual agreement that formally establishes a relationship that transcends the transaction. This might include, for example, the supplier providing ongoing services to accompany a traditional product offering in order to help the company achieve the best possible results from the supplier's product.

On the third "investment" rung, employees from the supplier become integrated into the company's operations and work as part of a team, side by side with the company's employees. This could be a temporary project-based arrangement such as a product development effort or improvement initiative or even as part of ongoing operations. At the highest rung, the company turns part of its activities over to a supplier, who takes ownership for the successful execution of those activities. These could be mundane back-office transactions such as payroll or entire business functions such as manufacturing or customer care. At this level of "ownership," companies are focusing on what they do best and are accessing all other capabilities through their suppliers. In these relationships, the supplier is given the greatest amount of latitude in terms of how the activities are conducted. Success requires not only the "soft" side of the relationship (i.e., trust and confidence) to be solid, but also the harder side: governance mechanisms that institute strong accountability by measuring and rewarding successful business outcomes. In the extreme, suppliers will in turn become solutions providers. It is important to note that a company will not have the same relationship with each of its suppliers and would therefore be likely to operate at several of the rungs simultaneously. Indeed, we observed that most firms maintain a portfolio of relationships that are on various rungs of the ladder. Firms may even operate simultaneously on multiple rungs with a given supplier for sourcing different commodities or services.[11]

Our survey highlighted the universal importance of close supplier relationships among our respondents (see Figure 4.7). A large percentage—88 percent of the total respondents—expected increas-

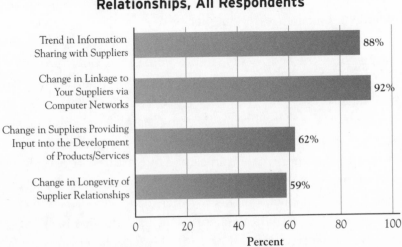

Figure 4.7 Trends in Supplier Relationships, All Respondents

ing information sharing with suppliers, and the vast majority—82 percent—was experiencing a tightening of computer network linkages with suppliers, more supplier input into development, and more involvement in suppliers' operations (as indicated by a response of five or greater on a seven-point scale on our survey questions). All of these specific behaviors point to a more intimate relationship with suppliers where product specifications and cost drivers are increasingly shared. As companies pinpoint where on the value chain they want to play and shed non-core operations, their relationships with suppliers become increasingly vital, especially where critical components and complementary offerings are concerned. Winning suppliers have also recognized this need among their important customers and have tried to work hard to climb this ladder with their customers. Not only have they learned to develop close communication channels and dedicated client teams, but in some instances have co-located staff on customer sites to simplify the coordination of tasks.

One of the ways to strengthen supplier relationships, and to move them from the lowest "transaction" level to one or more rungs farther up the ladder, is to develop and nurture trust between the company and its suppliers. Indeed, successful companies recognize the power of trust in all their business relationships, and they expend tremendous energy developing ways to institutionalize that trust in their procurement process in particular.[12]

Developing this level of trust is not easy, but relationship-centered organizations are finding ways to breach traditional organizational boundaries and outsource activities closer and closer to the core. Sustained performers among our survey respondents try to build long-term relationships with their suppliers. Our survey shows that while overall 59 percent of respondents anticipated an increase in the longevity of supplier relationships, the difference was stark between sustained performers and bottom-quartile companies in our survey: 75 percent of sustained performers intended to increase the duration and strength of supplier relationships, while only 55 percent of bottom-quartile companies intended to do so. We have observed again and again that leveraging relational capital with one's suppliers requires true collaboration, a working strategic partnership that transcends traditional product and service transactions as both organizations search for mutual value.

When it works, outsourcing operations to suppliers offers compelling strategic and economic benefits. It results in lower costs, greater flexibility, enhanced expertise and discipline, and the freedom to focus on core business capabilities. At first connected to non-strategic business activities such as cleaning, transport, and payroll, outsourcing is now encompassing even such functions as manufacturing. Not surprisingly, top-quartile companies often lead by example. In their own dealings with customers, they model the sort of supplier behavior that they have come to expect.

Sometimes the value in partnerships with suppliers is measured by both entities not by short-term individual gains but by long-term joint gains. Starbucks, for instance, has a great deal of brand equity invested in its reputation as a company focused on positively contributing to the economic, environmental, and social conditions in the Third World countries where its coffee originates. It works with Conservation International to develop environmentally sound sourcing guidelines designed to foster sustainable coffee farms. Moreover, it works with Fair Trade to help coffee growers form cooperatives and negotiate directly with coffee importers, who are also encouraged to foster long-term relationships with growers and to furnish financial credit. Starbucks pays Fair Trade prices for its Arabica beans regardless of market prices, which quite often fall below subsistence level. In fact, in October 2001 the company announced its intention to buy one million pounds of Fair Trade Certified coffee within the next eighteen months, a real commitment to improving the plight of coffee farmers who have sometimes seen the market price for their coffee drop as a result of oversupply.

The benefits of leveraging relationship capital with one's supply base are manifold. In successful partnerships, both firms gain as they move up their industry's value chain together. Value is not reapportioned; rather it is created and shared. The sharing is often the thorniest part. First of all, how do you fairly measure gains (from a total cost/benefit perspective) and divvy them up in such a way that both parties see a return on their investment, so that 2+2=5, instead of 2+2=3?

Relationship-centered organizations have wrestled with this central challenge longer than most and have developed best practices that help them establish win/win relationships with their suppliers. Ultimately, some form of "open book" arrangements combined with joint mutual dependence in which both parties need each other may furnish the transparency necessary to ensure true gain sharing.[13] Building the trust that facilitates that sort of arrangement is not a "feel good" exercise; it is a business imperative.

Starbucks has developed very clear standards and a rigorous process for selecting and maintaining its supply relationships with a wide range of vendors from the farmers who grow its beans to the manufacturer of its cups. Specific criteria, robust training programs, regularly scheduled business reviews, and a high degree of information exchange all distinguish and guide the procurement process. Starbucks takes a holistic approach, engaging representatives from not only its purchasing operations, but also its technical product development, category management, and even its business unit operations teams to understand—from an entire supply chain perspective—how a supply relationship will ultimately impact operations. Buck Hendrix, VP of Purchasing, says, "We are looking for, first and foremost, quality; service is #2 on our priority list; and cost is #3. Not that we want to pay more than we should, because we negotiate very hard, but we are not willing to compromise quality or service in order to get a lower price."

Once a supplier is selected, Starbucks works diligently to establish a mutually beneficial working relationship. If the relationship is strategic, senior management from both companies will meet face-to-face three or four times the first year and then semi-annually afterward. "Our biggest focus in these sessions is how to team with our suppliers," notes Hendrix. "We want to create a two-way dialog as opposed to dictating the conversation." Discussions encompass not only Starbucks' expectations, but supplier concerns and suggestions about how to improve the productivity and profitability of the relationship.

According to John Yamin, VP of Food, "We won't go into partnerships where the vendor won't make money or grow with us." Michelle Gass, VP of Beverages, adds, "Our vendors are willing to do what it takes to stay with us. I am amazed by the flexibility of our vendors, which is driven by our partnerships with them." For example, Solo, Starbucks' cup manufacturer, bought a company in Japan and a manufacturing facility in the UK so they could supply the coffee retailer's operations there. In return, Starbucks has committed to a long-term global supply agreement with the disposable products company. It's this sort of give-and-take that characterizes top-quartile supply relationships.

Third Dimension of Relational Capital: Alliances

The vast majority of the firms we surveyed universally placed a high magnitude of importance on entering into and carefully managing their strategic alliances. For example, 70 percent of firms were experiencing increasing linkages to their partners, and furthermore, partners were increasing their input into the development of products and/or services in 63 percent of the companies.

Increasingly, successful companies focus on what they do best and "alliance" the rest. Thus, as firms "expand the periphery" of their value proposition to customers, they increasingly rely upon greater connections with their alliance partners who may offer complementary offerings to their own to fill the gaps in their product or service offerings that may constitute an important part of their efforts to offer solutions. These partnerships can be not only with horizontal and vertical members of the value chain, but also diagonal when partners from disparate industries come together to tackle new opportunities. Our survey findings indicate that while 59 percent of bottom-quartile firms expect to increase involvement of alliance partners in product development, fully 75 percent of sustained performers plan such an increase. As they expand their network of alliances in this way, they move up a relationship ladder that parallels the customer and supplier ladders (see Figure 4.8). This ladder begins with one-off, mutually convenient agreements that are often sparked by a specific need or opportunity, but never evolve into anything greater. These "transactional" relationships are often quite simple and may not even involve any financial terms. The Maytag repairman who appears in a car commercial and talks about reliability can help build both brands—but the shared environment is unlikely to evolve into anything deeper between the two companies. At the next higher level, firms evolve towards creating what we call "contractual partnerships" in which firms agree to coordinate select activities that are typically non-critical with each other and stay close to narrowly specified contracts for those select activities. These "enhanced" partnerships can take many forms, such as distributing one company's product through the other's channel.

At the third rung of the ladder, the relationship shifts from simply coordinating tasks to active cooperation in which the partners begin to rely upon each other for more critical tasks. At the top of the

Figure 4.8 Alliance Relationship Ladder

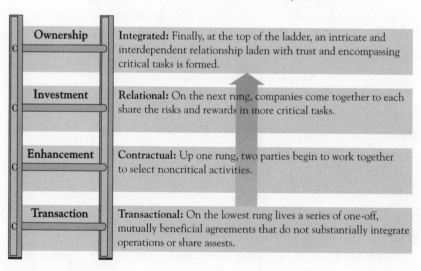

Ownership	**Integrated:** Finally, at the top of the ladder, an intricate and interdependent relationship laden with trust and encompassing critical tasks is formed.
Investment	**Relational:** On the next rung, companies come together to each share the risks and rewards in more critical tasks.
Enhancement	**Contractual:** Up one rung, two parties begin to work together to select noncritical activities.
Transaction	**Transactional:** On the lowest rung lives a series of one-off, mutually beneficial agreements that do not substantially integrate operations or share assests.

ladder, at what we call the "trusted partner" stage, true partnerships form and are sustained, where each company shares resources with one another toward a purpose neither company could achieve without the other.

As firms advance on this journey, they not only climb this ladder with specific partners, but they also begin to create an intricate and interdependent web of entities that deftly collaborate, with each entity possessing a shared stake in the success of others and the combined whole. Entire industries may form such groups of relationships that compete against each other (e.g., in the airline industry we now see competition between Star Alliance and OneWorld and SkyTeam).[14] As with both the customer and supplier ladders, many companies will operate at multiple points on the ladder, forming different strengths of alliances for different purposes.

Not only are successful firms demonstrating greater propensities to enter into alliances, the ties they are binding are qualitatively different. They are more strategic, deeper, and anything but conventional. Once again, it's all about leveraging relational capital. Successful firms recognize that alliances enable them to do more with less. As they expand their periphery, they need not do it all themselves and can instead leverage their partners' resource base much more broadly and effectively. As a result, they are becoming more creative in identifying alliance opportunities and potential partners with whom they can collectively serve certain target markets. The result is a web of business relationships populated with shifting alliances that relate to one another in new ways.

Alliances typically revolve around four distinct categories of partners that transcend horizontal and vertical boundaries: the channel, the licensee, the complementer, and (increasingly) the competitor. The implications of this expanded alliance building are profound in terms of organizational structure and behavior. The whole notion of "in-house" becomes suspended as companies contend with organizational boundaries that are newly fluid, transparent, and semipermeable. Web-based collaboration tools have accelerated this "boundarylessness" and enhanced the channels of communication between partners.[15] Among the firms that responded to our survey, 68 percent of firms are experiencing increasing links to their partners via computer networks, and 63 percent are experiencing greater input from partners in the development of products and services. With the availability of new communication tools, alliance partners around the world can inexpensively share product specifications, opportunity alerts, blueprints, sales figures, and expertise—all with the click of a mouse. The sharing of this knowledge, in turn, accelerates value creation.

Companies in this new context rely on external partners more and more, not only for cost reasons or to handle peripheral, narrowly circumscribed activities as in the past, but for strategic purposes, such as accessing new capabilities, improving quality, or sharing risk. New and powerful cooperatives are emerging, composed of multiple communities operating in a highly interdependent network and armed with a collective sense of purpose. At the extreme, we are witnessing unprecedented levels of cooperation between direct competitors, a phenomenon dubbed "co-opetition" by some observers.

While firms are exhibiting more enthusiasm towards alliances, there naturally remain hurdles to success. Like supplier relationships, governance and gain sharing are two of the enduring challenges companies must address. In a world where the boundaries within and among firms are collapsing and your business is everyone's business, defining the "rules of engagement" in alliances becomes a tricky issue. Previously guarded business processes are now open—either partially or entirely—to outside partners. Controls, operating protocols, and information technology standards must now be agreed upon and embedded in the processes of all participants to create the electronically linked, real-time information-sharing network needed to ensure success. Leadership and accountability need to be clearly defined in this space; otherwise, multiple points of contact overwhelm the efficient functioning of the alliance. Partners need to fully understand their respective roles and responsibilities.[16]

For all these reasons and more, several studies suggest that up to 60 to 70 percent of alliances ultimately fail. Those are odds most executives are not inclined to play. However, within those discouraging odds, some companies are struggling with an abysmal track record, while other companies are hitting 90 percent of their alliances out of the park. For companies who discover and hone the right success formula, the alliance game becomes one of increasing the odds rather than simply playing the averages. That success formula is commonsensical and yet eludes many firms. It consists of careful selection, jointly articulated expectations, management flexibility, and performance incentives designed to secure a win/win outcome.[17]

Over the years, Starbucks coffee has been served to millions of United, Horizon, and Canadian Airlines flyers as well as to Marriott, Sheraton, Westin, and Hyatt hotel guests through carefully constructed licensing agreements. Compass cafeterias, Barnes and Noble bookstores, HMS Host airports, and Safeway grocery stores all sell Starbucks coffee by the cup as *licensees*. The company has also extended its product line in logical directions through *complementary* alliances and joint ventures. Its highly successful bottled Frappucino beverage is marketed, manufactured, and distributed through a 50/50 joint venture agreement with Pepsi. Its ice cream—the #1 brand of coffee-flavored ice cream—is made and distributed by Dreyer's, and the packaged whole-bean and ground coffees you see in supermarkets are marketed and distributed by one of Starbucks' arch *competitors* in the at-home coffee consumption arena, Kraft. In stark contrast to its domestic retail stores, which are all company-owned, Starbucks has expanded internationally through joint venture agreements with well-established local players. Today, they have expanded aggressively in disparate markets outside North America sporting the Starbucks name and logo.

Not all of Starbucks' alliances have been so successful. Its early attempts with Pepsi to produce a coffee-flavored carbonated beverage called Mazagran flopped. Attempts to diversify beyond coffee-flavored ice creams to other flavors did not prove fruitful, and some of its more ambitious food-oriented ventures such as the Café Starbucks and Circadian restaurant concepts proved less than successful. Moreover, highly publicized plans to create a Starbucks destination/ affinity portal on the Web with all sorts of lifestyle links came to naught. However, in each of these well-calculated risks was embedded a tremendously valuable lesson. The same joint venture that launched Mazagran produced Frappucino, a fabulously successful incremental revenue stream for Starbucks. The experiments with non-coffee-flavored ice cream and full-service restaurant concepts helped Starbucks establish parameters on where its brand makes sense to consumers. While the Internet portal never came to pass, Starbucks used what it learned to design a wireless high-speed access network for its stores.

Maintaining these business alliances is, even at the best of times, a challenge, and Starbucks' approach has steadily evolved as its experience grows. According to Gregg Johnson, VP of Business Alliances, "Originally business alliances were intended to bring the Starbucks experience to places where retail could not go … a fairly simple mission with a number of complex components. First, the alliances we build need to be profitable for both partners. Second, they need to be designed around delivering the experience, whether it's through a consumer product (e.g., packaged coffee) or on a United flight. If we are not confident that we can do that, we don't go to the next place. (United, for example, had to replace the coffee-making equipment on all of its planes to meet Starbucks' exacting quality standards.) Third, it has to be a place where the consumer expects to find us. Yes, people expect to find Starbucks in Hyatt hotels, but not at Motel 6 at this point. But what we see is a very natural expansion of those boundaries year after year as consumers become more comfortable associating Starbucks with places and products they did not a few years back."

In developing solutions for its customers, Teradata frequently finds that it does not possess nor desire to possess all the missing links that may be critical for a solution that a distinct industry segment may require. In such instances, it seeks out alliance partners who often provide key components of the solution as well. Some of its alliance partners include firms such as Siebel, SAS, Cognos, FairIsaac, and Tibco. The offerings obtained from its partners can vary and include elements such as specific consulting services, specialized tools, or applications. Successful partnering is critical to its aggressive growth plans. As a result, even when there is conflict with its partners, they try to retain focus on the bigger picture. Sometimes that takes sacrificing something for the greater good.

With the passage of the Sarbanes-Oxley Act, most companies have quickly learned that changing accounting processes alone will not address these areas sufficiently and that the timely availability of financial information on an ongoing basis across the enterprise is critical. For this enterprises are turning to technology to make their financial information readily available, auditable, and analyzable. Teradata saw this opportunity but also realized that they did not have all the key applications to serve this market in an effective manner. They teamed up with Hyperion, a leading provider of financial applications, to provide their customers greater insight into financial performance. The agreement will allow businesses using a Teradata data warehouse and analytical solutions to link to Hyperion's Essbase XTD platform and applications. The partnership focused on two keys deliverables: drive core technology integration and optimization, and developing products that enable customers to analyze their business results easier and faster. Since 2000, the companies worked together to integrate their respective products by building a Teradata Analytic Accelerator: a set of prebuilt analytics and reports centered on a subject area such as General Ledger or Accounts Receivable. The objective of an Accelerator is to get analytics up faster and at less cost than by building analytic applications in the traditional way. A Financial Analyst can look at business results easily via graphs and reports at the summary level using information from the Teradata Enterprise Data Warehouse. Implementing an Accelerator can shorten the normal development and deployment of an analytic application by up to two months. The two companies have also worked closely in defining how they will support their joint customers in a coordinated manner. The support strategy involves having experts from both companies address customer issues through a single point of contact in a coordinated manner. A customer contacts Hyperion for initial support for technical questions about the Accelerator. If these questions relate to certain specific technical aspects of the solution, an escalation process defines how they pass to Teradata's support organization.

In some instances, it is a customer that forces two firms to work together. One such alliance is Teradata's partnership with Siebel systems to align their suite of applications and make them compatible with Teradata's data warehouse. Both shared a customer—DirectTV, who urged them to work together to make life easier for their customers. As a result of these joint efforts, Siebel provides the analytic tools and related consulting while Teradata provides the data-oriented expertise and consulting.

Fourth Dimension of Relational Capital: Internal Units

Relationship-centered organizations that succeed in the marketplace typically follow the same relational instincts with their own business units and discover the relational capital that is in their very own backyards. This form of capital results from promoting greater collaboration among the firm's own internal business units, which in turn can lead to significant external benefits. Firms must not only create a seamless connection with their external suppliers and alliance partners, but also with their internal business units, which need to come together in a harmonious fashion to offer customers an integrated experience. Hence a similar ladder of increasing responsibility and commitment can be applied to internal relationships at high-performing companies (see Figure 4.9).[18] In the weakest internal relationships, organizational subunits are treated as separate entities, perhaps even as independent profit centers. There is little interaction among them, with limited sharing of intellectual

Figure 4.9 Organizational Subunit Relationship Ladder

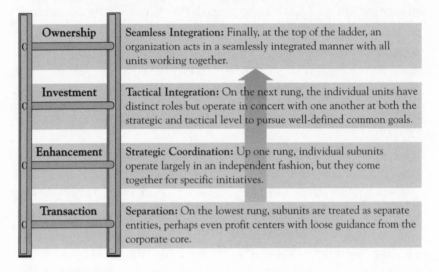

or human capital. The relationship between the business units and the corporate core is more akin to that of a holding company. At the second rung the organizations operate in a largely independent fashion, but they come together for specific strategic initiatives, where focused pooling of capital and other resources is drawn from to drive to a single corporate objective.

On the third rung, business units are integrated, working towards a common corporate goal. They may have the power to independently define how they reach that goal and are often left by senior management to meet their targets using their own devices. However, they are communally accountable for corporate success; they share capital, infrastructure, and talent across organizational boundaries; and they communicate on a regular basis. The final rung represents a wholly integrated company with "no walls." Information, capital, and talent flow freely across organizational boundaries, if any still exist. While the first two stages afford some basic levels of coordination, the higher levels demonstrate greater levels of active cooperation.[19] The intensity of interaction increases, as does the interweaving of operations and outcomes across the units.

None of this comes easy, and several executives we interviewed hinted at the fact that sometimes cooperation with internal business units can be harder than with external partners.

Different levels of the ladder are appropriate for different companies at different stages of their life cycle and based on their specific strategic goals. Furthermore, the level of interaction may vary among the different business units of a single firm as well as depend on the nature of underlying synergy among their respective operations. Regardless of the level of the ladder, the relationship-centered organizations in our study perform better than do fourth-quartile companies. Business units in high-performing firms communicate more with each other than in low-performing firms (58 percent vs. 35 percent) and best practices are deployed with greater frequency across groups/locations (83 percent vs. 55 percent—as indicated by a response of five or greater on a seven-point scale). This elevated level of effective communication and coordination fosters accelerated innovation.

One instance of a firm that has successfully invested in enhancing internal collaboration and benefited from it is Jones Lang LaSalle (JLL). In 2001, JLL was one of the largest commercial real estate services companies in the world. The product of a 1999 merger of London-based Jones Lang Wooten and Chicago-based LaSalle Partners, JLL was a global company with more than 680 million square feet of property and more than $20 billion in real estate funds under management in the United States, Europe, and Asia. The previous few years had been financially difficult for JLL. By early 2001, the company's stock price warranted a market capitalization less than the valuation of either of the two original firms. In addition to the lackluster stock performance, the economic downturn in the United States was further depressing sales. Senior management realized that change was needed to halt the slide in margins and to boost revenue.

In the marketplace, corporate clients were beginning to demand more from their real estate service providers. On the one hand, increasing globalization combined with heightened concerns about fees meant that the real estate marketplace was increasingly com-moditized. On the other hand, many companies were no longer sat-isfied with just being sold a product or service; they wanted a complete solution for their real estate needs. Some of JLL's largest customers—especially the prized global multinationals—sought more integrated services across the globe as an increasing number sought to outsource their entire real estate operations.

Meeting such diverse requests strained JLL's historically inde-pendent business units, which offered disparate real estate services and operated autonomously. The company's management realized that significant changes to their traditionally silo-based organization were needed in order to successfully compete on price and integrate their services. Consequently, in 2001 JLL's Americas region under-went a dramatic reorganization, dividing its nine business units into two groups—Corporate Solutions and Investor Services—according to the types of clients they served. Along with bringing its disparate services targeted to large multinational clients under the one roof of corporate solutions, senior management created a new account man-ager function to better provide JLL's clients with full-service inte-grated solutions. By establishing a single point-of-contact for JLL's largest clients along with shared accountability, senior management hoped to provide flexible and scalable resources for clients, enabling them to draw on the resources of JLL. In establishing this new orga-nizational arrangement, however, JLL had to tackle several critical internal issues. Most of these revolved around getting the internal business units to collaborate with each other and with the integrat-ing unit that worked with the customers directly. Results so far have been excellent and are a testimony to the efforts put into building a more collaborative internal environment.

In their efforts to differentiate themselves from their competi-tion by providing customers with integrated solutions, Teradata has recognized the importance of aligning their internal business units to create a seamless experience for the customer. To harmonize their internal efforts, they have shifted most of their resources, including technical specialists and industry specialists, into their sales organization. Further, they have devised what management calls a three-legged stool. The first leg of the stool is the sales account manager who owns the relationship with the customer organization and remains the point person for that firm throughout their interaction with Teradata. The second leg of the stool is the architectural technology specialist who helps specify the customers needs and decides which components of Teradata's offering may make sense for that customer. The third leg is an industry specialist (who also typically resides within the sales organization). This person helps define the industry-specific applications that would allow Teradata to customize the solution for the customer. While the sales account manager is the key point person, she or he works closely with the other two legs of the stool to ensure that the customer has a seamless experience. Along with incentive alignment to ensure that these disparate individuals work closely with customers, the customer-oriented culture is also key. As Bob Fair, Chief Marketing Officer at Teradata, suggests, "The glue here is the culture. Since we are trying to embark on a lifelong journey with our customers, we know clearly that the customer is critical and that we all need to work together to help solve the customer's problems."

Combining the Four Dimensions of Relational Capital

To achieve a shrinking core and expanding periphery, successful organizations recognize the mutually reinforcing nature of activities on each of the four dimensions of the relational architecture. Hence, collaboration with customers to offer them solutions necessitates close collaboration with alliance partners, with suppliers, and among internal business units. As a result, what is noteworthy about the relationships built by exemplary firms is their breadth and degree of integration. Winning organizations have moved beyond a single-minded focus on perhaps one or two facets of individual customer, supplier, or alliance relationships and are now developing a more holistic and multidimensional view of their entire network of relationships, one that takes into account the other relationships the firm may have on different dimensions that can create new opportunities for leverage and economies of scale. More and more, these companies' perspectives encompass a broader universe of involved and interacting players who move into and out of the organization with an unprecedented degree of freedom and flexibility.

In this new model, critical relationships along these three external dimensions—customer, supplier, and alliance partner—are no longer distinct and separate from the organization but rather interconnected and synergistic. In developing a total solution for a customer, for example, a relationship-centered organization will readily draw on such resources as complementary capabilities of its alliance partners or its network of key suppliers. Recognizing that its internal subunits and the employees within them are its ambassadors to customers, a relationship-centered organization will focus on optimizing the former to serve the latter. Top performers build multifaceted relationships that are interdependent and thus more than "the sum of the parts." Therein lies the difference.

Conclusion

This study sheds light on the particular strategies that top-performing relationship-centered organizations utilize to achieve superior performance by optimizing the architecture of their network of relationships. Our survey indicates that in each of four key relationships—customers, suppliers, alliance partners, and internal business units—what clearly sets sustained performers apart from their peers is a higher willingness to engage these entities and a greater focus on increasing the longevity of the relationships. Our research suggests that the relational capital unleashed through collaboration not only improves operating performance, but its vehicles—be they solutions, strategic outsourcing agreements, alliances, or acquisitions—help companies leverage assets more effectively, expand into new markets, mitigate risk, and increase market agility. Together, these efforts shape their success by shrinking their core and expanding their periphery to achieve market success.

No one relationship suffices to bring success in today's top competitive environment. Instead, it is a *combination* of distinct and critical relationships and the way they interact across a seamless and transparent organization as a *network* that leads to competitive advantage and value creation. Ultimately, companies want to build operating models that enable customer orders to automatically trigger supplier orders or that appropriately leverage employees as the conduit to the customer. Think of the Starbucks barista or the Harley Davidson dealer or the Jones Lang LaSalle account manager and you have a compelling image of the powerful circle of relationships that winning organizations create and foster. Organizations today are all too often the impediment to their own long-term success when they create barriers rather than facilitate communication and coordination. The relationship-centered organization is, in contrast, moving towards becoming a friction-free facilitator.

Where the emphasis in recent years has typically been on a single dimension—such as outsourcing agreements with suppliers, joint ventures with alliance partners, vision and values exercises with employees to align goals of internal subunits and achieve greater synergy, CRM tools for aligning with customers—now top performing organizations are operating on all dimensions at once to build a coherent and enduring whole that is greater than the sum of its parts. While the attributes and behaviors of the relationship-centered organization are by no means a guarantee of success, they do tend to differentiate the winners in many industries from the rest of the field. Just as companies manage, monitor, and measure their financial capital, so should they actively manage, monitor, and measure their relational capital. Relationships are a mission-critical asset, and should be treated as such. Relationship-centered organizations recognize this reality and organize in such a way to react to it.

Chapter 5

Product Leadership in a Network Era

N. Venkatraman

David J. McGrath Jr. Professor of Management
Boston University School of Management

Consider the following:

1. A high-end automobile has nearly twice the number of lines of software code as Windows XP; yet we think of cars like the GM Cadillac or BMW 5 Series as the first and foremost electro-mechanical device that runs on gasoline. Few would describe a car as a "computer on wheels" connected to the network through GPS and telematics—although most high-end cars already have more computer capability than personal computers with remote diagnostics functionality.

2. Apple's iPod transformed not just digital music players but the broader music sector with iPod serving as the primary gateway through which consumers search, access, acquire, consume, and share music. Although other MP3 players existed before, Apple treated iPod not as another product in the traditional electronics market but as a means to influence the competitive dynamics of the music sector.

3. Health-monitoring devices are no longer just standalone tools for recording vital signs but are becoming part of the digital, connected healthcare networks. The healthcare sector is in the midst of a business transformation that calls for different products

and services to interoperate with each other. For example, Lifeshirt is a product from Vivometrics (www.vivometrics.com) designed to continually collect, record, and analyze cardiopulmonary information through sensors embedded in garments. The current version may be suited for laboratory use but the product concept could emerge as a key node in the transforming healthcare marketplace while Microsoft HealthVault, Google Health, and others seek to transform healthcare delivery.

Thus, a Cadillac is a node in the transportation network, an iPod is a node in the music network, and a Lifeshirt is a node in the healthcare network. All three products are key parts of the business network transformations under way in these three sectors. These three examples—neither comprehensive nor exhaustive—illustrate the importance of recognizing the opportunities and challenges when products become nodes in evolving value networks. The time is right for managers to strategize about how individual products transform their roles and functions when interconnected with other products in complex business networks. This chapter highlights new challenges of product leadership in a network era: leadership in networks calls for recognizing the role of individual products, both in isolation and when interacting with other complementary parts of dynamic ecosystems to deliver compelling value to end-consumers.

Emergence of New Business Landscape

We are in the midst of a steady transformation away from the familiar business landscape, rooted in industrial age ideas, and towards a new business landscape shaped by networks of computers and communication technologies. The locus of value creation is shifting from points of production (upstream) to points of consumption (downstream). Furthermore, products are becoming digital and therefore connected in a global business infrastructure. Lack of recognition of this fundamental shift will surely limit managers in product companies as they seek to innovate and grow out of the current economic crisis.

For the purpose of simplicity, I describe the emerging business landscape facing product companies at the confluence of three technology laws: (1) Moore's Law, (2) Metcalfe's Law, and (3) Bandwidth Law*. These laws—taken together—create the core characteristics of the new business landscape (see Figure 5.1). My thesis in this chapter is that business network transformation is about effectively recognizing and responding to the characteristics

Figure 5.1 The New Business Landscape for Product Companies

Moore's Law

Forces Shaping the Business Landcape

Metcalfe's Law

Bandwidth Law

---

*In simple terms, Moore's Law states that "the number of transistors that can be placed inexpensively (at constant dollars) on an integrated circuit has increased exponentially, doubling approximately every two years." For more details, see http://www.intel.com/technology/mooreslaw/index.htm.

In simple terms, Metcalfe's Law states that "the value of a network grows as the square of the number of users." For a good discussion from a managerial perspective, see Carl Shapiro and Hal Varian, *Information Rules: A Strategic Guide to the Network Economy,* Harvard Business School Press, Boston, 1988.

For a technical discussion on Bandwidth Law, see Cherry, S., "Edholm's law of bandwidth," *Spectrum,* IEEE , vol. 41, no. 7, pp. 58–60, July 2004. George Gilder put it relative to computer power by proposing that "bandwidth rises three times faster than computer power, implying that speed of communication doubles every six months."

of this new landscape. I discuss the relevance of these laws as they relate to the three examples introduced above.

Telematics and the Automotive Sector

Ask anyone to make an educated guess on the number of software lines of code in a Windows XP operating system and they would consider that to be a legitimate question, even if they may not guess it right (the answer is: approximately 40 million lines of code). However, if you ask anyone to wager a guess on the number of lines of software code in a high-end automobile today, many are surprised by that question. Some even think it is a trick question. This reaction happens because we do not normally associate an automobile with software code, but high-end automobiles could have as many as 100 million lines of code! Yet, we do not generally consider an automobile as a computer or, for that matter, a networked electronic device.

Look at telematics. Viewing an automobile as "a computer on wheels" impacts the design architecture and the specification of how various modules and subsystems work together. Going beyond emergency services connected to airbag deployment, GM cars enabled with OnStar have embedded computer power that allows for remote unlocking of doors, diagnosis of engine performance, and instant capturing of accident details (e.g., rollover sensors). This computer power can also track the oil change requirements and monitor tire pressure (www.onstar.com). Providing this suite of services calls for rethinking the electrical and electronic connections in the car as well as re-specifying the data models within the automobile design. The transformation is about shifting from logic of automotive design to one that follows principles of hardware-software–services interdependence. This shift also implies the same shift from coordinated networks of suppliers surrounding the automakers towards more collaborative networks and will require new levels of trust and information sharing between automakers over these new network relationships. (See Chapter 1 for Geoffrey

Moore and Philip Lay's discussion of business network architectures and Chapter 9 for Jeffrey Dyer's discussion of the role of trust in business networks.)

GM OnStar is not the only case in telematics but it is the current leading example. Not to be left behind, Ford and Microsoft teamed up to create Sync (www.syncmyride.com). Although it does not impact the core features of the car as directly as GM OnStar, Sync enables smooth connectivity of multiple devices within the cabin of the car. Ford cars incorporate voice recognition and the ability to plug in multiple different mobile phones and digital music devices including Apple iPod and Microsoft Zune. By making sure that the car's cabin allows for integration and interoperability of different devices, this initiative highlights a thorny question facing companies during business network transformation—how do you ensure compatibility and interoperability across different products used by consumers?

GM OnStar and Ford-Microsoft Sync highlight two different avenues for business network transformation in the auto sector. OnStar impacts the core design of automobiles to create and deliver an integrated set of services. On the other hand, with Sync, Ford is striving to deliver services to the driver (and passengers) in terms of convenience when using different devices, while not directly impacting the core design features of the car. More importantly, both of these initiatives are clearly designed to improve the overall product experience for consumers and require the automakers to develop very different types of relationships with new partners in order to develop these new features and support them over time.

So, an automobile is not just a car traveling independently on roads but one that is connected to the network—which changes the features and functionality, expands the scope of services delivered, and requires an extended set of business partners to deliver those services. The transformation is possible because the cars have: (a) computer power that would be unimaginable even a decade back, at price points that make this feasible (Moore's Law); (b) a connection to the network (Metcalfe's Law); and (c) high-bandwidth connection speeds that allow for data- and media-rich interactions (Bandwidth Law) with wireless routers embedded within automobiles.

Once the car is seen as a "node" on the network, auto companies are able to wrap services around the core product in new and innovative ways. Value-added services are aimed differentially at the driver (e.g., turn-by-turn directions, remote door unlock, engine performance) and passengers (e.g., wireless Internet connectivity in the car). Some services are provided proactively (warning of low tire pressure or impending oil change through e-mail) while others can be provided on demand when requested (engine diagnostics and turn-by-turn navigation). The car becomes a product platform for delivering customized services based on mining detailed data collected from sensors embedded in cars. Ultimately, such network connections provide opportunities for new streams of revenue and profit.

So, what will business transformation in the auto sector look like? Figure 5.2 depicts the impact of the "three laws" on the auto industry. It will undoubtedly focus on alternative fuel sources (gasoline, electric, and hybrid). Beyond different fuel sources, it will also involve restructuring the business network. The design of the car will not be entirely controlled by traditional automakers such as GM, Toyota, Ford, and Mercedes Benz. Cars will be co-created and co-designed within a web of relationships involving modules that interoperate such that the end-consumer has far more options to customize the car to personal specifications. We could well see the emergence of specialist design firms with core capabilities at the intersection of automotive and computerization. More importantly, insurance coverage will involve a detailed understanding of driving patterns of individual drivers and road conditions. Simply put: technology is at the core of business network transformation in the auto sector not as an end but as a means to create new business models. The economic crisis of 2008 may be the catalyst to compel auto executives to move beyond incremental adjustments to the industrial-era business models and create a more effective, collaborative, and dynamic industry architecture.

Figure 5.2 Telematics and the Auto Sector

Bandwidth Law through connections to
GPS expanding the range of possible services

Metcalfe's Law of
Connectivity
reflected in the
installed base of
cars connected
on the network

Moore's Law impacting the
design features and functionality of the
automobile as a "computer on wheels"

iPod and Apple's Dominance in the Music Sector

In the twenty-first century, the music sector's transformation threatened the big music labels (Warner Music, EMI, Sony Music, etc.). Managers in the music label segment of this sector do not find such shifts comforting. The reason is simple: the traditional product manufacturers no longer control the key parts of the business model in the digital, networked era as the new landscape has marginalized their core competencies. Figure 5.3 depicts the impact of the "three laws" on the music industry. In the transformation of business models away from bundled music (albums sold physically on CDs) towards digital downloads of individual songs directly to digital devices or through computers, the music labels have allowed new entrants such as Apple, Amazon, WalMart and others to establish

Figure 5.3 iPod and the Music Sector

Bandwidth Law through connections to the network expands
the range of media and entertainment possible

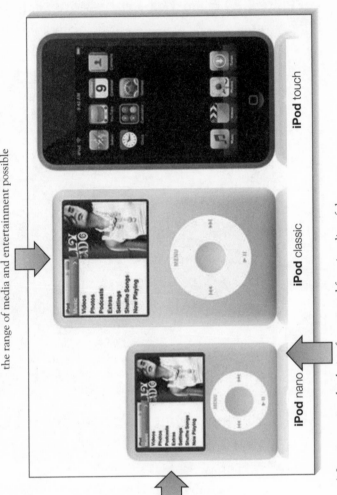

iPod touch

iPod classic

iPod nano

Metcalfe's Law reflected in
connections to both Windows
and Macintosh operating systems,
thereby expanding the potential
installed base of consumers

Moore's Law impacting the design features and functionality of the
product family and the evolution of the product architecture

dominant positions over the distribution and sales of music. These new entrants dictate pricing logic, specify key conditions (e.g., digital rights management), and develop closer relationships with consumers using superior recommendation engines that mine vast amounts of data to glean likely preferences. Essentially, new entrants are able to master the requisite new competencies and develop superior strategies based on understanding how consumers search, access, consume, and share music in the newly transforming marketplace. Therefore, the music labels find that their core competencies are mismatched with the new requirements and they find it difficult to adapt. Their challenge is not to become like Apple or Amazon but explore ways to work together.

The transformation in the music industry is fueled by technology but the end result is far more than a technical shift. It is not simply one of an evolution from selling music in the analog era (albums and cassette players) to the digital era (tracks downloaded to MP3 players). Looking at it as a technical shift (with minimal business impacts) misses a broader point of business model transformation that involves key dimensions such as: (1) manufacturing (producing single-track music versus producing albums), (2) pricing (single track versus bundled albums), (3) analytic recommendation engines (proactively suggesting songs based on superior data-mining functionality), and (4) social network–based endorsements (relying on social networks such as MySpace and Facebook for peer-to-peer endorsements to complement other advertising avenues). Those in the music sector—who saw this shift in technical terms and believed that the new entrants were illegitimately usurping power (as in the early days of Napster)—now find themselves at a strategic disadvantage in the new, networked business landscape.

Apple's dominance in such a short time period shows how it used its product (iPod) to master the evolving business network in music. Analyzing the product architecture from a hardware-software perspective, it is easy to see that it is proprietary and closed (iTunes requires iPod and vice versa). However, Apple strategically made iTunes compatible with Windows in addition to Macintosh. Apple did not compel users to buy Apple Mac OS in order to take advantage of its iPod and iTunes. By making it strategically open (Windows and Mac compatibility), Steve Jobs capitalized on the network effects enjoyed by Windows OS (Metcalfe's Law of Connectivity) while keeping other facets of the business network closed and proprietary to provide consistent and streamlined service. This example highlights important new requirements of understanding the complex role of closed versus open systems, as products become part of different networks of value creation. More critically, this case highlights that there is no absolute demarcation of open versus closed business architecture and that every product company should assess *when* and *where* to be open versus closed within dynamic business networks.

It is by no means certain that Apple will continue to dominate the music sector as it battles against companies such as Microsoft, Yahoo, MySpace, and others. Thus far, Apple has used its product design superiority and dual distribution/consumption (iTunes/iPod) capability to create a distinct appeal to end-consumers and to establish different business network architecture with iPod/iTunes as the anchor. Apple rode the digital network wave not as a leader but as a fast-follower that defined and controlled the new business network. With over 150 million units of iPod sold in five years, and over 4 billion downloads, Apple redefined the way individuals search, purchase, consume, and share music in the transformed music network.

Apple's evolving leadership role in the music network offers useful lessons for other sectors: it grasped the role of the iPod and iTunes as part of the business network transformation. While Sony led with Walkman in the analog age (using cassette tapes) and with Discman in the early part of the digital age (CD-ROM), it did not successfully transform its business models to the network era. It let Apple specify the rules. Apple capitalized on the network effects of connectivity by making iPod compatible with both Mac and Windows operating systems. Then, it further extended its reach of network effects with iPhone and expanded the scope of influence beyond music to mobile telephony as well.

Transformations in the Healthcare Sector

There is little doubt that the characteristics of the healthcare sector in the next five years will be very different from today. The unfolding transformation to the network era poses profound challenges but also offers opportunities for companies involved in every facet of this sector. Given the thrust of this chapter on product leadership, I focus on those companies that design and deliver medical devices. These companies are required to transform away from standalone devices towards crafting strategies to capture value, with such devices becoming part of the critical information flow and service delivery. Figure 5.4 depicts the impact of the "three laws" in the healthcare sector.

Take the case of a device manufacturer such as Nonin, which designs and delivers a pulse oximeter medical device that indirectly measures the oxygen saturation of a patient's blood. Nonin and other companies producing similar devices have historically offered standalone oximeters but now are required to connect their devices to evolving healthcare networks. They need to assess how to effectively connect their devices to online network initiatives such as Microsoft's HealthVault (www.healthvault.com). Such network connections change value propositions to different constituencies in the ecosystem. Patients get freedom and independence to go about their daily activities without being tied to monitoring meters; the data can be sent through mobile phones and other personal devices without excessive intervention. Healthcare service providers obtain real-time data on patients for diagnosis and preventive intervention. With the HealthVault platform in place, device manufacturers allow consumers to move their data from a device to the Web, share it with others, and use it with other applications linked on the same platform. This case example highlights links involving three actors—consumers, healthcare providers, and

Figure 5.4   Healthcare Network

Bandwidth Law through connections to the network expands the range of healthcare diagnostics and telemedicine services possible

Metcalfe's Law reflected in connections to a broad range of patients and devices enabling interoperability and expanded services

Moore's Law impacting the design features and functionality of health monitoring devices and the evolution of the product architecture

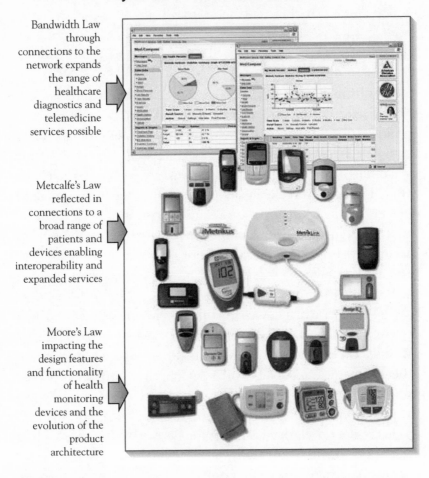

device manufacturers but could logically be expanded to cover a much broader healthcare network. From the point of view of product leadership in the network era, connectivity is compelling device manufacturers to rethink their role and value propositions in healthcare delivery.

This case example highlights strategic choices facing product companies about maintaining compatibility in networks. Now, look at the product compatibility choices facing Nonin (and other device manufacturers in healthcare): it has made its oximeter compatible with Bluetooth functionality (industry standard) and in line with Microsoft's HealthVault protocols. At some future point, when alternative protocols to Microsoft emerge, it has to decide whether to make its product preferentially connect with one or more systems or make them connect to all alternative platforms. Just as independent software product companies decide about compatibility choices (Windows versus Macintosh versus Linux), product companies in the healthcare sector will be called upon to make their products compatible with one or more competing healthcare platforms. Here, healthcare product companies should look to how software product companies have made choices about compatibility and interoperability as benchmarks since decisions about interconnections and interoperability will be central to marketplace success.

Now look at the transformation of healthcare from Microsoft's point of view. Microsoft is capitalizing on the trend that several health-monitoring devices are becoming digital (Moore's Law) with enhanced connection capabilities (Metcalfe's Law) that allow for systematic collection and analysis of complex data across diverse locations (thanks to Bandwidth Law). Its success will ultimately depend on the vibrancy of the ecosystem with multiple different device makers enabling their products to be compatible with HealthVault. Here, it brings its extensive experience to orchestrating platforms in software to the healthcare arena just as Apple brought its design superiority to the music sector.

This example shows the symbiotic nature of the interrelationships between the platform (e.g., Microsoft) and those manufacturing health-monitoring devices (e.g., Nonin). And as different alternative platforms in healthcare emerge (Google has already entered the fray and others are likely to follow), the transformation challenges become more complex and will impact how value is created and captured. Multiple different entities will be part of the transformation as healthcare delivery becomes more efficient and effective in the coming years.

Beyond Examples: Three Questions

The three examples provide initial ideas on how products transform their roles and functions when seen as part of the broader network of complementary products and service delivery ecosystems. The three laws discussed as part of the examples are at the core of the business network transformation. Some sectors may be slightly ahead but eventually, the three laws will impact every sector—albeit not in the same manner. Such shifts are not limited to these three examples but can apply in numerous settings. Instead of enumerating more examples, I pose a set of questions to motivate managers to think about their business strategy challenges in a network era.

1. What opportunities and challenges do you see to differentiate your products through digital technologies? Digital features can be added to more products than may appear plausible at first blush. Core product features can be enhanced and transformed with computer power as in Nonin's oximeters, GM cars with OnStar functionality, Ford cars with Sync features, and Apple with iPod and iPhone devices. Features and functionality of everyday products such as refrigerators and home alarm systems have increasingly embedded digital features.

So, examine ways to embed digital features within the core design of your products.

2. What opportunities and challenges exist to interconnect your products as part of emerging business ecosystems? Increasingly, products are embedded with other complementary products as part of evolving service and solution ecosystems. Lack of recognition products playing a role in business ecosystems means that companies continue to fine-tune their core competencies and may lose to companies that exploit their core connections in the ecosystems. Seeing products as part of the business ecosystems implies recognition that value lies not only in the core features of the product (see the previous question and discussion) but also in how the products interconnect and interoperate with other parts of the larger system. Nobuyuki Idei, Ex-Chairman of Sony Corporation, said it best: "Old Sony sold devices. New Sony will sell connections."[1] This vision is compelling as Sony is in the midst of a steady transformation away from a leader in selling electronic gadgets (TVs, music players, etc.) to one that is a key player in the broadband entertainment network. Idei's successor, Sir Howard Stringer, is navigating Sony through this tough and challenging transformation while many other consumer electronics companies who competed against Sony in the 1980s, such as Sanyo, Sharp, Philips, and others, have not so fared as well. Even in the case of Sony, the jury is still out on whether it has made a successful transformation to a network era.

So, examine how your products connect with other products and evaluate whether such interconnections enhance or diminish the value of your products.

3. What opportunities and challenges are possible when products are connected to the network with increased bandwidth? Many product managers may be well aware of the role their products play in emerging business ecosystems and may have already transformed their strategies and tactics to adapt to those requirements. This question expands their strategic thinking to recognize the transformation possibilities when products are connected through high bandwidth to the network. Take for instance, Dell's recent service offering—remote access.[2] For an additional fee, consumers can remotely access the computers on their home network, share files, access and manage their computer files through mobile phones, as well as use computers for home security, etc. What Dell has done is to shift the basis of customer value from the core product—which is being steadily commoditized—to services wrapped around the product that can be delivered thanks to the impressive improvements in the bandwidth speed in fixed and mobile networks. While other PC manufacturers—essentially delivering devices embracing the Windows platform—strive to differentiate on the basis of limited design features, Dell is pushing beyond the core product to creating new value features through connections. Such services need not necessarily be limited to only PCs but can be extended logically to other settings as in the case of GM OnStar's ability to deliver remote diagnostics and related services.

So, examine how high bandwidth connections alter product features and create new avenues for service delivery.

These three questions serve to examine opportunities as well as challenges faced by companies that are in the middle of shifting away from the established approaches and practices of the industrial age. We need to go beyond prescriptions that call for refinements within an industrial-era rulebook without placing information technology—digitization, connectivity, and bandwidth—at the center. In contrast, I urge managers to place the context of transformation (the shift from industrial age to network era) at the center of strategic discussions while still recognizing the importance of outsourcing non-core activities, global offshoring of business processes, and restructured supply chains as appropriate.

The three questions are to be addressed together because focusing on any one is incomplete and unlikely to yield robust new insights. For example: the Internet-enabled refrigerator from LG Electronics launched in 2003 has not been a success. Now Whirlpool has launched a variation on the idea that shows an understanding of the importance of the product architecture (open instead of closed) with more attention on how the refrigerator is part of the broader network of kitchen and cooking. Whirlpool refrigerators have a docking station that accommodates different digital devices[3] and is similar to Ford Motors accommodating different devices within the cabin of its cars. Over time, refrigerators will become nodes to influence the kitchen network. However, more building blocks need to be implemented to receive seamless integration of supply chains, beginning with the requirements in the kitchen and ending with the delivery of required supplies back in the kitchen. The kitchen network will connect with consumer products goods and logistics and will evolve to deliver more compelling value propositions in the future.

So, the central message of this chapter is: most managers today formulate their strategies by allocating critical resources to strengthen their core competencies and maximizing their firm-specific strengths. Firms competed as autonomous entities with competition between autonomous firms within well-defined industry boundaries. Such firm-centric views of strategy may have recognized the first question posed above but may not have focused on the two other questions. Taken together, these three questions shift the frame of strategic choices of product companies to a network-centric perspective with a more compelling view of business transformation.

Now, many firms find themselves in situations where their strategies are becoming network-centric. As firms are embedded within networks of relationships, their drivers of competitive advantage are not wholly limited to what they control within their boundaries. A corporation is not an isolated entity but is embedded in a network of relationships tied through joint ventures, cooperative R&D, marketing agreements, complementary product connections, patent licensing, equity investments, and interlocked memberships on boards. Firms are no longer just portfolios of products (or businesses); they are portfolios of capabilities assembled and orchestrated through a wide range of business relationships in dynamic ecosystems.

Embarking on Business Network Transformation: Call for Action

In order to take advantage of the emerging opportunities for network-centric products, companies must take four key steps towards transforming their business networks. Companies must carefully consider each of the following steps individually yet maintain a coherent overall strategy to achieve them in parallel. Additionally, the analysis in each step must include a plan for managing the IT resources that will be required to successfully implement each step.

1. Influencing the Key Shifts in Product Architecture

Business network transformation is shaped by shifts in product architecture—especially when the three laws together impact the features and functions of products. The case for business transformation of product companies begins with the recognition that the product architecture will undergo major changes with digital add-on features and services wrapped around core products. Thus, the rationale for transformation is made not to merely rectify incremental weaknesses in the current ways of organizing; it is made to create new ways of organizing the activities inside a firm and with partners in ecosystems. The transformation agenda is about envisioning different avenues for winning in the emerging networked landscape and developing a plan of action to assemble the required capabilities through relationships.

Start by sketching out how the three laws are likely to impact the product architecture of your portfolio. Some changes may be under your control while others may be impacted by actions of your competitors and complementors, as well as new entrants in your market. Just as competitive analysis in terms of "five forces" shaped strategic actions in the industrial age, mapping the impact of three technology laws as drivers of business network transformation guides strategic alternatives and actions in the network era.

The three laws impact the architecture of a single product line as well as the entire portfolio. For example, in the case of Sony, the three laws influence a product line such as televisions as well as the entire product portfolio. Newer televisions from Sony linked to the Net make possible the convergence between television and Internet, thus challenging traditional business models in media and entertainment. The product architecture of television transforms to recognize the role of complementary devices and seamless connectivity to different sources of entertainment. Beyond television, the three laws impact the trajectory of evolution of the architecture of Sony's product portfolio that includes computers, music players, videogame consoles, and others. Linking this evolution to the transformation of business strategy is fundamental to Sony's business performance. So, Sony's ultimate success will depend on how well its business network transformation plans are aligned with its product portfolio's architectural shifts. Looking at the shift in the architecture of single products provides detailed insights into how specific products transform for the network era. Correspondingly, analyzing the architectural shift of the portfolio in its entirety provides insights into broader strategic capabilities required to win in the transformed marketplace.

So, a company such as Sony can influence the architectural shifts in two different ways. One is to focus on product architecture *in design* as in Sony's specification of how it seeks to create interoperability across products within its product portfolio. The other is to focus on product architecture *in use*. Dell's introduction of remote services has not changed the design architecture of the personal computers or the laptops. Nor has it really changed how it sources, manufactures, and distributes the computers, but it has impacted the architecture in use. By understanding how end-consumers use their products in different situations, Dell has been able to deliver new services that take advantage of the fundamental principles of Metcalfe's Law of Connectivity and Bandwidth Law of Speed of connections and interactions on the Web. While the product architecture in design may still be controlled by Microsoft (and Intel), Dell is seeking to influence the architecture in use. In a similar vein, my assessment is that Sony has focused on architecture in-design more than on architecture in-use thus far.[4]

In a similar vein, the architecture of the automobile is changing with more computerization and network connections. GM OnStar is focused on delivering services related to safety (linked to the car) and convenience (for the driver and passengers). In contrast, Ford Sync (in partnership with Microsoft) does not directly impact the car while providing entertainment and convenience features for the driver and passengers. Taking the three laws together, we can conceive of automobiles in terms of three-layered product architecture: hardware layer (the "chassis"), the software layer ("electronics"), and services layer (navigation, entertainment, safety and maintenance, insurance, etc.) with GM and Ford adopting different approaches.

And over time, there will be further shifts in the architecture of the automobile as a product and the broader industry itself. We are in the early stages of business network transformation as the automotive industry shifts away from designs for gasoline-powered vehicles towards designs for hybrid and electric-powered vehicles with greater role for digitization and connectivity. The larger question, then, is: who gets to control and influence the product architecture in the automotive industry—the traditional automakers or software companies such as Microsoft or other new entrants?

So, think about influencing the shifts in product architecture for offensive reasons: what can you proactively deliver to enhance the scope of services and reap additional revenue as in the case of GM OnStar and Dell? Think about it also for defensive purposes: will your competitive advantage be eroded and marginalized by someone else designing the new product architecture as in the case of Apple against traditional music labels? Treating product architecture as if it is entirely controlled by any single firm is myopic and does not recognize the broader shifts to how products are embedded in complex, dynamic business ecosystems.

2. Maintaining Control of the Cash Register

Business network transformation is not just about enhancing operational efficiency. It's equally about seizing control of the cash register as the network transforms. So, the call for action should focus on the likely shifts in value creation and capture. The way to engage senior business managers in discussions of business transformation is to sketch out how the discontinuities might impact drivers of revenue and margins. Nothing gets the attention of senior managers more than a compelling presentation of how the current sources of profits could be challenged and threatened. Those product companies—historically comfortable charging for stand-alone products—need to rethink the location of cash registers when products are embedded as part of service and solution ecosystems. The shift in cash registers also implies corresponding changes in the competencies that are required for success and relative roles and positions of different entities within the ecosystems.

Consider the transformation under way in the digital music business. Apple has usurped control over pricing decisions away from the music labels. In doing so, it has shifted the location of cash registers away from the point of production and packaging (traditionally under the control of the music labels responsible for bundling songs in an album or CD) to the point of consumption (at the time of downloading the music track on an individual basis). Apple's ability to mastermind this shift is due to its fundamental control over the evolving industry architecture influenced by the three laws discussed in this chapter.

The healthcare sector is prime for major shifts in the cash registers as part of the business network transformation under way. Initiatives such as Microsoft HealthVault, Google Health, WebMD, and others are challenging the traditional modes of charging fees for services. A casual look at these initiatives may lead one to conclude that these initiatives focus on capture and consolidation of information. A deeper look into how companies seek to monetize these initiatives (beyond advertising) may yield clues into how streams of cash flow (and value capture) could change. Just as telematics influence auto insurance premiums indirectly, these initiatives could restructure the distribution of revenue and margin among different players in the evolving healthcare delivery network.

The burning platform for business network transformation is the shift in drivers of revenue and profit margins. So, map the current model of financial flows not just focused on your company but on the entire ecosystem. Then, examine how the shifts in the product architecture (as discussed earlier) impact financial flows and more specifically, your profit margins. Microsoft faces this challenge as it struggles to figure out a profitable way to migrate its suite of services online (cloud computing). Television networks face the challenge of maintaining control over advertising revenue under conditions of personal digital video recorders (e.g., TiVo) and online streaming over the Net. The call for action in business network transformation is that it creates discontinuities in patterns of value creation and capture within ecosystems.

3. Positioning in Dual Ecosystems

Business network transformation challenges how firms position themselves in different ecosystems to acquire complementary resources for success. Under steady-state conditions, network positions are relatively easy to structure and manage. However, under transformative conditions, there are at least two equally critical ecosystems—one for supporting the implementation of the current product architecture and another for shaping the new product architecture. The first type is familiar to most companies that have used partnerships and sourcing relationships. Dell's global supply chain is a good example as is Nike's arrangements with different tiers of manufacturing partners for translating their distinctive designs into physical products. However, as Nike recognizes sneakers not as a standalone product but one connected to Apple iPod, the scope and boundary of ecosystems change to recognize the shifting product architecture. The new product architecture involves not just Nike (and its traditional supply chain) but also newer players such as Apple. And over time, Nike (and Apple) will have to decide if the functionality will remain exclusive to their respective products or will become more open to others. Nike's positions in these dual ecosystems specify how it makes superior profits with physical products (Nike) and digital connections (Nike +).

Structuring and managing positions in dual ecosystems is not limited to Nike. Similar challenges exist for every company that finds itself in complex, fast-changing ecosystems. Take, for instance, the videogame sector. Companies such as Sony, Microsoft, and Nintendo need support from videogame developers for their current generation of videogames on their specific hardware consoles (PS/3,

Xbox/360, and Wii, respectively) while at the same time striving to create different ecosystems as they transform their business models to online gaming. In this transformation, the game developers that support the sales of hardware consoles may be different from those whose collaboration may be required to transform to the next generation of gaming online. The transformation cannot be achieved alone but requires the cooperation of selected complementors. This is mainly because the competencies that are required for games that run on consoles may be different from those for online games. The challenge facing product companies is the need to manage the delicate dance between these two generations of games, since some game developers themselves may be wanting to transform from consoles to online gaming but may not have the requisite level of competencies as seen by the videogame platform players such as Microsoft or Nintendo. So, managing conflicting requirements and capabilities within these different ecosystems is a key challenge for business network transformation.

So, map your key current relationships to understand your positions of advantage in the current ecosystem. Then, map how shifts in product architecture realign positions in emerging ecosystems. I have found such maps to be useful to identify how some partners play useful roles in supporting the current business model while others play critical roles in shaping new business models. The map also highlights those few players that function as hubs with core capabilities across both ecosystems. Recognizing the differential roles of partners in contributing capabilities for success and managing the portfolio of relationships is a key requirement for success in networks.

4. Defining Business Footprint

Network transformation ultimately changes the business footprint of corporations. Hence, it is legitimately on the senior management agenda and involves specification of core activities to be carried out within firm boundaries (scope), investments in those capabilities that drive uniqueness and differential value creation (capabilities), activities that need to be coordinated with partners across the dual ecosystems (relationships), and patterns of global offshoring and outsourcing activities to be pursued (sourcing).

Successful firms fail because they do not adapt to the changing requirements: they stick to their erstwhile model of success even as the business landscape has shifted, and they continue to rely on a prior set of partners even as their contribution has waned. They incrementally modify their business footprint while the business conditions have radically changed. In short, they trap themselves into their known repertoires, which have outlived their relevance and currency.

Take a look at Apple's products engraved with the slogan: "Designed by Apple in California...Made in China." With this slogan, Apple's bold statement is that "design" is a high-value activity (its scope and capabilities), leaving manufacturing to its global supply chain partners (relationships and sourcing). Increasingly, every company is to make strategic choices about scope, capabilities, relationships, and sourcing as it sheds unproductive assets and outmoded business practices. The core message of this chapter is that a company needs to think of itself not as a portfolio of independent products but as a portfolio of interdependent products created and delivered through a portfolio of relationships with partners in networks.

Time is right for product companies to systematically analyze their business models to recognize the role of three important technology laws. Such analysis will ultimately result in changes to the business footprint that will specify how choices of scope, capabilities, relationships, and governance impact business performance in the network era. Over the last decade, we have seen companies embrace outsourcing, partnerships, offshoring, and related business practices without an overarching vision for the transformed marketplace. Embracing such practices in a shotgun manner has not yielded sustained benefits. Pursuing them within a broader framework of business transformation fueled by technology laws will help product companies to craft winning business models.[5]

Conclusion

The first decade of the twenty-first century is marked by profound shifts and uncertainties: companies find themselves in a global marketplace with fierce competition for resources, talent, technologies, and customers. The logic of winning that worked well in the last decades of the twentieth century seems ill-tuned to the requirements of the twenty-first century. The financial crisis during the second half of 2008 has compelled many to question core assumptions about strategy, organization, competition, and value creation. Managers, analysts, venture capitalists, and entrepreneurs are looking for robust principles that guide and govern business successes in the twenty-first century. The many rules based on how companies succeeded during the last century do not guide enterprises into the uncharted territories of today.

The future is not an extrapolation of the past. Success in the past is no longer adequate to guarantee success in the future. This chapter focused on product leadership in the network era shaped by three technology laws. Using telematics, music, and healthcare as case examples, this chapter motivated the need for product companies to think urgently to look at business network transformation. More products will connect to the network as cloud computing becomes a reality, and business network transformation will be a requirement for success. The call for action is based on shifts in product architecture, new drivers of revenue and margins, differential positioning in ecosystems, and changes in business footprint.

Chapter 6

Driving Collaborative Success in Global Process Networks

John Hagel III, John Seely Brown, and Gautam Kasthurirangan

Deloitte Center for Edge Innovation

The increasing competitiveness of the global business environment, the emergence of a flattening world,[1] and the surfacing of new business practices such as open innovation have forced firms to look beyond their existing boundaries for sources of competitive advantage. (See Chapter 8 for Henry Chesbrough's discussion of open innovation networks.) In recent years, informal networks have emerged as a new organizational form that helps firms to tap into the specialized capabilities of other firms in their ecosystem. The overall objective for firms behind these kinds of external collaborative efforts has been clear: to make their business activities more effective, efficient, and speedy.

The majority of companies, especially in the West, believe that the right way to manage their collaborative activities is to exercise a high degree of control and tightly manage the activities in their network. This high degree of monitoring and control of their network partners tends to limit the number of partners that a firm can manage at any time as complexity overheads and transaction costs escalate with the addition of large numbers of participants. (See Chapter 9 for Jeffrey Dyer's discussion on the role of trust in business networks.)

The other disadvantage associated with this kind of tightly controlled activities is loss of flexibility. Take, for instance, a factory fire at LG Chemicals, one of the primary battery suppliers for

HP's laptops, that shuts down production for an extended time period. The shortage of batteries significantly cripples HP's laptop assembly line, resulting in production delays that in turn trigger domino effects with logistics providers and retailers. In tightly controlled networks firms can end up making significant investments in platforms or infrastructures that are very specific to the transactions involved. These investments that are tightly customized to individual business partners increase the risk of introducing an inertia that significantly impedes the firm's flexibility to react to any significant technology or market shifts. For example, investments in expensive infrastructures specific to the collaboration, which cannot be easily redeployed to other operations, can significantly increase the exit barriers that firms encounter in the collaboration. The firm may perceive that they are "locked in" to the particular relationships and may be unable to leave the collaboration even if the collaborative environment turns out to be unfavorable.

Compared to the drastic consequences experienced by HP, Hong Kong–based apparel manufacturer called Li & Fung was able to deliver on their deadlines to customers spread all over the world, even following the September 11 attacks when the global transportation system was crippled for a few weeks.

So what do companies like Li & Fung do differently to avoid the downside risks of outsourcing critical parts of their production and supply chain processes? In this chapter, we will explore the ways that leading companies leverage the power of their business networks by putting into place the right business processes, incentives, and relationship management techniques to flexibly adapt to changes rapidly and exploit the value-creation capabilities of their entire network for competitive advantage.[2]

Li & Fung: An Example of a Classic Orchestrator

Li & Fung is one of the largest supply chain management companies in the world, managing the supply of high-volume, time-sensitive goods through a network of more than 10,000 partners located all over the world. Li & Fung began as a small company in Guangzhou province in China in 1906 and specialized in trading classical Chinese items such as porcelain and bamboo. The company remained small in its first 50 years. During the 1960s, the company relocated to Hong Kong and began exporting clothes, toys, and other products. In the early 1970s, two brothers, Victor Fung and William Fung, who were the third generation of the Fung family, took over the reins to run the family business. Through a series of transformations, the company expanded rapidly. Today the Li & Fung Group is a multinational group of companies with staff based in offices in 40 countries worldwide and enjoying total revenues of close to US$14 billion. They are also one of the leading suppliers to almost all the top apparel brands in the U.S.

What really sets Li & Fung apart from any other apparel manufacturer is that they do not operate or own a single manufacturing facility. They execute projects by leveraging a rich network of more than 10,000 providers in over 50 countries. For every project, they assemble a set of specialized network participants who each manage different stages of the integrated Buy-Make-Sell process—from procurement of raw material and various production and assembly operations to export and shipping operations. As an example, to assemble a sweater requested by a European retailer, Li & Fung may procure a specific kind of wool from New Zealand, acquire zippers or buttons from a supplier in Indonesia, and may get it knitted and assembled by a manufacturer in India, who would then ship it to the European end-customer. Design capabilities are also part of their network.[3,4]

Key to Li & Fung's success are the loosely coupled interactions they manage across their growing network of partners. Li & Fung would have never been able to develop this scale of global network if they had to tightly define and monitor the specific activities of each of their providers. The nature of this loose coupling and the operational approaches required for its success will be discussed later.

Li & Fung is a classic example of a pure orchestrator who excels at managing end-to-end networks from generation of the order to delivery of the finished goods. (See Chapter 1 for Geoffrey Moore and Philip Lay's discussion of orchestrators in collaborative networks.) All activities of the buy-make-ship processes are executed by specialists external to Li & Fung. We describe these kinds of collaborative arrangements as *global process networks* (GPNs), a variant of the collaborative networks described by Geoffrey Moore and Philip Lay in their introductory chapter. These networks are actively managed by an orchestrator who mobilizes a large and diverse set of highly specialized companies on an end-to-end basis across the extended core operating processes of a business through loosely coupled interactions shaped by long-term, trust-based relationships. As a result, they are a distinctive subcategory of business networks, offering key advantages of scalability in coordinating the activities required to deliver high performance in core operating processes.

Difference Between Process Networks and More Traditional Management Approaches

Western companies generally tend to adopt a very risk-averse and short-term view towards managing their business collaborations. They do not spend significant time or resources in building long-term trust-based relationships. Instead they generally focus on short-term value maximization strategies. Long-term trust-based relationships help firms minimize costly monitoring and control mechanisms, thereby allowing firms to collaborate with a larger number of partners with lower transaction costs. (See Chapter 9 for Jeffrey Dyer's discussion on the value of trust in business networks.)

Western companies, in their pursuit of efficiencies, also tend to develop hard-wired approaches in managing their external partnerships. Activities are specified in high detail (usually through service-level agreements and contracts) and monitored with equal precision to ensure performance. While this approach has helped managers become more efficient in their internal operations, severe limitations crop up when this approach is applied to managing their external partnerships. The degree of monitoring and control of their network partners can significantly limit the number of external collaborations a firm may manage at any time. As the number and diversity of the external participants increase, these hardwired approaches to managing the collaborations can become expensive and very easily break down.

By employing loosely coupled systems, global process networks can help firms retain select benefits of these hard-wired approaches while also benefiting from advantages of scalability, flexibility, and rapid performance improvement in their network operations. This distinctive combination of loosely coupled interactions and long-term trust-based relationships tend to differentiate process networks from many of the most common examples of open innovation, which tend to be much more focused on isolated transactions within a much more broadly defined product development process. (See Chapter 8 for Henry Chesbrough's discussion of open innovation in business networks.) Global process networks also provide the management capability to extend loose business collaborations across geographic boundaries, differentiating them from the kind of localized collaboration networks that one typically finds in individual geographic clusters like Silicon Valley.

Process networks can be employed across a wide range of core operating processes of a business ranging from supply chain processes as we had seen in the Li & Fung case to employing process networks for product development efforts. Two such cases that we will discuss are Dachangjiang, a Chinese motorcycle manufacturer, and Portal Player, a Silicon Valley company developing platforms for MP3 players. Process networks can be used by firms to coordinate complex customer relationship management (CRM) processes. Cisco Connection Online (CCO) is designed to be a one-stop-shop package for customers. The portal provides configuration tools that help customers identify their needs and customize the Cisco products they would like to use. Cisco maintains collaborative relationships with over 40,000 specialized providers who offer complementary products or services supporting Cisco's platform. CCO provides qualified leads to appropriate network participants and helps to orchestrate on behalf of the customer a broad range of services extending from site preparation, delivery, and installation to helping customers get more value out of the products once installed. Cisco guarantees the quality of the products and services offered by their providers by setting stringent qualification criteria and having them go through a rigorous training and certification program. In this way the CCO program has allowed Cisco to add unique value to their products or services while also allowing them to strengthen their relationships with customers.

Global Process Networks Have Been Successful in Many Diverse Industries

Since the early 1990s, the Chinese motorcycle industry has witnessed rapid expansion. Rising from almost negligible exports in the 1980s, today Chinese motorcycle manufacturers account for almost 50 percent of the world's supply of motorcycles and prove to be significant competitors for the Japanese leaders in the motorcycle industry. The motorcycle industry in China during the early 1980s was dominated by tightly controlled state-owned enterprises where almost the entire process from design to manufacturing took place in-house. Today, there is a large number of private manufacturers who produce brands such as Jialing, Jianshe, Sun, and Qingqi (Light Ride). Many of these manufacturers tend to be clustered in the Chonqing province in Central China. This province is also home to a large number of motorcycle part manufacturers who contribute to this growing ecosystem.

One leading motorcycle manufacturer located in this province is Dachangjiang. Established in 1991, the company has grown rapidly to become a leading motorcycle manufacturer. Very early on, Dachangjiang realized that to be competitive, they would have to provide low-cost products while at the same time maintain a high degree of quality. They began by taking the tightly integrated product architectures of traditional Japanese motorcycle manufacturers and unbundling these architectures into relatively self-contained independent modules with well-defined interfaces. But the real innovation of these manufacturers was to develop a modular approach to the design process, mobilizing a large number of specialized subsystem and component manufacturers in the design process. Dachangjiang provides rough design sketches to the participants in its network along with very aggressive performance targets in terms of price points and quality metrics that each component had to meet. The individual participants then have the autonomy to make significant improvements to their components as long as they are consistent with the overall product specifications. Participants are expected to identify and independently resolve any interdependencies in design across the various components.

A high degree of competition among participants in the network helps drive significant cost and performance improvement. Independent of Dachangjiang's intervention, the suppliers coordinate with each other, ensuring that their components are compatible with each other and thus minimizing costly delays due to unnecessary iterations. The local restaurants and tea shops in the vicinity of the firm serve as hotbeds for social networking among the participants while also facilitating coordination of activity. In an informal setting, the participants share among each other important design information necessary for interoperability between their parts and also iterate over alternate designs and prototypes.

This approach of recruiting large numbers of highly specialized providers and orchestrating the interactions in these process networks allows Dachangjiang to develop low-cost, high-quality motorcycles at a rapid pace. The result has been Dachangjiang's emergence as one of the largest motorcycle brands in the domestic market. Dachangjiang's motorcycle brands have also been voted as the top motorcycle brand in China for three years in succession since 2006.[5]

More broadly, largely as a result of the initiative of process orchestrators like Dachangjiang, China has come to be known as a major exporter of motorcycles in the world. The average export price of a motorcycle has fallen from $700 in the late 1990s to as low as

$200 in 2002 without any meaningful decline in performance or reliability. Faced with this kind of competition in high growth export markets such as Vietnam, Chinese motorcycle manufacturers have been aggressively taking share from traditional Japanese manufacturers. For example, Honda's market share in Vietnam fell from 90 percent to 30 percent in three years since the entry of Chinese motorcycles in 1997. Between January and September of 2008, the combined production of all the Chinese motorcycle manufacturing firms stood at about 8.6 million units, and production is expected to go up to 10 million units for the next year.[6]

PortalPlayer is another company that proved to be an exemplar in successfully orchestrating a process network to support its product development efforts. Few people have heard of PortalPlayer but everyone is familiar with the iPod, one of the most successful consumer products of the 2000s. Tony Fadell, an independent contractor and engineer, pitched the idea of combining a Napster-like music service with a hard drive–based MP3 player to Apple in 2001. Tony was soon hired and given the responsibility of developing this player, later to be known as iPod. Fadell approached a firm called PortalPlayer, a smaller entrepreneurial start-up in Silicon Valley, to leverage the global design network PortalPlayer had been cultivating for several years to drive aggressive product innovation in the emerging MP3 player product category. The collaboration with PortalPlayer was a key factor in delivering a successful product to the marketplace in a compressed time frame of about nine months. In terms of the iPod product itself, Apple focused on the external design and the design of the user interface, while relying heavily on PortalPlayer and its global process network to deliver the high-performance platform within the iPod.

PortalPlayer, a technology development company headquartered in Santa Clara, California, has major offices in the U.S. and India and employs a little more than 200 employees worldwide. PortalPlayer, Inc. had been founded with the goal of developing robust product platforms for the emerging MP3 player product category and licensing these platforms to major consumer electronics companies to commercialize under their own brand names. They first developed a robust product architecture for the controller chip that supported modular development of the various components required to deliver a high-performance music experience.

Once again, though, the real breakthrough for PortalPlayer was to take this modular product architecture and use it to move to a much more modular approach to the design process itself. This enabled PortalPlayer to mobilize a global network of deeply specialized technology players to engage on the difficult performance challenges of designing a small, portable music player with high-quality sound and low power consumption at an affordable price. Among many other participants, Wolfson Electronics and ARM technologies in the UK were assigned the task of the chip design, LSI Logic performed the product testing, Toshiba and Sony in Japan undertook development of the hard disks and the battery technologies, respectively, and finally a few Taiwanese companies were contracted to fabricate and manufacture the chip. After delivering the first prototype, PortalPlayer continued delivering newer versions in rapid waves, with each version becoming cheaper and superior in performance relative to the previous versions.

Platforms like PortalPlayer, in which systems are designed and verified by a range of specialist companies who possess deep knowledge and expertise in their respective fields, offer fewer worries to a company that is in a rush to market. The three cases presented above represent companies that significantly leveraged global process networks in industries ranging from the low-technology apparel industry to the emerging technology products in the electronics industry. All these companies can be classified as pure orchestrators, since they rely on their network participants to undertake either product development or manufacturing efforts in their entirety. Once the product architectures are modularized and the interfaces are defined, the participants take full responsibility for each of the modules. Making the transition from traditional management approaches to a much more innovative set of network-oriented management techniques will be challenging for most established companies, given the need for fundamental changes in their business processes, operating cultures, and mindsets. However, observing these orchestrators offers important lessons for all firms in the way they operate their networks and partnerships.

Key Operational Elements of Global Process Networks

All businesses involve some sort of collaboration; however, GPNs are highly effective and flexible due to a few key elements that differentiate them from traditional forms of collaboration. The following section outlines the core elements of a GPN.

Element 1: Product and Process Modularity. Modularity emerges as one of the key elements necessary for successful execution of these process networks. *Modularity* is generally defined as the property of a system where components can be separated and recombined. Typically, the modules tend to be structurally independent of one another while being functionally integrated with each other.

Modularity can be of two types—product and process modularity. *Product modularity* allows a product to be decomposed into a number of components and then these components can be mixed and matched in a variety of configurations. *Process modularity*, a relatively new concept, is the key element to successfully executing these GPNs. The modular approach begins with the orchestrator breaking the process into discrete modules of activities containing relatively independent clusters of activities. These modules can then be pulled apart and assigned to participants based on their expertise in that specific activity. Finally, the orchestrator takes the important responsibility of coordinating activities across these modules, with a particular focus on ensuring that the performance requirements are met as each hand-off occurs across modules to deliver the end product or service reliably while optimizing performance across the end-to-end process. Figure 6.1 illustrates this concept.

Figure 6.1 Depicting the Process Modularity Approach of the Orchestrator

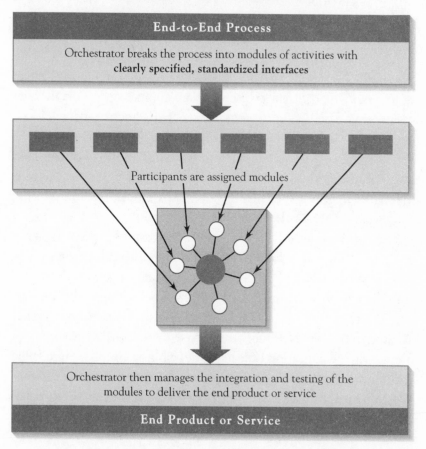

In all our examples, companies were seen to adopt a modular approach in their operations. While Li & Fung adopted a modular approach to its global supply processes, Dachangjiang and PortalPlayer adopted a modular approach to both their products and their development processes.

The modules must be designed in such a way that they are self-contained and the interdependencies between them are minimized. This strategy will allow the teams to independently work on the module and also minimize costly coordination costs between the teams working on the different modules. In the example of

PortalPlayer, the process modularization was performed in such a way that each company was given considerable latitude in the design of its individual components, coordinating with each other to address and resolve inevitable interdependencies. In this way, for example, ARM provided the core processor chip design while Sharp Electronics focused on developing the flash memory. Rather than specifying the design of individual components, PortalPlayer concentrated on defining overall system performance specifications and helping individual participants to coordinate with each other in resolving performance issues across components. PortalPlayer also coordinated all the project management activities such as managing deadlines, ensuring smooth interactions, and making timely payments for the participants' efforts.

Process modularity offers firms the opportunity to become more specialized, allowing them to effectively tap into their "core" capabilities while relying on specialist providers to supply the other complementary, or "context," resources. (See Chapter 1 for Geoffrey Moore and Philip Lay's concept of core and context processes.) Western companies have begun to wrestle with the threat of increasing specialization of firms in developing countries like India and China. Rather than trying to replicate these specializations, Western firms can create higher value by using process networks to access these specializations while concentrating their resources on honing their own core skills and competencies.

Element 2: Loosely Coupled Processes. The concept of loose coupling emerges as the key ingredient necessary for successful execution of these process networks. Loose coupling operates in stark contrast to other traditional ways through which firms manage their relationships with external entities. Typically, firms adopt a hardwired approach to managing their external relationships. Firms engage in extensive negotiations, draft out detailed and well-defined legal contracts with their partners specifying the activities and how they will be performed, and, once the agreement is put into effect, carefully monitor their partner's activities to ensure compliance. These challenges of micromanaging their partner's operations can quickly get aggravated as the number and diversity of participants increase.

Managers often confuse "loose coupling" with "loss of control." However, while these process networks tend to be loose in one dimension—the freedom to innovate—they are remarkably tight on another dimension: defining clear interfaces or "action points," where participants must come together and deliver outputs. By not overly influencing or controlling the activities of their partner's operations, process networks allow the orchestrator to fully tap into the capabilities of its partnering firm. For example, Dachangjiang is aggressive about defining specific output parameters for the modules being developed by the supplier. They, however, do not set any constraints on the development process that the supplier would be employing to make the subassemblies. Dachangjiang does not micromanage the development process, thus giving the suppliers the freedom to develop innovative solutions for the problem at hand. Hence, this kind of loose coupling helps maintain integrity and autonomy in the provider's operations, ensuring that the provider is able to effectively contribute in the design process.

For example, Li & Fung may give a Chinese yarn manufacturer the expected output specifications such as color of the yarn, thickness, grade, etc. Li & Fung would also clearly state the due date and output quantities that need to be shipped to another provider specializing in providing weaving services. Li & Fung undertakes a comprehensive due-diligence process to assess the capabilities of a prospective participant in their network. This assessment gives Li & Fung the confidence to rely on the provider's capabilities, thereby allowing it to monitor only the outputs (quality, due dates, etc.) from the modules of activity of each participant without continuously monitoring the internal activities of each participant.

When a diverse set of providers works together, there is also some likelihood that the providers may not have consensus on standards used in the collaborative process. For instance, do yarn buyers in Indonesia and yarn suppliers in Malaysia have a common way of determining what the color red should look like? Traditionally, in tightly coupled systems, the procuring company specifies unique terms for each purchase and treats each transaction as an independent event with its own uniquely defined requirements. However, in loosely coupled systems, orchestrators concentrate on defining inputs and outputs for each module of activities in ways that allow the orchestrator to quickly move companies in and out of specific processes. Hence, at the outset, it becomes imperative for the orchestrator to standardize the definition of module outputs and invest significant time in building shared meaning across all participants.

Once shared meaning is established within the network, the orchestrator can focus on rigorous specification of performance outputs for each process module. Li & Fung, for example, does this through a design kit. The design kit originates with the customer, who specifies the required specifications. In the case of a design kit for a particular type of linen, the specifications are typically composed of: the design name, sewing requirements, color chip, and yarn sample. Once Li & Fung receives the kit, it begins what is called a fabric creation process that involves multiple discussions with the customer design team or contract designer to finalize color, yarn size, and industrial feasibility (consisting of the feasibility of factories in the network to produce the fabric and color specified by the client's yarn requirement). Once the specifications in the kit are agreed upon, Li & Fung will begin the manufacturing process utilizing the kit specifications to guide the manufacturing activities.

Standardizing evaluation criteria for recruiting and assessing the performance of providers also helps bring more transparency and clarity in the system. Dachangjiang has a very transparent performance evaluation, and quality expectations are clearly communicated to the providers. This helps minimize unnecessary altercations and misunderstandings.

Loose coupling is a very scalable approach allowing firms to collaborate with a large number of participants with relatively little effort. The absence of extensive legal agreements, lengthy negotiations, and reliance on market-based incentives that can be tailored to shifting demand conditions allow firms to accommodate a significantly larger number of participants and lower transaction costs.

Conventional hard-wired approaches that firms adopt could never work in managing the network operations of more than 10,000 diverse specialists with rigorous performance requirements. Using loosely coupled processes may also have the advantage of being better able to manage fluctuating demand conditions. Firms can adopt an improvised approach, where depending on fluctuating demand conditions, they can increase or decrease the number of partners.

The traditional approach of managing a network is based on a push model where resources are made available dependent on anticipation of demand. In contrast, process networks offer a pull model, where resources are flexibly made available in response to changing market conditions. This gives the firm better flexibility to sense and adapt to external shocks in the environment. For instance, during the late 1990s when the Indian rupee began to rise against the dollar, Li & Fung were able to quickly redeploy their operations from India to Bangladesh and Pakistan, thus allowing them to keep the overall cost of production down. Similarly, after the September 11 attacks, Li & Fung quickly realized that they had a fairly high degree of exposure in countries that had a high degree of political instability. Within three weeks they redeployed their operations to other countries that were more politically stable. Li & Fung's operations are set up in such a way that if problems arise in any one provider, it can with minimum effort shift the activity from one provider to another. The absence of long-term binding contractual relationships also offers the orchestrator the convenience of an easy exit strategy from the transaction in case the conditions turn out to be unfavorable.

Element 3: Trust in the Collaboration.   As the operating environments for firms become even more complex, firms within a network must not just deal with broader uncertainty but also the inherent risk from each other's activities. Establishing trust throughout these networks has become an important way to deal with relationship risk and uncertainty. Trust serves as an important organizing principle in global process networks and gains fundamental importance in the management of these loosely coupled processes. (See Chapter 9 for Jeffrey Dyer's analysis of trust in business networks.)

The traditional assumption among managers is that trust is built organically as a consequence of repeated interactions and inevitably takes a long time to develop. This is a very static view of trust and may not be very useful to our case of network collaboration where the orchestrating company needs to establish a forward-looking way of establishing trust in the network. Since orchestrators rely on re-configurable networks, where they continually attempt to recruit new participants depending on the changing market conditions, approaches to promote trust may have to differ from the traditional approaches where trust evolved through prior interactions occurring over extended periods of time.

A high degree of dependence of one party on the other can negatively influence the degree of trust in this relationship. This is especially true when parties perceive that they do not have alternate options and that they have been forcefully locked into a relationship. This can lead to unhealthy dependency across firms, making it much harder to build and maintain trust.

To counteract the high dependency and risk that can develop over extended partner relationships, Li & Fung commits to never utilize more than 70 percent of a participant's capacity in their network, while at the same time committing to always engage at least 30 percent of a partner's capacity in any given year. This ensures that Li & Fung will have priority in its dealings with the participant, without the risk of the participant becoming totally dependent on Li & Fung. By engaging in operations outside of Li & Fung's, the participant is exposed to a wider range of other practices and thus has an opportunity to advance their capabilities as well as bring new learning into the network. Similarly, Dachangjiang works closely with their network participants to upgrade them and help them hone their technical capabilities.

In another example, Li & Fung saw a market opportunity for bathroom fixtures in the mid-market niche of an upscale retailer's home products line. The Li & Fung executive responsible for this client (Li & Fung also sourced a number of other products for this customer) connected this client to their network partner that had experience supplying low-end bathroom fixtures. This brokering move by Li & Fung helped the retailer secure a high-quality source of supply while also helping their supplier augment their customer base. Such acts by the orchestrators, where they are known to go beyond their contractual obligations and involve themselves in the provider's operations, help develop norms of trust and reciprocity and help minimize incidences of opportunistic behavior.

Long-term trust relationships also help maintain the stability of the network by minimizing the need to unnecessarily recruit new participants. Even though a participant might be excluded from one generation of PortalPlayer's platform, the participant was encouraged to remain in PortalPlayer's development network by the prospect of winning a spot in the next generation, which would be just around the corner. PortalPlayer continued to share with all of its participants key lessons from the current development effort, allowing them to keep abreast of the most recent development efforts.

Process networks, while allowing the orchestrator to leverage the specialized capabilities of their providers, also require the orchestrator to specialize. To successfully orchestrate a complex network, the orchestrator must have deep and specialized capabilities in their own domains as well as having a deep understanding of the domains of its participants. This helps develop trust and respect for the orchestrator's competencies.

Take, for example, Li & Fung. The participants recognized Li & Fung's deep expertise in the apparel industry, driven in part by Li & Fung's decision to hire in a group of managers who had run apparel manufacturing operations before. These executives could do a walkthrough of a prospective partner's operations and within 15 minutes tell exactly what this partner would be capable of executing even if the partner management team claimed otherwise. This experience and expertise helped to quickly build trust among partners that they were dealing with someone who knew what they needed and what would contribute to their success. These relationship managers could be very helpful to participants in troubleshooting their own operations and addressing any performance gaps that might exist.

Similarly, PortalPlayer would not have been able to assume a leadership position and successfully orchestrate the product development in less than nine months if they did not have a deep understanding of music compression technologies and unique power management issues encountered in small, portable electronic devices. Their deep understanding of MP3 technology allowed them to recruit the right partners, structure the interactions among the participants, and provide quick and accurate performance feedback to the participants.

Firms can undertake activities to accelerate trust building. The migration path towards establishment of trust lies along two dimensions designed to minimize unnecessary risk. On one dimension, firms may have the uncertainty that the provider may not adequately deliver and hence outsource low-value, noncritical tasks. On the other dimension, firms can instead begin with specifying all parameters of the process with a high degree of monitoring and gradually migrate to just specifying critical outputs. Depending on their requirements, firms can begin the migration process along any dimension, but the migration path will resemble the staircase model, which alternates along the two dimensions as shown in Figure 6.2. The migration transitions from outsourced activities that have limited value, with all parameters of the activity being tightly specified, to high-value activities that are loosely coupled and outsourced across a large number of participants.

Element 4: Productive Friction Among the Players. Bringing together specialized players and having them work collectively is not an easy task. The different participants bring with them unique perspectives and capabilities. When these participants work together on real problems, there can be a clash of ideas and opinions between the participants. This friction can quickly turn dysfunctional, characterized by conflict, mistrust, and misunderstanding among the

Figure 6.2 A Staircase-Model Explaining the Development of Trust

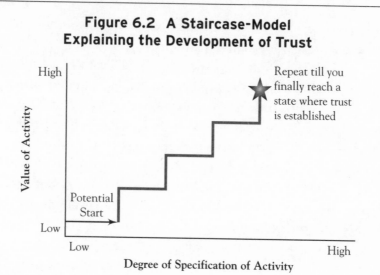

partners. The challenge for management will lie in avoiding this kind of dysfunctional behavior and harnessing this friction to create value for the firm. When these situations are managed properly, the interactions among the participants will be challenging, stimulating, and catalytic and it can lead to a multitude of new ideas and alternate options that can be explored and evaluated.

Process networks offer orchestrators the potential for harnessing productive friction as they bring together a very large and diverse set of participants who possess specialist skills in their respective domains. Early on, PortalPlayer's founders, who had experience developing technology for notebook computers, recognized the importance of developing components that had lower power consumption. Subsequently, PortalPlayer orchestrated joint problem-solving sessions, where the engineering teams from the different participants met, argued, and reviewed each other's ideas and designs leading to innovative solutions and ideas to solve the power consumption problems. In the same way, one of the DRM vendors had a technology that forced a long dead-space between songs, which became annoying to consumers. To solve this problem, PortalPlayer convened on their premises a group of experts in MP3 technology who worked with the DRM vendor to diagnose the cause and suggest alternative solutions.

Similarly, Dachangjiang was able to successfully harness productive friction among their specialized component and subsystem assemblers. Once the set of participants is recruited into the network and the output parameters were specified, the participants engaged with each other in parallel development efforts to develop new designs. Frequently, the parts developed by the suppliers failed to meet the stringent specifications set by Dachangjiang. Subsequently, the participants interacted and iterated over prototypes to develop alternate solutions.

Li & Fung was also successfully able to leverage the benefits of productive friction. In one instance, Li & Fung quality personnel discovered that there was a difference in the color of a fabric produced by three different factories even though the specification given to each factory was the same. To solve this problem, Li & Fung brought personnel from all three factories together in a brainstorming session to discover the root cause of the problem. The personnel jointly reviewed each other's manufacturing process and a joint solution was agreed upon.

The examples above show the benefits that firms may gain by bringing together a diverse set of specialists and encouraging an atmosphere of productive friction between them. However, in their quest for operational efficiency, Western executives have been conditioned to view friction as a wasteful activity and undertake efforts to remove any friction that occurs in these operating processes. Executives must learn to not just embrace this friction but more importantly to promote it and effectively harness it.

Achieving Productive Friction. Four key elements contribute to adequately building productive friction between the participants:

First, a strategy to generate productive friction begins with recruiting the participants who possess the right skill sets and capabilities and can bring to the table new and creative solutions to the problem at hand. As mentioned previously, loosely coupled platforms, where the scope and terms of the interactions are not strictly defined, allow firms to recruit a large number of participants and quickly scale up their operations. Second, the orchestrator must then explicitly state aggressive performance and output criteria that the providers are required to meet while not setting constraints on how this is to be achieved. This step is also synonymous with the design criteria for loosely coupled systems, which tend to be loose in one dimension, giving participants the freedom to innovate in their respective modules, and tight in other dimensions, defining clear interfaces or "action points." The next two key characteristics that help foster productive friction revolve around structuring and managing the interactions among the participants. The participants must be given the opportunity to interact with each other, allowing them to discuss and iterate around competing options for solving the problem at hand. Finally, to effectively harness and manage this friction among the participants and to bring resolution to the conflicts, orchestrators must set appropriate action points where participants must come together and resolve any potential disagreements that may prevent effective integration of the components and subsystem.

Possible Misconceptions Regarding Process Networks

To date, very few firms can be characterized as pure orchestrators—in other words, all activities of the value chain are undertaken by specialized entities who are external to the firm. We expect this will change as more firms begin to recognize the benefits from these process networks and begin to transform their business networks. The slow adoption of these process networks is partly due to the misconceptions that managers hold with regard to the usage of these process networks. Following are a few misconceptions that managers are likely to have regarding the usage of these global process networks.

Misconception 1: Process networks are better suited to commodity sectors where the product/process technology is not complex. My product or development process is way too complex for usage of process networks.

While some process networks operate in commodity-based or low-technology industries, there are other firms in high-technology sectors that are beginning to employ process networks in their product development activities. (See Chapter 1 for Geoffrey Moore and Philip Lay's discussion of volume operations versus complex systems.) PortalPlayer engaged in developing a robust platform for MP3 players, using relatively new technologies in an emerging technology and product category.

Similarly, a Silicon Valley not-for-profit organization called Myelin Research Foundation[7] (MRF) has begun to pursue research designed to help develop drugs to combat multiple sclerosis. MRF is undertaking this basic research and development effort by mobilizing academic researchers across traditional boundaries and developing relationships with commercial entities. The primary researchers in the MRF network had jointly accumulated about 125 years of research experience. While continuing to maintain their individual institutional affiliations, the researchers work together under MRF's collaboration infrastructure, which organizes data/video links, monthly conference calls, and joint research workshops conducted about three times a year. Conventional research techniques typically take about 15 to 30 years to identify and validate a single target suitable for drug development. However, MRF is hoping to cut the development cycle to about five years and seems to be on track towards meeting this goal.

An increase in the technological complexity of the product can increase the coordination costs as firms may feel the need for increased monitoring and control of the participant's operations. This may automatically discourage firms from outsourcing the effort to external entities. However, outsourcing these complex activities to external specialists may prove to be more economical and efficient using the innovative modular and loosely coupled management techniques of global process networks when compared to undertaking these high-risk and high-incidence of failure activities in house.

Misconception 2: My product is not modular—or not yet modular—and hence not ready for a process network approach.

In functions where high levels of technical uncertainty exist (e.g., early phase innovation) modularity can be inhibited and process networks may not prove to be very effective. However, PortalPlayer and the Myelin Repair Foundation are examples of firms who employed process networks in early phases of new technology development. Once a rough blueprint of the product architecture was developed, they managed to outsource the modules to specialist firms while continuing to work with these firms to refine the modules and the architecture.

For process networks to be applicable, it is essential that the process is modular. Product modularity is important but not essential. Take the example of Li & Fung in the apparel industry, where a typical product such as a shirt cannot be categorized as modular. Li & Fung was fully able to realize the benefits of process networks by taking a modular approach to the supply chain process. The supply chain was broken into distinct modules and specialists were employed to work on these modules. This example shows the importance of a modular approach and the potential value of adopting a modular strategy in the early stages of product design efforts. Even in cases when the product is not modular, firms often have the opportunity to break up other core operating processes like supply chain management or customer relationship management into individual modules and utilize the skill sets of specialists to develop these modules.

Misconception 3: I have intellectual property (IP) concerns and I am worried that my process network will lead to IP leakage or IP theft.

Successful execution of process networks entails some degree of knowledge sharing with the participants. In countries where the IP regime is considered weak, managers may fear that deploying process networks can increase the risk of IP theft. However, firms must take a balanced approach with regard to managing their IP. Fearing the risk of IP leakage, they can run the risk of becoming too closed and thereby not sharing critical information that may be necessary to access world-class specialization in complementary areas.

PortalPlayer had a balanced approach towards managing its IP strategy. PortalPlayer split the IP into two components—a "core" element and an "interfacing" element. PortalPlayer retained control over the core IP element, which was mostly comprised of the firmware in the controller chip. The interfacing components and the specifications that were essential for the participants to develop conforming technologies or products supporting the main platform were shared in the entirety with the providers.

Previously, we addressed the importance of modularity and the subsequent benefits of breaking the product or process into smaller modules with minimum interdependencies. Depending on the sensitivity of the IP information, the manager can choose the modules that need to be kept in house or outsourced under high supervision and control versus those modules that can be more readily shared. We have argued that trust is a key organizing element in managing these loosely coupled processes. The presence of trust helps develop confidence among the network participants, helping to minimize possible concerns that participants may improperly use the critical knowledge for their own benefit. Once again, the staircase of trust may provide an important tool in helping management to become more comfortable with sharing higher-value IP over time.

Pursuing a Pragmatic Migration Path Towards Orchestration

The large-scale global process networks that we observed in our examples were not created overnight. They tended to emerge gradually as firms undertook systematic efforts towards becoming an orchestrator. Following are some of the common steps that each orchestrator followed in its business network transformation journey.

Step 1: Identify the key operating processes: Most firms have three core operating processes—supply chain management, product innovation and commercialization, and customer relationship management. Typically, a company performs relatively better in one of these three core operating processes. If the company is under severe market-driven performance pressure in this core operating process, it might choose to focus on this one to launch its global process network initiatives in order to strengthen its performance by more effectively connecting with world-class performers. On the other hand, if it is performing extremely well relative to other firms in this core operating process, it may choose to focus on one of the two other core operating processes that are tending to drag down the overall performance of the firm. In this context, global process network initiatives may be viewed as a program to outsource increasing portions of this core operating process. Over time, as management skills are honed, the global process network approach can be extended to all three of the core operating processes of the firm.

Step 2: Define leadership accountability: Designate a senior executive with accountability for this core operating process to drive the global process network initiative. Make certain that this executive is held accountable for all end-to-end activities in the extended core operating process, not just the activities performed within the firm. The transition to a global process network approach will require significant organizational change and will likely run into resistance along the way, so a senior champion for these efforts will be key to ensure that difficult changes are executed successfully. This senior executive must enjoy status and visibility and command respect from the rest of the top management team members if he is to successfully champion this effort. The executive must also have adequate management control over the resources required to support a transition to global process networks.

Step 3: Modularize process activities: One of the first tasks of the senior executive will be to re-conceive the core operating process activities within the firm by clustering them into relatively independent and self-contained modules. Interfaces for each module will need to be carefully defined and standards established for specifying performance requirements from each of the modules. Management responsibilities may need to be reassigned to correspond more effectively to these new module boundaries and new, more tailored performance measurement and incentive systems may need to be implemented.

Step 4: Begin with existing partners: As the executive team gets more comfortable with the approach to loosely coupled modular management of core operating process activities within their own operations, they can begin by extending these management practices to their existing business partners in the extended core operating process. The modular clustering of activities and careful consideration of interface design and performance specification will be extended to the activities of adjacent business partners. In many cases, new relationship managers may need to be designated to provide relevant expertise in their partners' operations rather than simply being good at negotiating deals. These relationship managers will be pivotal in building long-term, trust-based relationships with these partners in addition to managing the loosely coupled interactions on a day-to-day basis. By pursuing the staircase of trust approach outlined earlier, they can more rapidly build trust while managing near-term risk as they gradually move from the monitoring of tightly specified activities to management of performance outputs.

As trust and shared understanding are strengthened, the relationship managers can begin to catalyze productive friction by specifying more aggressive performance targets. Particularly at the outset, they will need to orchestrate the interactions among their own personnel and the personnel of relevant partners in addressing these performance challenges to ensure that appropriate diversity of perspectives is engaged and that participants have reasonable action points when resolution of differences is required.

Step 5: Expand scope of process network: As the firm gains experience in applying these management techniques to existing partners, the management team can begin to expand the scope of its orchestration activities beyond its existing partners. Typically, this takes three forms. On one dimension, the firm can start to adopt a broader end-to-end view of the core operating process, reaching out to connect with participants in more distant levels or layers of the process. For example, rather than simply coordinating the activities of first-tier suppliers in a supply chain operation, the firm might begin to take a more active coordination role upstream until it ultimately connects with suppliers of key raw materials. On a second dimension, the firm can begin to identify key modules of external activity within the process where more specialized capability might be required to tailor the activities to specific market needs. For example, in customer relationship management, there may be a need for a broader range of expertise to deal with the different needs of customers operating in different industries. On a third dimension, the firm may become so confident with the advantages of global process networks that it may choose to outsource to specialized providers more of the modules of activities currently performed internally.

Few firms will ever become pure global process network orchestrators, shedding all of their own activities. On the other hand, most firms will find some way to profit from the advantages offered by these new network formations in terms of access to more specialized capabilities and the ability to accelerate performance improvement and learning both within and across participants. At a time when we are all discovering the downside of financial leverage, perhaps more companies will choose to explore the significant upside of capability leverage and learning leverage. Global process networks provide a powerful platform for exploiting this opportunity.

Note: The authors would like to thank Chetan Desai, Dieter Ernst, Jayant Lakshmikanthan, Leonard Lane, and Scott Wilson for their help in conducting and synthesizing research to support the development of this material. The data and information for all cases used in this study come from interviews conducted with executives in these firms. John Hagel III is co-chairman and John Seely Brown is independent co-chairman of the Deloitte LLP Center for Edge Innovation, where Gautam Kasthurirangan is a research fellow.

Step 1	**Identify the key operating processes to be used for deploying GPNs.** • Identify if the orchestration process is primarily going to be in supply chain management, product development, or customer relationship management activities. • Initial initiatives should be targeted against core operating process with greatest performance challenges.
Step 2	**Define leadership accountability.** • Identify a senior executive who can be given management control over all the resources required to support a transition to global process networks.
Step 3	**Modularize process activities.** • Develop relatively independent and self-contained modules. Interfaces for each module will need to be carefully defined.
Step 4	**Begin with existing partners.** • Develop necessary management experience by applying global process network practices to existing business partners.
Step 5	**Expand the scope of the network.** The firm can expand the orchestration activities by • Connecting to multiple layers of the process activities, or • Identifying key modules within the process where more specialized capability may be required and recruiting appropriate additional partners, or • Outsourcing to specialized providers more of the modules of activities currently performed internally.

Chapter 7

Operational Excellence

The New Lever for Profitability and
Competitive Advantage in a Networked World

Randall H. Russell

*Vice President and Director of Research,
Palladium Group, Inc.,
Executive Editor, Balanced Scorecard Report
(published by Harvard Business Publishing)*

Better. Faster. Cheaper. Every organization is grappling with these concepts today as economic uncertainty spreads around the globe. Instead of pursuing ambitious expansion plans, many organizations are focusing their efforts on short-term results. They are trying to identify what can be trimmed or eliminated in their operations to protect their profit margin or simply survive in the global marketplace.

But the current economy also offers a unique opportunity for businesses to transform their operations into an instrument of strategic competitive advantage. We observe that leading organizations are redoubling their efforts to find new ways to execute with greater efficiency and effectiveness—to achieve operational excellence without sacrificing the value their customers expect.

In the fall of 2008, prompted by emergent new thinking on business network transformations, innovative management processes, and powerful, next-generation technology, we embarked on a multistage research project to explore operational excellence with a fresh eye, repositioning the concept within the new context of linking strategy and operations across the entire business network. We initiated this research to show chief operating officers and key senior executives how to respond quickly to the near-term pressure to reduce costs without losing their ability to take advantage of future growth opportunities. As our research confirmed, cost efficiencies are the main source of profitability for companies, while improving the customer experience is the primary source of revenue growth. Both of these findings were confirmed by the 2008 Economist Intelligence Unit report, "The Collaboration Advantage," in which they found that cost savings and customer intimacy were the primary drivers for business network transformation initiatives. Certainly, achieving short-term survival is essential. But establishing a foundation for repeating these kinds of operational successes, while preserving the ability to pursue longer-term strategic objectives, is key to sustaining superior operational performance and competitiveness.

In this chapter we provide a brief overview of a six-stage model for building an operational strategy management system as described by Drs. Kaplan and Norton in their new book, *The Execution Premium*. We will discuss how the strategy management system extends into operational management and decision making by leveraging three key components: people, processes, and technology.

Our research also involved surveying 101 organizations representing a wide range of industries in order to explore the relationship between their management practices and the performance results they have achieved. Among our most important findings: IT, if aligned well with strategy, plays a very significant role in determining the ultimate chance of execution success. Integrated, end-to-end software solutions, together with operations governed by robust strategy management systems, constitute a proven method by which organizations and their entire business networks can achieve the Execution Premium.

As Jeffrey Liker has shown in his book *The Toyota Way*, "Toyota has turned operational excellence into a strategic weapon." More interestingly, Jeff Dyer's research on trust in partner relationships (see Chapter 9) shows that Toyota has extended that operational excellence into its shared processes with its suppliers and has reaped significant strategic rewards from those efforts. It is our hope that, by absorbing the insights from this chapter, you will have a much clearer understanding as to how you can quickly enable your organization to achieve operational excellence throughout your business network—and reach new levels of profitability and competitive advantage now.

Linking Strategy and Operations

Survey after survey shows that business leaders are increasingly recognizing the paramount importance of strategy execution. According to the Conference Board's 2007 CEO Challenge, "execution excellence" has surpassed profit and top-line growth as a focus for CEOs around the world. This recognition comes in the wake of numerous other studies over the past two decades demonstrating the widespread failure of organizations to execute strategy, from the two seminal *Fortune* articles that revealed that 90 percent of organizations failed to execute strategy,[1] to *Profit from the Core* author Chris Zook's finding that only 12 percent of companies successfully execute their strategy.[2] The public sector suffers the same failure rates, according to a recent Barron's survey that found that only 15 percent of federal government programs executed their strategies as intended.[3]

Those who don't merely recognize the importance of strategy execution, but act on it, get results. A 2006 Palladium Group survey of 143 organizations showed that of the more than half the respondents that were using a formal strategy execution management process, nearly 75 percent were outperforming their peer group. Among those without such a formal process, 75 percent were underperforming, or at most, matching the average performance of their peers.[4]

Executing strategy depends on a number of factors including, and perhaps most importantly, its effective integration with operations. As Balanced Scorecard creators Robert Kaplan and David Norton noted:

> A visionary strategy that is not linked to excellent operational and governance processes cannot be implemented. Conversely, operational excellence may lower costs, improve quality, and reduce process and lead times; but without a strategy's vision and guidance, a company is not likely to enjoy sustainable success from its operational improvements alone...

Companies generally fail at implementing a strategy or managing operations because they lack an overarching management system to integrate and align these two vital processes.[5]

Alignment between all the moving parts is crucial—from sharing a common understanding of the strategy and its goals to relying on an integrated model to design, measure, and monitor performance of day-to-day activities and strategic initiatives alike. Alignment—of people, processes, and technology—helps the organization optimize internal and network resources, opportunities, and performance. It enables the whole to create value that exceeds the sum of its parts.

All three components must be well established and well connected in order to achieve the following:

1. Ensure alignment between strategy and operations through the use of "strategic themes"
2. Transform existing processes (or introduce missing processes) across the business network by selecting the appropriate process transformation tools
3. Engage operational excellence "theme" teams
4. Optimize strategic decision making

Most experts concur: alignment is vital to successful, sustainable strategy execution. Alignment requires having a management process that integrates activities across traditional functional lines, along with information systems that enable and promote alignment. It depends on transparency.

This suggests that organizations today need a broader definition of operational excellence, one that takes into account operations' integral tie to strategy, one that looks at the overall operations of the business network, and one that considers strategy management itself as a process warranting performance excellence. And because we know that high-performing organizations review, refresh, and adapt strategy continuously, as the environment changes—whether, for example, due to internal innovation or a shifting competitive landscape—so must operations have a built-in capacity for ongoing improvement.

The Evolution of Operational Excellence

Traditionally, operational excellence has meant optimizing business processes, generally production and manufacturing. Its purpose has been to satisfy customer demand, improve quality, or boost productivity and efficiency. Over the past few decades, it has evolved to include not just process improvement (through quality programs, Lean manufacturing, or Six Sigma, for example), but also process automation (IT), or outright process redesign or reengineering à la Michael Hammer—the wholesale top-down deconstruction and reconstruction of a process to streamline and optimize it to best serve customer needs.

Certainly, operational excellence applies not only to manufacturing but equally to service-based businesses, many of which have adopted the rigorous disciplines of Six Sigma. It is also important in shared services and other internal partnerships. With the rise of the extended enterprise—businesses and their networks of interdependent relationships—it also applies to integrating with partners. Where these relationships include outsourcing agreements, the risks as well as the increasingly higher-level and higher-value processes involved demand attention to, and new requirements for, process management and operational excellence.

What Is Operational Excellence—
And Why Is It So Critical Today?

Operational excellence is, and has always been, about reaching the height of operational efficiency—doing things better, faster, and cheaper. No organization can afford inefficiency and waste, particularly in periods of belt-tightening. The tightly run, highly efficient organization can undercut competitors and win market share. Moreover, the ability of a company and its business network to respond and adapt to rapidly changing market conditions becomes a matter of survival.

But today, operational excellence means much more—and its implications are more far-reaching. While not a strategy in and of itself, operational excellence has enormous implications for strategy management and execution. Whether your strategy entails being the low-total-cost provider, being a product or service leader, or focusing more on customer intimacy, operational excellence as a supporting strategic theme is not just a foundation for survival (in good times or bad)—it's a key lever for improving profitability and competitive advantage.

The Three Components of
Operational Excellence

As we see it, operational excellence involves three factors. First, it means having the strategy management capability to identify and focus on the "right things"—those that will provide differentiated value to your customers. Second, it involves being excellent in executing that strategy—consistently doing these right things better, faster, and cheaper. Finally, and perhaps most importantly, it involves having the ability to ensure continuous improvement over the long term, for that is how operational excellence enables organizations to sustain operational performance and ongoing competitive advantage.

Often strategy management and operations management occur at different levels of the organization, with little interaction and, in some cases, no interdependence. Operations, quality, and engineering executives must recognize their link to strategy. Perhaps more important, senior executives must begin to acknowledge the role of process management in strategy execution—that operational excellence is inextricably tied to strategy excellence. And management itself must be viewed as a process (or set of processes) unto itself, one that often requires new processes and that encompasses the broad definition of operational excellence.

Like innovation (see Chapter 8), operational excellence need no longer be confined to a discrete role in product development or manufacturing. It can touch every organizational function and process inside and outside the company. Instead of a siloed approach—pursuing efficiencies within discrete areas (e.g., manufacturing, sales, procurement)—organizations can adopt an end-to-end approach that links business processes throughout the network, not merely internal functional areas, and that does so seamlessly across internal and external boundaries. In other words, organizations can unify all their operations—for example, manufacturing, procurement, and after-sales service—to run them as one. This end-to-end approach both requires and provides complete visibility throughout the process chain, which, in turn, promotes greater efficiency than could be achieved independently by silos. In fact, the 2008 Economist Intelligence Unit survey "Sustained Growth Through Operational Excellence" reported that 45 percent of responding senior executives chose "end-to-end visibility" into operations as the most important contributor to operational excellence. For example, organizations that close the loop in integrating the sourcing and procurement processes can maximize savings in four important ways: by being able to quickly identify savings opportunities, source the best supply base, optimize the value of the contract, and sustain the achieved savings. By instituting efficiencies in its entire procurement cycle, a major chemicals specialty manufacturer cut annual costs by nearly $6 million and increased on-time payments by more than 87 percent.

But operational excellence is not just about managing day-to-day operations with efficiency. Operational excellence is a way to foster continuous improvement. Achieving this benefit level, however, requires a fact-based understanding of operational performance. To address today's challenges and capitalize on tomorrow's opportunities, the COO and key operations executives must be able to define, monitor, and adjust actions aligned with the operational strategy and objectives (through, for example, the use of metrics and key performance indicators, or KPIs)—and, when necessary, change the organization's processes and performance objectives.

And here again, IT plays a central, strategic role.

Integrated applications—such as enterprise resource planning (ERP), supply chain management, and customer relationship management systems—coupled with performance management systems and advanced business intelligence systems and analytics, have triggered greater advances in operational excellence. Successful businesses go beyond delivering functional efficiency by bringing together all these applications to unify operations and ensure tight linkage between strategy and execution. This dynamic IT architecture helps to seamlessly link end-to-end business processes together, creating a holistic view of operations across the entire business network. By ensuring complete visibility across the business network, it also allows organizations to achieve extraordinary results. Not only does this transparency improve coordination and efficiencies, but it also enables real-time information flow, feedback, and adjustments. The net result: a closed-loop approach to strategy and execution that enhances collaboration, improves the quality of decision making—and heightens performance. A leading petrochemical company provides a perfect example. By streamlining its end-to-end operational processes with integrated software, the company was able to vault into the top ten position in its industry—just three years after it was founded. This world-class company enhanced its competitiveness and realized extraordinary bottom-line results, including eliminating more than $7 million in direct operating costs within a few months.

Today, integrated software delivered through open, service-enabled business process platforms enables companies to transcend corporate and national boundaries to manage entire business networks of customers, partners, and suppliers. These platforms can help create further competitive differentiation by allowing companies to reuse software capabilities, rapidly develop new processes, integrate with their partners, and drive cross-enterprise operational performance.

There's clearly no one formula for operational excellence. How your organization embraces it—whether as a top-to-bottom, pan-organizational, "meta" process, or as an approach that resides within prescribed internal processes—depends on the nature of your business, your business network, your organizational structure, and the processes you employ. Likewise, the benefits can be multidimensional, extending beyond cost savings to enhanced customer service, predictable compliance, indeed to enhanced overall (enterprise-wide) operational performance.

Key Obstacles to Achieving Operational Excellence

In many enterprises, operational silos, which have evolved organically as the organization has grown, represent the greatest single obstacle to allowing a holistic view of operations across processes and throughout the business network—and thus to achieving operational excellence. Silos affect manufacturing and service businesses alike. The resulting poor visibility applies not just to the lack of visibility of operational activities across the business network, but to the lack of visibility of the strategy as well as of performance. Without visibility, the organization cannot react quickly to change. Long-term planning is impaired. Among the many critical impacts of this inability is missed on-time delivery targets.

Inefficiencies in execution represent another obstacle. These include time-consuming manual and paper-based tasks (and the high number of errors that can result from non-automated processes), poor communication, redundant steps, and the inability to replicate efficiency globally. The result is costlier operations that erode margins.

Compliance and risk management are another problem area that can impede operational excellence. Some companies lack internal and/or external controls. Others may unknowingly be committing violations, or suffering from product quality or safety issues. This can lead to complaints, regulatory investigations, and high added cost from warranty claims, penalties, and even lawsuits. Recall the serious impact on U.S. toy manufacturers in 2007 when it was discovered that their manufacturing partners in Asia had used lead-based paint on children's toys without their knowledge.

Finally, a reactive and tactical operational culture, along with resource constraints, impairs operational excellence. Companies focus on day-to-day operations to the exclusion of the long-term, strategic view. They take a reactive, rather than proactive, approach to improvement and innovation. These attitudes and ways are often exacerbated by the lack of tools, resources, or skills. The result: a lack of competitiveness that translates into weaker performance against industry peers.

Linking Strategy and Operations: How the Execution Premium Model Can Help Organizations Achieve Operational Excellence

Kaplan and Norton's new architecture for a comprehensive and integrated management system explicitly links strategy formulation and planning with operational execution. In doing so, it helps organizations map all of the places where operational excellence should reside.[6] This architecture consists of a six-stage system (see Figure 7.1).

• **Stage 1: Develop the Strategy.** The organization clarifies its mission, vision, and values; articulates key issues and challenges; and identifies ways in which it can best compete.

Figure 7.1 Linking Strategy and Operations: A Six-Stage System

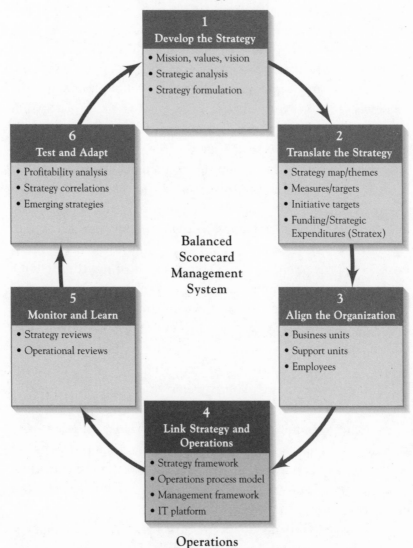

Strategy

1
Develop the Strategy
- Mission, values, vision
- Strategic analysis
- Strategy formulation

2
Translate the Strategy
- Strategy map/themes
- Measures/targets
- Initiative targets
- Funding/Strategic Expenditures (Stratex)

3
Align the Organization
- Business units
- Support units
- Employees

4
Link Strategy and Operations
- Strategy framework
- Operations process model
- Management framework
- IT platform

5
Monitor and Learn
- Strategy reviews
- Operational reviews

6
Test and Adapt
- Profitability analysis
- Strategy correlations
- Emerging strategies

Balanced Scorecard Management System

Operations

- **Stage 2: Translate the Strategy.** The organization describes its strategy (through a strategy map); develops strategic objectives, measures, targets, and initiatives, as well as budgets that guide action and resource allocation. It also creates cross-functional strategic "theme teams" to lead strategy execution.

- **Stage 3: Align the Organization with the Strategy.** Here, the organization aligns all business units, aligns support units with business unit and corporate strategies, and aligns and motivates employees to help execute the strategy.

- **Stage 4: Link Strategy and Operations (Plan and Execute Operations).** This stage is ground zero for linking long-term strategy with day-to-day operations. It includes creating an operational process model, linking strategy and operations through the use of a sales and operational planning process (matching demand and supply), budgeting to align strategic initiatives with operational processes, and identifying the most critical business process improvements. It also entails establishing the right IT platform to support the management of strategic processes and reporting and review capabilities—leveraging strategic dashboards and KPIs along with operational dashboards and KPIs. This chapter focuses primarily on this stage of the model, since it is here that the so-called "rubber" (the strategy) meets the "road" (operations)—and, thus, where operational excellence opportunities arise.

- **Stage 5: Monitor and Learn ("Is the strategy in place—and working?").** The organization ensures operational processes are under control; confirms that the strategy is being implemented; monitors and learns from strategic performance feedback; and ensures continuous improvement.

- **Stage 6: Test and Adapt the Strategy ("Do the fundamental strategic assumptions remain valid?").** This involves running profitability analytics to identify sources and size of profit contribution; testing the causal model of the strategy; and identifying and recommending strategic alternatives.

A Process Model: A Prerequisite for Process Management

To manage processes, the organization must have a process model. With a process view of its "universe" (encompassing itself and its network of customers and partners), the organization can determine whether instituting change to a given process or subprocess involves implementing a quality program or other improvement initiative, shifting responsibility for a piece of a process to a partner, or reengineering the process altogether.

Which model an organization uses is necessarily determined by the nature of its business, the capabilities of its network and its strategy. Different schools of thought prevail, from the more traditional or mechanical view (emphasizing the core processes, those focused on creating and delivering the products/services) to those encompassing all processes—including management, support, and ancillary processes such as overseeing regulatory compliance. The process-based view, first espoused by Michael Porter (with his value chain)[7] and reengineering guru Michael Hammer, identifies primary activities (such as inbound logistics, operations, marketing, and sales) and support activities (such as procurement, HR management, and technology development). More recently, the American Productivity and Quality Center (APQC), a leading organization dedicated to process improvement and benchmarking, developed its Process Classification Framework, a generic enterprise process model that identifies a whole taxonomy of operating, management, and support processes.

Four Mechanisms for Linking Strategy to Operations

To link strategy and operations across a business network, organizations need the following four key mechanisms:

1. **An Integrating Framework:** A common framework that allows for the integrated design of the strategy/operations

management system. The strategy map, with its strategic themes, is a useful framework because it describes the strategy and its components in a cause-and-effect manner, depicting the component themes across the functional areas implicated.

2. **A Linked Process/Measure Model:** An integrated model of the organization's operational processes (including specific activities demanded by the strategy), along with the relevant measures and targets. The Balanced Scorecard can be used to link strategic objectives and measures to the operational KPIs. This provides the mechanism for joining strategic scorecards with operational dashboards. Initiatives represent the activities that are used to introduce new processes or transform existing ones.

3. **An Integrated Management Process:** A mechanism that facilitates the integration of activities across traditional organizational silos, such as theme teams (governors) of the cross-functional strategic themes.

4. **An Integrated Information System:** Information systems designed to provide top-to-bottom and end-to-end alignment by strategic theme and process—and thus visibility throughout the business network. These integrated systems can help to align all operations to drive efficiency and effectiveness across the operational continuum and to facilitate decision-making by providing the right insights in the right business context.

Operational Excellence: Our Research Hypotheses

Our new expanded definition of operational excellence, and of the role of linking strategy to operations, is based on several hypotheses:

- The role of the strategy map, created by Kaplan and Norton as part of the Balanced Scorecard management system, in helping achieve higher levels of understanding and commitment among management team members through its depiction of operational excellence objectives.

- The importance of aligning strategy and execution to achieve operational excellence objectives.
- The need to align all operations, processes, and systems to achieve organizational excellence.
- The role of cross-functional strategic "theme teams" in managing operational excellence objectives, improving operational performance, and ultimately in achieving strategic goals.
- The importance of standardized, integrated, and networked technology in reporting and managing performance to enhance decision making.

To test our hypotheses, in mid-2008 we conducted an online survey of organizations that can be described as either generally interested in the Balanced Scorecard (i.e., those thinking about getting started) or those that are already somewhere along the road to a full-scale implementation. While ours is clearly a self-selected sample, we consider it representative of the general population of organizations since 61 percent of the respondents are already using a Balanced Scorecard as a management tool. This percentage approximates the global penetration rates reported by others (other broad-based surveys show 60 to 65 percent usage rates).

Correlating the Model and Performance Excellence

Survey Findings

1. An Integrating Framework. As Figure 7.2 shows, three of the six Execution Premium stages are especially relevant to our current investigation. Stage 2, Translate the Strategy, entails using strategy maps and scorecards to describe and measure the strategy, identifying action programs (initiatives) required by the strategy, funding these

**Figure 7.2   General Management Principles:
The Execution Premium Model**

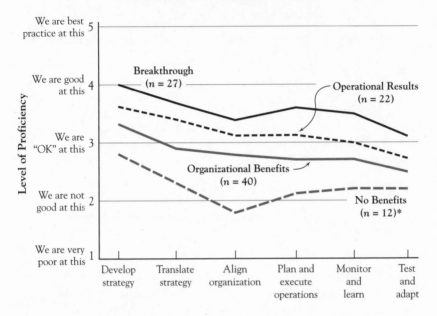

action programs, and leading their successful execution. Organizations that are using or have begun to use these tools are in a better
position to execute their strategy and, in turn, achieve better results.
Both the Breakthrough Results and Operational Results groups report
significantly better performance than the other two outcome groups.

Stage 4 of the Execution Premium model, Link Strategy and
Operations, represents the intersection of planning and operational
execution. A high score in this stage indicates that an organization is
able to develop and leverage an operational process model of the business, identify the business process improvements most critical for execution, link the strategy with operating plans and budgets, and
establish the IT requirements that will enable this integrated approach
to function effectively. By "function effectively," we also mean generating feedback in the system to allow for continuous improvement in
all affected areas. We will explore this fourth stage in the next section.

Stage 6, Test and Adapt, is where IT enablement is most important in terms of helping an organization address the most critical

question of all: whether the strategy is the right one—the most effective one—for achieving the organization's mission and vision. Here, again, we find that most organizations achieving Breakthrough Results report higher levels of conformance to the Execution Premium model. However, even this group's scores are the lowest when compared to its scores in the other five stages. That's not surprising, though. Typically, organizations that do well in testing and adapting their strategy have been actively implementing this strategy management approach for three or more years. It takes time for an organization to mature to the point of effectively taking advantage of each of the six Execution Premium stages. Moreover, the IT requirements in terms of tools and skillsets are high once an organization approaches Stage 6. You need professionals with capabilities in such tasks as profitability analysis, causal modeling, identifying alternative strategy scenarios, and recommending alternatives based on the feedback evidence. Many organizations lack expertise in these areas and are still too limited in their IT capabilities to be proficient at this stage.

2. A Linked Process/Measure Model. Earlier, we observed that managing strategic initiatives provides the critical linkage between strategy and operations. This activity is part of the Execution Premium, found in Stage 2, Translate the Strategy, with strategy maps and scorecards, and Stage 4, Planning and Executing Operations. Of all the governance activities involving initiatives—funding the initiatives, managing the initiative portfolio, and aligning the initiatives with strategy, the last has the greatest impact on achieving strategic success. But if initiatives must be aligned to be effective, a mechanism for understanding the process model of the organization must be in place. Simply put, in order to align initiatives with processes, the organization needs a process model as a reference, so that strategic initiative investments (including changes to existing processes or the introduction of new processes) can be directed appropriately.

Figure 7.3 illustrates that the likelihood of achieving breakthrough results is a function of two factors: key process management

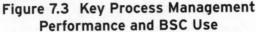

**Figure 7.3 Key Process Management
Performance and BSC Use**

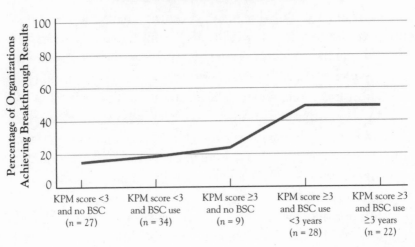

capability (ranked on a scale of 1 to 5) and length of Balanced Scorecard use. There is no question that managing key processes competently through such approaches as quality management, Lean Manufacturing or Lean Six Sigma, and continuous improvement techniques delivers benefits. But for organizations that rated their key process management capabilities a 3 ("OK") or above—absent the use of a Balanced Scorecard—the odds of success were limited: no better than one in five. However, when the Balanced Scorecard is added to the mix, the likelihood of success more than doubles to 50 percent. In this case, the duration of use is not a differentiator, so we can conclude that the combination of an "OK" or better ranking in key process management, combined with Balanced Scorecard usage, markedly improves outcomes.

In other words, optimizing operational performance—true operational excellence—requires a strong link between strategy and operations management.

Now that we know that strategy management, when combined with key process management, yields a markedly higher payoff, the next question is: Which processes receive the most attention in terms of strategy and/or operational management? Figure 7.4 shows

Figure 7.4 How Critical Processes Are Managed

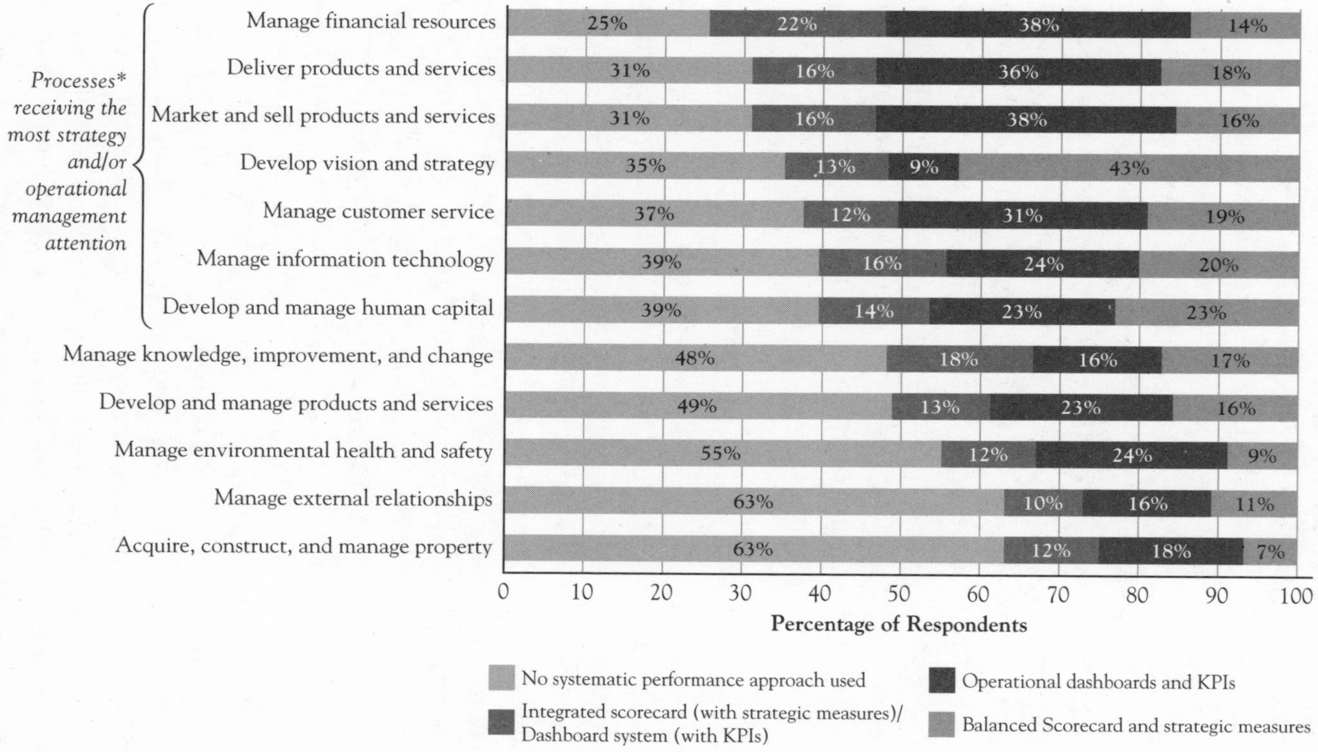

Processes* receiving the most strategy and/or operational management attention

Manage financial resources: 25%, 22%, 38%, 14%
Deliver products and services: 31%, 16%, 36%, 18%
Market and sell products and services: 31%, 16%, 38%, 16%
Develop vision and strategy: 35%, 13%, 9%, 43%
Manage customer service: 37%, 12%, 31%, 19%
Manage information technology: 39%, 16%, 24%, 20%
Develop and manage human capital: 39%, 14%, 23%, 23%
Manage knowledge, improvement, and change: 48%, 18%, 16%, 17%
Develop and manage products and services: 49%, 13%, 23%, 16%
Manage environmental health and safety: 55%, 12%, 24%, 9%
Manage external relationships: 63%, 10%, 16%, 11%
Acquire, construct, and manage property: 63%, 12%, 18%, 7%

Percentage of Respondents

■ No systematic performance approach used
■ Integrated scorecard (with strategic measures)/ Dashboard system (with KPIs)
■ Operational dashboards and KPIs
■ Balanced Scorecard and strategic measures

where organizations have made investments in creating scorecards to manage the strategy or dashboards to manage operations, or where they have done both (or neither). The number one area in which we find both approaches is in managing financial resources (used by 22 percent of respondents). This is also one of two areas where dashboards are most frequently used. Since the combined use of scorecards and dashboards is present in only a relatively small percentage of all processes, it seems reasonable to argue that this is a major area of opportunity for organizations that want to improve their chances of achieving breakthrough results. Without access to management tools such as strategy scorecards and information management platforms such as operational dashboards, organizations tend to manage operational processes the old-fashioned way: by fiat, gut feel, or "the way we do things around here!"

3. An Integrated Management Process. It almost goes without saying that to achieve significant strategic results, an organization needs strong leadership. Unless your organization happens to be lucky enough to be an early entrant in an emerging rapid-growth sector where excess profits are easily available, you are more than likely struggling just to stay even. Given the current global market turbulence and increasing risks at every turn, the task is even harder. Thus, leadership is correctly seen as being critical to survival. The same is true when looking for reasons why performance management programs succeed or fail. Why is it that anywhere from 25 percent to 63 percent of the major processes in organizations are not managed with either a scorecard, dashboard, or both? Certainly the difficulty in instituting such systems helps explain this management deficit. Moreover, the discipline of measurement-based performance management is still in its early years. While quality management has been applied to many operational processes over the past several decades, strategy management is still relatively new—and the discipline of applying an integrated approach to strategy and operations performance management can be considered in its infancy.

Nonetheless, new approaches for effective strategy execution continue to emerge, showing the way forward for those seeking competitive advantage. One such approach is the use of theme teams (described earlier) to manage strategy across traditional organizational lines, such as processes or functions. Our research focuses on one strategic theme—operational excellence, arguably the most common theme, especially in a down market.

Strategic themes require strong executive-level leadership to secure adequate resources and ensure continued visibility, action, and review. Typically, one or two members of the executive team are assigned to each theme as theme "owners"—those responsible for overseeing execution of their individual theme. The original idea of the theme team needs to be expanded when we begin to formalize the linkage between strategy and operations. Theme teams that will be accountable for linking strategy and operations require broader representation from across the organization. Specifically, members of the operational management team should be added to the theme team in the interest of achieving strategic objectives driven by specific processes that link to the strategy map.

4. An Integrated Information System. IT enablement is the remaining critical component of the execution foundation. When we look at the worlds of strategy management and operations management from the perspective of IT, we see two very different developmental histories. The path to strategy management via the use of the Balanced Scorecard is characterized by face-to-face discussion between executives to achieve consensus on the organization's mission, vision, and strategic objectives. Early on in the development life cycle of organizations implementing this management system, technology use is generally limited to desktop productivity tools, such as spreadsheets and presentation applications. Enabling an executive team to get its collective head around a set of strategic objectives doesn't require much in the way of technology—at least not in the beginning. Certainly, more technology-centric companies may rely on their information platforms to help inform their strategy development discussions. However, implementing a strategic measurement system—even one that requires only a modest set of 20 or so strategic measures—is where the challenge of integrating the management process with the data arises. Many organizations that began with rudimentary tools, and that achieved early success, often find themselves bumping up against the limits of their technology choices. Their reliance on spreadsheets begins to test the patience and bandwidth of the team members responsible for capturing, reporting, and analyzing the data. The challenge of relying on inadequate technology grows exponentially for a large and/or complex organization. When such organizations enter their second year of Balanced Scorecard implementation, they often discover that the technology choices that got them to where they are will not get them to the next level of performance. They require more robust tools at each point—from core, traditional transactional (e.g., ERP) systems all the way to specialty performance management systems—to automate more of the management and reporting processes and enable them to spend more time on value-adding activities, rather than on merely managing the data. To get there, they also need an IT governance program—to ensure the needed data is being collected, to ensure data accuracy and process integrity, and to establish common formats based on corporate standards. And they need the right IT competencies and tools.

The evolutionary cycle of an organization's management of operations, on the other hand, is typically quite different from its strategy management evolution. Large-scale ERP systems have been in place in many organizations for quite some time. These implementations often followed major reengineering efforts. Thus, operational and information management systems—and their associated analytical applications—are prominent features in the world of operations. It is fair to say that, in most organizations, the level of maturity of operations management far exceeds that of strategy management. And yet it is the connection between these two worlds that makes all the difference in terms of executing strategy and achieving Breakthrough Results.

We began to explore the connections between strategy and operations from an IT perspective by examining the primary technology solutions used to capture and report performance metrics that link to the strategy. While research has repeatedly shown that the length of Balanced Scorecard use correlates with the likelihood of achieving increased shareholder returns,[8] we wanted to see what relationship, if any, exists between the tools used and improvements in results. Figure 7.5 shows the distribution of tool usage by major category: desktop productivity tools, packaged software (e.g., SAP Business Suite software) and specialty packaged performance management software (e.g., Business Objects enterprise performance management software), and independently developed custom applications. Respondents were allowed to record all tools that are in use. The data show how ubiquitous desktop tools are (Excel, for example, with its 97 percent penetration rate) and how other tools are relied on less frequently to capture and report performance data.

The real story lies in observing which tools the more advanced organizations rely on. Figure 7.6 shows the results that organizations expect to achieve over the next three years. More than 90 percent

Figure 7.5 Primary Technology Used to Capture and Report the Performance Metrics Linked to the Strategy

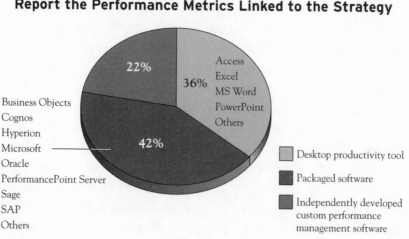

Figure 7.6 Primary Technology Solution Used to Capture and Report Performance Metrics That Link to the Strategy, by View of Performance over the Next Three Years

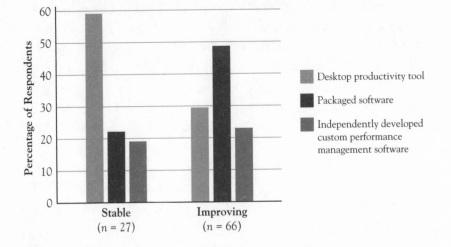

of the survey respondents expect their organization's performance over the next three years to be either consistent with current performance levels (27 respondents) or to improve (66 respondents). Only eight of the study participants expect their organization's performance over the next three years to drop below current levels. Figure 7.6 also shows the data for the "stable" performance group and the "improving" performance group broken down by software category. Here, we see that while custom software use grows somewhat (from 19 percent to 23 percent), the big story lies in packaged and specialty performance management packaged software. Reliance on packaged software increases from 22 percent to nearly 50 percent of all organizations who expect to see their business performance improving over the next three years. The desktop tool category fades considerably (from 59 percent to 29 percent) for those anticipating performance improvements over the next three years.

Clearly, alternatives to the desktop solution are more attractive. Beyond efficiency and scalability, systems need the capacity to gather data from multiple sources, linking dashboards and strategy performance systems across the enterprise. The resulting end-to-end visibility across the business network not only enhances data analysis, but helps support—and accelerate—decision making and planning. This is where operational excellence translates into competitive advantage. But the benefits even accrue in a local way: in a leading pharmaceutical's R&D group, enhanced visibility of performance metrics enables individual project work streams to conduct their own analysis and implement localized process improvements.

A final point concerning the role of IT. One of the important drivers of ongoing strategic success is how well an organization leverages its decision analytics in the last two stages of the Execution Premium model (Monitor and Learn, and Test and Adapt). To help us understand the role of decision analytics in achieving strategic success, we developed a composite score of an organization's ability to perform decision analytics based on data access, organizational maturity, use of analytics, scenario analysis capabilities, and several other dimensions.

The results of this analysis are presented in Figure 7.7. Here, we believe, is the most striking finding of our entire study. The use of decision analytics alone does little to improve the chances of

Figure 7.7   Decision Analytics Performance and BSC Use

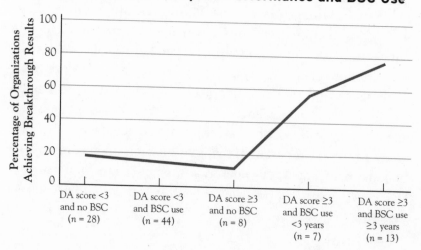

strategic success for an organization (less than 20 percent report Breakthrough Results). However, when decision analytics is paired with Balanced Scorecard use, the odds of success rise dramatically to a 57 percent chance of Breakthrough Results (when Balanced Scorecard usage is fewer than three years) and to 77 percent when the Balanced Scorecard has been in use for more than three years. Interestingly, the three greatest contributors to the decision analytics composite score were (1) organizational maturity, (2) the organization's commitment to utilizing analytics for making business decisions, and (3) IT's responsiveness to changes within the business and how well it supports the information needs required to make decisions. These last two items—both relating to the impact of analytics on improved decision making—yielded the highest ratings for Breakthrough Results organizations!

This compelling finding parallels our earlier observation concerning the role of key process management. Having a middling-to-strong capability in either key process management or decision analytics doesn't do much to improve an organization's chance of strategic success. Think of these as silver bullets that can only travel so far. But when these are paired with a solid strategy management approach—based on the Balanced Scorecard—your chances of success improve many times over.

By creating an operationally driven IT architecture based on integrated, end-to-end software solutions, organizations can transcend silos to unify operations and create transparency across the enterprise. This end-to-end visibility can help augment the traditional notions of operational excellence—greater automation, standardization, and integrated controls for compliance, to name a few—to create new sources of value. Whether the results are improved customer service and satisfaction, cost reductions, quicker access to critical information that informs decision making, or continuous improvement that enables best-practice innovation, today's IT-enabled operational excellence has more enterprise-wide impact than ever before.

A Strategic Imperative: Turning Operational Excellence into Sustainable Success

As more organizations recognize the primacy of formal strategy management, embrace the notion of optimizing the strategy-operations connection, embark on business network transformation, and begin to take advantage of powerful new technologies that provide end-to-end linkage of organizational processes, operational excellence takes on new meaning. As a way of supporting strategy execution, operational excellence is an important lever in boosting profitability and sustaining competitive advantage. But on a fundamental level, we cannot lose sight of the role operational excellence plays in helping organizations—and their entire business networks—weather volatile markets. In today's uncertain economic environment, as organizations seek to shore up their defenses and strengths, trimming costs and driving greater efficiencies assume new importance. Operational excellence is not only a lever to a promising future, but it can represent a lifeline in a turbulent present.

Certainly, combining all three factors—a strategy management framework; solid key-process-management capability; and strong IT enablement based on integrated, end-to-end software solutions that link strategy to operations—is the best recommendation we can make to those organizations that want to turn operational excellence into sustainable success.

Note: The author would like to thank Janice Koch for her contribution to an earlier version of this material that appeared as a white paper upon which this chapter is based.

Chapter 8

Constructing and Managing Innovation in Business Networks

Henry Chesbrough

*Executive Director,
Center for Open Innovation,
Haas School of Business, UC Berkeley*

As this book illustrates, business networks are increasingly vital to competitive advantage. This means that a company must not focus exclusively upon its internal capabilities and processes as it strives to compete in a globally interconnected company. Instead, the company must also examine the network of companies that exist around the company, from its suppliers (and their own suppliers), to its customers (and often their own customers), and also third parties that makes goods and services that complement the company's own offering.

In this chapter, we will explore innovation within business networks. This is a key aspect of how business networks transform. Parts of this innovation process can be actively directed by a leading firm in the network. Yet other parts of this innovation process can only be nurtured by that leading firm, and the actual innovation must be performed by others in the network. We will examine the innovation process in business networks in detail in the semiconductor industry.

Before developing the argument in detail, let's consider an initial example that will motivate the points in this chapter. Many readers will be familiar with the Apple iPod music player. iPod users are familiar with loading their favorite CDs onto the device, and then purchasing additional music from the iTunes online store. Most iPod users have also purchased additional earphones and accessories such as cases, car chargers, and other useful items.

This constellation of goods and services can be thought of as an ecosystem or a business network. Apple provides some of the elements in the network, such as the player and the iTunes store. But many others contribute additional items. The music, videos, and other content for the iPod are all created by others. All of the accessories for the iPod are made by other companies, not Apple. Companies like Nike have combined chips in their footwear with online services through iTunes that record a runner's workout and allow that runner to chart her progress through days and weeks of exercise.

One of the most recent additions to the iPod network has been Kleiner Perkins's (a well-respected Silicon Valley Venture Capital firm) decision to launch a new VC fund called iFund.[1] This $100 million fund is dedicated to investing in new ventures that are building upon the iPod/iPhone device platform. You know you have a powerful business network when a leading venture capital firm decides to invest its own money to help grow that network.

Many companies have tried to compete against the iPod by Apple, so far without much success. This includes smaller companies like Real Networks, but also very large companies like Dell and Microsoft. One of the most daunting challenges facing a challenger to iPod is that the rival company cannot simply make a better device in order to win. In order to compete effectively, the rival must develop its own ecosystem or business network to provide the same offerings as the iPod ecosystem, and perhaps innovate new kinds of offerings. That means convincing other companies to put their own talent and resources to work for the new ecosystem. And many of the best companies to join the new ecosystem may already be thriving in Apple's highly successful network. So why would they agree to join your new fledgling network?

Business Networks Are Networks of Compatible Business Models

Motivating others to join your business network gets to a core issue in constructing and managing innovation in business networks. Business networks are comprised of firms, but also of the business models of those firms. Businesses will make the necessary investments to join your network if and only if they have found a business model that allows them to profit from doing so. To grow and sustain a network of firms over time, the business models of these differing firms must be compatible.

To understand this better, let's begin by defining the term "business model." At its most basic, a business model must perform two critical tasks:

- First, it must create value in the value chain of activities from the raw materials through to the final consumer. Without a net addition of new value, others will not see any benefit in joining in.
- Second, it must allow the firm to capture at least a portion of the value created for itself. This allows the firm to sustain its position in the network and continue to invest in future innovations.

Companies seeking to establish and grow their own business networks must keep these two properties clearly in mind. In Apple's case, the iPod clearly created a superior user experience and allowed new ways for music and other content to be enjoyed. Yet Apple must also be careful not to take all of this created value for itself. By leaving some value on the table, other parties will be attracted to joining the network to compete for that remaining available value. And the success of these other network participants increases the value of the iPod network as a whole, not least to the final consumers of the iPod, who appreciate having more choices and options for how to utilize, decorate, and otherwise enjoy it.

The process of innovating business networks can be seen in more detail by considering the innovations in those networks in the semiconductor industry. In particular, we will consider a new initiative by Taiwan Semiconductor Manufacturing Corporation (TSMC), the world's leading semiconductor foundry. This new initiative is its Open Innovation Platform. As we shall see, the Open Innovation Platform is an attempt to transform TSMC's business network, a business model innovation. We turn now to a detailed examination of this process, starting with a review of business models in the semiconductor industry. Later, we will consider the new wrinkles in TSMC's business model that result from its adoption of the Open Innovation Platform.

Prior Business Models in the Semiconductor Industry

Historically, the semiconductor industry has witnessed a progression of business models, which have given rise to a variety of business networks. This progression starts with entirely vertically integrated models with relatively sparse business networks, and has evolved into a highly vertically specialized series of coordinated business models with a rich, robust set of business networks.

The Vertically Integrated Model

In the beginning, the experiments of Bardeen and Shockley at AT&T's Bell Labs, which led to the discovery of the semiconductor, were motivated by finding a lower cost and more reliable replacement technology for the vacuum tube. AT&T commercialized its technology entirely through its own products as semiconductors became part of AT&T switches, exchanges, and later, handset products. Other early uses were by the military for its defense weapons, particularly the Minuteman I and II missiles (Moore, 1995). These were made by a prime contractor, who provided the entire system to the military. IBM, which was one such contractor, also built its highly vertically integrated System 360 mainframe computer around captively manufactured semiconductor devices (Pugh, 1995).

This was the initially dominant business model for semiconductors. In order to make them, one had to create a captive subsidiary within a systems company and design the system and the semiconductors within that system at the same time. This vertically integrated systems model pioneered by AT&T and later by IBM was copied by leading Japanese companies (Hitachi, Fujitsu, NEC, Toshiba) and also by leading European companies (Siemens, Philips, Bull, Olivetti).

Note that most of the business network of such companies was inside the firm. Sister divisions making different parts of the system had to coordinate with one another to deliver systems that met specifications of customers. The information that allowed these sister divisions to coordinate was kept inside the firm, usually as trade secrets. This made it exceedingly difficult for external companies to join the network. Unless the systems company wanted another company to join, it could effectively exclude it from the network. IBM, for example, not only sold the hardware system, it also sold the operating system, the applications for the system, and provided the installation, service, support, and even financing for the system.

As the semiconductor technology diffused and became better understood, the information that linked the many parts of the system became available outside the systems firm. Small startup companies began to emerge. These companies did not follow the vertically integrated business model. Instead, they became merchant market suppliers of semiconductor products that were designed to plug and play with the systems architectures established by the vertically integrated firms. The external business network began to grow, though in the early days it grew in spite of the dominant systems firm, not because that firm actively encouraged it.

Intel is one important example of this. Its first products were memory products for IBM mainframe computers. They later invented the DRAM circuit as a replacement for the core memory that IBM was using in its 360 computers (Moore, 1995). These merchant suppliers soon included other small companies like Intersil, Mostek, Signetics, and National. This business model later became known as an Integrated Device Manufacturer (IDM) model because the company did not make the final system, but did make all of the elements in the semiconductor device used in the system.

The systems company did not necessarily welcome these new entrants into their business network. They could typically make more margin if they could provide the functionality offered by the entrants themselves. Over time, though, the entrants pioneered new technologies not available from the systems company that worked with the systems architecture of the systems company. These new technologies were valuable to customers, and even to the systems company, because they helped that system compete against rival systems.

The IDM Model

The IDM business model competed for many years against the vertically integrated systems model in the semiconductor industry. In the beginning, the vertically integrated model had tremendous advantages over the IDM model. The deep knowledge of the design of the system helped captive producers design products that would work in those systems. Semiconductor design and manufacturing was something of a black art, and having control over all the interactions between the memory and the rest of the system was a huge advantage.

However, the knowledge of how to make semiconductors later matured and diffused, reducing the amount of black art necessary to design a functional component. System architectures also became better understood, and de facto interface standards began to develop that would enable customers to plug in memory modules and have them work in the system. As these developments took root, the vertically integrated business model's weaknesses became more apparent. Perhaps the biggest weakness was that the high fixed development costs of the captive semiconductors could only be spread over the shipping volumes of the systems of the vertically integrated company. A second, more subtle weakness is that the captive producer could not develop all of the possible offerings that could be created through a market of competing firms. The largely internal business network of the vertically integrated firm lacked the scale and scope economies of the more diverse IDM business network.

By contrast, IDMs could ship their products to a range of customers, enabling them to reduce their fixed costs by spreading them across a broad customer base. This ability to aggregate volume across the market through serving many customers had a second order effect as well: IDMs often justify the addition of new capacity sooner than could many of the vertically integrated companies. This gave IDMs access to the latest fabrication technologies, further enhancing their cost advantage. Eventually, the combination of higher market volumes (in relation to captive volumes) and lower costs pushed most systems companies to abandon their captive semiconductor efforts, or to spin them out into independent companies, who effectively became IDMs.

The IDM model gradually took over the industry from the vertically integrated model in most of the semiconductor industry. This shift first occurred in DRAMs, and later to other types of semiconductors. The rise of the Japanese semiconductor firms and later, the Korean firms, resulted from the rise of the IDM model. This is also typical: business model innovations often trigger far-reaching shifts in industry structure.

One particular impetus for this shift was the fabulous success of Intel's microprocessor business. Intel initially positioned its 8088 and 80286 processors as components within the IBM PC architecture. IBM had built a powerful business network around its IBM PC architecture, with thousands of hardware and software manufacturers creating products that were "IBM compatible," and fostered the emergence of thousands of retail outlets that stocked these myriad products for sale to customers. A fabulous business network had been established.

By the time of Intel's 80386 processor, however, IBM was dragging its feet in buying Intel's latest and greatest chip. Another company in the network, Compaq Computer Corporation, was eager to launch an IBM compatible computer with this latest Intel chip under the hood. It became a big success, and Intel began to realize that it could lead the business network that IBM had initially created. Over time, IBM lost leadership over its own business network, ceding that leadership to Intel in semiconductors and Microsoft in operating systems.

Even as Intel's microprocessor was reaching enormous volumes through the IDM business network, though, yet another business model was beginning to emerge, the so-called fabless model. This business model would create a very different business network from that of the IDM model.

TSMC's Fabless Business Model

The fabless semiconductor model emerged from the efforts of Morris Cheng and his colleagues at TSMC, supported by extensive government assistance in Taiwan and the talents of a centralized government research lab, ITRI. Cheng was a veteran of Silicon Valley and knew well the economics of the semiconductor business. He knew that for every Intel microprocessor product success, there were dozens of products that never could achieve sufficient volumes to justify their own dedicated manufacturing facilities. As the costs of building new fabrication facilities (called "fabs" in industry parlance) grew, more and more companies' products would have to be manufactured in a different way. Moreover, new design methodologies and tools from firms (such as VLSI's Verilog product) offered the promise of being able to build multiple different product designs on the same semiconductor fabrication equipment. So long as the same design tools were used, the resulting chip could be manufactured on TSMC's equipment.

Initially, Cheng thought that he could build other companies' semiconductor designs as a stepping stone to developing the scale and capital equipment he would need to develop and manufacture his own designs. Events soon caused him to change his plans. The external fabless customers with designs ready to be manufactured were lining up at the door, while his internal designs were struggling to get finished. Cheng soon determined that TSMC's future would rest upon a new business model, the fabless model (Saxenian, 2005; Hu interview, 2004).

The fabless model by its construction was even more of an external business network than the earlier IDM model. The IDM had to worry about plugging into the system it was designing chips for, but all of the aspects for designing, developing, manufacturing, and testing the chip were the responsibility of people inside the IDM. By contrast, the fabless model required TSMC to work with a variety of customers' designs. As we will see, over time many other companies got involved in the process of assuring design customers that their designs would work on TMSC's processes and then in the market. The foundry model thus led to a global model of vertical specialization.

TSMC's business soon took off. Its foundry model was rapidly imitated by other companies, including Chartered Semiconductor in Singapore, UMC and Grace Semiconductor Manufacturing Corporation in Taiwan, and more recently, SMIC in China. Another company in San Jose, California, Silicon Valley Technology Corporation, now even applies the foundry model to process development. This means that companies can develop the processes required to build a new design and then transfer those to a foundry to make the chip. So the business network is expanding into the design area of process development as well.

Further network expansion has arisen in the chip design industry. Freed from the constraints of designing for one company alone, companies like Cadence and Synopsys provide development tools that can be used to create many different kinds of chips. They even maintain "libraries" of designs that have been proven to work in the past, and (for a price) will allow customers to re-use those designs as part of a new design. This creates an expansion of the business network in yet another direction. Still other companies provide testing, packaging, and other functions that previously were performed entirely inside a single IDM—another expansion of the network.

Today, the foundry manufacturing business model accounts for more than 25 percent of all semiconductor manufacturing. And TSMC enjoys more than 50 percent of the market for foundries making semiconductor products.

Is the fabless model therefore better than the IDM model? It is a competition between two kinds of business networks. Prior academic research has documented the competition between the IDM business model and that of the foundry. Jeff Macher's research program (Macher, 2003; Macher and Mowery, 2003) has documented the differences in manufacturing efficiencies between foundries and IDMs. He has found persuasive evidence that each business model has comparative advantages in different product categories. IDMs, in Macher's work, have strong advantages in products with high volumes and long production runs, which require the latest production technologies. Using a transaction cost lens, Macher finds strong support for IDM advantages when the design of the product is tightly coupled to the design of the production process. A similar logic sustained the earlier business model of the vertically integrated business model against the IDM model, at least in the early days of the industry.

Marcin Strojwas's recent dissertation (2005) further refines Macher's conclusions. He finds that the IDM model functions best when both technological newness and high technical challenge are involved in the design and manufacture of a semiconductor product. Like Macher, Strojwas finds that each business model is best adapted to certain product classes. IDM's are best suited to memory products, while foundries are better adapted to analog and ASIC product classes. In these latter product classes, product volumes are smaller per design, and there are many more kinds of designs sold in the market.

Robert Leachman's research (2002) analyzed the comparative manufacturing efficiencies of IDMs and foundries at the level of individual projects and facilities. Using data on the yields of the production process, Leachman finds that IDMs' processes produce higher initial yields and are able to reduce yield loss faster than foundries. However, this advantage diminishes over time and similarly diminishes as the production technology becomes more mature.

As of this writing, the IDM business model continues to compete with that of the foundry. In the next section, we will examine the forces that are influencing this competition and examine new trends in the fabless business model and the supporting Open Innovation Platform business network that TSMC is constructing.

Forces Driving the Competition Between Semiconductor Business Models

In this section, we examine the economic and technical forces that are influencing the competition between the IDM and foundry business models. We begin with the forces supporting the IDM model.

The Integrated Manufacturer: Real Men Have Fabs

One robust finding from the prior academic research is that the level of the interdependencies between design and manufacturing play a critical role in the competition between the two business models. When semiconductor products require the latest designs at the smallest feasible geometries, which in turn require the latest production technologies, the IDM model is likely to dominate in the market. It is clear that IDMs enjoy a comparative advantage in their ability to tune the design of the product to the design of the process. This careful mutual adjustment process involves substantial amounts of informal and unstructured technical dialog (Monteverde, 1995). It is very difficult to accomplish this level of tacit collaboration through market contracting (as with foundries). In these contexts, IDMs will be able to bring up latest generation processes faster, with higher yield, than foundries making the same part.

At leading edge line widths used in the industry today, the interdependencies are even greater. IDMs such as Intel and Samsung are now building and shipping parts using 45 nanometer line widths. It is taking enormous amounts of informal, unstructured interaction to resolve the myriad problems that are arising at these geometries. This has been called the "crisis in complexity" by IBM, among others (source: Bernie Meyerson interview on video with Dan Hutcheson of VLSI Research). As line widths advance to 45 nanometer and 30 nanometer geometries, circuit designs and materials will need to account for quantum level interactions, a new kind of interdependency not previously encountered by the industry at commercial scale production.

This is not mere marketing rhetoric. Research at UC Berkeley shows that, as line-widths narrow, the defect rates of chips made on those processes have deteriorated.[2] This complexity has increased exponentially, even since the time of the UC Berkeley study, which benchmarked process performance through 0.25 micron line widths while the leading edge processes today are at 45 nanometers, five generations further on (after 180, 135, 90, and 65 nanometers). The greater arms-length nature of design-only firms with foundry partners necessarily limits their ability to master these issues as quickly as the IDMs can.

One area where the management of these interdependencies can be seen most clearly is in the development of design rules for new generations of process technology. Internal design rules are better tuned to the intricacies of leading edge manufacturing processes than fab design rules, which must necessarily serve a much wider customer base. Foundries have to gravitate to a lower common denominator vs. IDMs, which can optimize processes for specific leading-edge applications. It is for this reason that microprocessors and especially DRAMs are made almost exclusively with IDMs, because these products must push the limits of the technology beyond what foundries can accommodate.

The IDMs can use their highest volume designs as the process driver to bring up these latest generation processes. By focusing upon a single product or product family to build, the IDMs' task is made simpler. They only have to make the latest process technology work for that single product. Foundries, by comparison, must be able to build a variety of products upon a single process technology. They lack a single product with sufficient volume to act as the process driver. Instead, they must employ some average based upon multiple product designs to bring up their processes and make further adaptations to the process as each new product enters into production.

A second force that is driving the IDM business model forward is the relentless increase in the capital equipment costs for semiconductor processes. The cost to build a new semiconductor plant, or "fab" in industry parlance, is now over $3 billion. Indeed, Intel's recent announcements of new fabs in Arizona and Israel noted that each facility would cost in excess of $3 billion.

As the capital costs to build a new fab continue to increase, only the largest and most successful semiconductor companies will be able to build these new fabs. This amounts to a barrier to entry for other competitors. Economists call these advantages *economies of scale*. Competitors without their own fabs must settle for whatever fab capacity they can arrange from others, such as foundries. However, the demand pattern for semiconductors has been cyclical, so in periods of high demand, there is inevitably a shortage of production capacity, precisely when prices are highest and margins are greatest for those who obtain capacity. When demand is low, there is plenty of capacity available, precisely when chip designers don't need it.

The Foundry Model: Why Own When You Can Rent?

Notwithstanding the forces favoring the IDMs noted above, there are other powerful forces driving the foundry business model forward. The technical interdependencies noted above are actually greater within the fab from one production line to another when making different products than they are between the fab and the design of the product (Hu, 2004). The way to manage these complexities is to understand and fully characterize the equipment configurations and "recipes" for making different chip designs. This is actually a key advantage for foundries. Economists call this advantage *economies of scope*.

Because foundries make a broader variety of products than IDMs on their production processes, they accumulate a richer set of experiences in developing and executing recipes that configure their processes properly for new products. This broader product range exposes process issues more rapidly to foundries. It lets foundries develop the capabilities of their process equipment more fully and more deeply than the IDMs, who are limited by a narrow mix of products. To use an ecological metaphor, the IDM environment is a monoculture in which a narrow range of products is made repeatedly. The foundry environment is a more diverse and heterogeneous culture. To translate this into economic terms, the IDM model is more efficient, while the foundry model is more flexible and adaptive.

As you might expect, the business network for the fabless company is more robust, more diverse, and less dependent upon a single product or market for continued prosperity. Because foundries can make small-volume products, more experimentation can be conducted by its customers. New trends and new markets are identified and exploited more quickly. Even large IDMs like Intel now use foundries for smaller-volume products, such as Intel's communications chips.

Relatedly, the foundry model is benefiting from a shift in the process equipment technologies that they purchase (along with IDMs) from equipment suppliers. Equipment manufacturers such as Applied Materials now create their products in an architecture of entire systems and processes, rather than as individual piece parts the way that they used to do. They now offer entire recipes and reference process designs along with their equipment for foundry manufacturers. In a real sense, equipment makers are adding more value to their equipment than they used to. This makes their equipment more capable over a broader range of functions than was true a decade ago. It subtly shifts the balance of knowledge away from IDMs (who buy the same equipment as foundries but employ their own proprietary processes to utilize it) towards foundries. There is less of a process knowledge advantage wielded by IDMs today in the deployment of leading-edge production processes using the latest equipment.

Foundry design rules have now caught up to the design rules of IDMs, as they relate to getting leading-edge process equipment up and running with high uptime and high yield. The diversity of customers has caused foundries to create far more robust libraries, and foundries have become expert at searching effectively to advance these design rules.

Foundries now claim that they no longer need a single design to be the process driver to bring up a new process. They now assert that all that is required is a gate-intensive design that needs high performance from the smaller line widths. For example, TSMC brought up its 0.25 micron process at the same time that Intel brought its process up. TSMC made graphics processors and similar logic products and believes that its yields compare favorably to those of IDMs.

The growing success of foundries like TSMC in certain market segments is creating an expanding business network with regard to design tools and libraries. According to Marco Iansiti of Harvard, TSMC has become the standard setter for semiconductor processing tools and libraries for ASICs and similar products. Other foundries like UMC, Grace, and SMIC follow many of the process standards that TSMC sets. Interestingly, even IDMs now work to comply with TSMC design process standards. Why? The answer is that even very large companies like Intel and TI recognize that many of their products will not be huge-volume products, so they must be designed to allow the IDM to transfer a product from an internal fab to an external foundry. By adhering to the design standards of the external foundry, they greatly simplify the transfer of an internal product to the external process. This lets them utilize external foundry fab capacity as additional capacity or buffer capacity for their products, increasing their capital efficiency.

As a result, we are seeing some surprising developments in the evolution of business models in the competition between the IDM model and the foundry model. Notwithstanding the issues around process complexity, foundries have nearly caught up to the IDMs in process capability, at least as measured by line widths employed in product manufacture. While Intel remains the process leader, TSMC is now close behind. Figure 8.1 depicts this evolution of business models in the semiconductor industry.

The Most Recent Transformation: TSMC's Open Innovation Platform

TSMC is rightly celebrated as the pioneer of the new fabless model. What is equally impressive is that the company has not stopped its business model innovation activities. As the foundry

Figure 8.1 Evolution of Semiconductor Business Networks

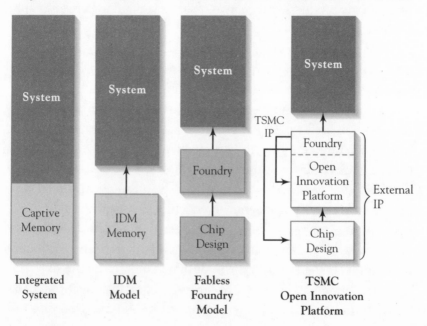

market begins to mature and as competitors improve their own foundry capabilities, TSMC has decided to develop some new wrinkles to its business model. Here, we will focus on its Open Innovation Platform.

It is not easy to describe the Open Innovation Platform in a single sentence. Here is TSMC's description:

> The TSMC Open Innovation Platform™ efficiently and openly encourages the speedy implementation of innovation amongst the semiconductor design community, its ecosystem partners, and TSMC's IP, design implementation and DFM capabilities, process technology and backend services. A key element of the Open Innovation Platform™ is a set of ecosystem interfaces and collaborative components initiated and supported by TSMC that more efficiently empowers innovation throughout the supply chain and which enables the creation and sharing of newly created revenue and profitability. TSMC's Active Accuracy Assurance (AAA) initiative is a critical part of the Open Innovation Platform™, providing the accuracy and quality required by the ecosystem interfaces and collaborative components.[3]

That is a rather dense explanation of the platform, and only those savvy in the intricacies of semiconductor design and manufacturing will get much out of it. Here is a more helpful description for the layperson from a Gartner analyst:

> OIP is a program that involves more "collaboration between the foundry and its clients at the early stages of the design phase," said Jim Walker, an analyst with Gartner, in Gartner's e-mail newsletter. "TSMC's OIP consists of a platform of design tools and IP to help customers with their design-to-manufacturing efforts. OIP integrates TSMC's manufacturing technologies, silicon IP, massive manufacturing database, and compatible third-party silicon IP and design tools. Through OIP, TSMC can offer vertically integrated services, from designing and manufacturing to testing and packaging, thus

shortening clients' IC development processes and reducing their manufacturing costs.[4]

What is new here is the level of integration that TSMC is providing to its design customers. In the beginning, TSMC simply performed the manufacturing of the customer's design. Soon, though, the company learned to impose certain design restrictions on its customers so that the designs would conform to the requirements of TSMC's manufacturing processes. These early design restrictions were housed largely inside of TSMC.

With the growth of TSMC's business network, many other third-party companies who made design tools, process recipes, testing, and packaging all began to take steps to ensure customers that their offerings would run on TSMC's processes. By being such a large factor in the foundry market, TSMC became the de facto standard for all third parties to develop for. This explosion in third party offerings creates more design options for TSMC's customers—a clear benefit. However, these new offerings also increase the complexity for TSMC's customers to manage, and this complexity risks causing new chips to require redesigns or other expensive modifications to be manufactured correctly.

The Open Innovation Platform addresses this complexity by providing a new level of integration and coordination. TSMC now provides documented interfaces for its ecosystem (i.e., its business network), so that these third parties can be confident that their offerings will comply with TSMC's process requirements. And with compliant offerings that conform to these interfaces, TSMC, in turn, certifies to customers of those offerings that they can use these tools with confidence to design for TSMC manufacturing, and that the chip will turn out properly the first time through the process. This avoids very expensive "turns" of the chip design, whereby the chip must be redesigned in order to be manufactured properly in volume. The result is faster time to market for TSMC's customers at a lower cost of design.

This is where business network transformation must begin: by delivering more value for customers. But TSMC benefits from this in important ways itself as well. First, by developing its own IP, TSMC can lock foundry customers into its own internal fab processes. While the IP provided by TSMC's third-party partners works across several competitive foundries, TSMC's proprietary IP does not work in competitive fabs. Second, by providing the assurance that conforming products will work the first time through, TSMC removes some of the anxiety and risk faced by its customers.

Both of these features (TSMC's own IP and assurance programs) raise the bar for TSMC competitors, making it harder to unseat TSMC as the foundry of choice. While the Open Innovation Platform has only been in existence for a year, it is likely to cement TSMC's position as the market leader in the foundry business. Like any effective business model innovation, the Open Innovation Platform seems to create value for customers and allow TSMC to capture a portion of the value created for itself.

And while Andrew McAfee's Chapter 10 will explore the importance of SAP's enterprise management software to companies' business processes in general, we can also see how SAP has contributed to TSMC's success. For doing all the functions implied in the Open Innovation Platform requires very strict process control, and the ability to document that control. In particular, the increased emphasis in the Open Innovation Platform upon both internal and external IP requires SAP's ability to "tag" the various TSMC processes with the IP associated with each process. This creates confidence in external IP providers that they will be compensated for the use of their IP in TSMC's foundries. And it provides a definitive listing of IP used in the event of any later litigation around the misappropriation of IP. Thus, litigation risk is reduced, both for TSMC and its customers, through SAP's ability to collect and manage the metadata involved in utilizing internal and external IP in its foundry processes.

Practical Lessons for Business Network Innovators

The first lesson for aspiring companies who wish to transform their own business networks is to think more openly about the business. A business network is far more than the business itself. As we have seen, it incorporates suppliers, customers, third-party developers, distributors, and others. These outsiders must have a reason to support your network and remain active in it. Be sure that they have compelling reasons to do so. Look at their business models, and get them aligned with yours.

The second lesson is that business networks grow over time. You don't need to start with the complete network on day one. In fact, only over time, as your network grows, will you find out who many of your network members are, as they self-select into your network. So make a plan to get started, but plan to adapt that over time, as new events, new companies, and new commitments unfold.

The third lesson is to think first about value creation and only then consider value capture. Business networks that do not provide sufficient value creation will fail to attract the critical mass of outside support, investment, and innovation that you want to deliver to your customers. It is often the case that you may need to restrain your own value capture a bit, in order to promote the growth and vitality of the network. If so, take comfort in the following aphorism: a smaller piece of a big pie is worth a great deal more than a large piece of a small pie.

The last lesson is that even strong business networks need more innovation. TSMC could have rested on its laurels from its successful fabless business model. But it has chosen instead to take the chance to innovate further. This is risky, and may not work over time. But it is a safe bet that any business network will stagnate over time unless there are new innovations and new sources of value creation and value capture to sustain it. In this way, TSMC's initiative may be less risky than simply standing still.

Chapter 9

The Value of Trust in Business Networks

Jeffrey Dyer

Chair, Organizational Leadership & Strategy Department
Horace Beesley Professor of Strategy
Brigham Young University

The management literature is full of testimonials about companies that claim they benefited by building trust with suppliers or customers. But does trust really pay off in *significant* bottom-line results, or does this feel-good approach only bring marginal benefits? And how do you build inter-firm trust? In this chapter, we will demonstrate that trust within business networks can be a valuable economic asset that does pay off in significant bottom-line results. More specifically, trust lowers transaction costs and increases information sharing, thereby improving performance. We also introduce *process-based trust* as a concept that is critical for companies who hope to build higher levels of trust within their business network.

> "Interactions—the searching, coordinating, and monitoring that people and firms do when they exchange goods, services, or ideas—account for over a third of economic activity in the United States."
> —*Report by McKinsey & Company*[1]

> "[Foreign-based manufacturers] squeeze you, but they're fair... [U.S. companies] want to beat you to

death. If somebody comes in one penny cheaper,
they'll replace you in a minute."
—*Tommie Burns, U.S. auto supplier, quoted July 2002*

Like motherhood and apple pie, trust is one of life's indisputable wholesome ideals. Indeed, the management literature is full of testimonials about companies that claim they benefited by building trust with suppliers or customers. Some scholars even claim that national economic efficiency is highly correlated with the existence of a high-trust institutional environment. For example, Francis Fukuyama (1995, p. 7) has argued that the economic success of a nation, "as well as its ability to compete, is conditioned by ... the level of trust inherent in the society."[2] But does trust really pay off in *significant* bottom-line results, or does this feel-good approach only bring marginal benefits? Most "research" on trust is anecdotal with little evidence of hard economic benefits. And even if the benefits are significant, how does a company best go about building trust within its business network (defined as the team of companies in the value chain that it collaborates with to produce a product/service)?

This chapter demonstrates that supplier-buyer trust can be a valuable economic asset that pays off in significant bottom-line results. More specifically, trust is valuable within the business network because it

- Lowers transaction costs, and
- Leads to superior knowledge sharing

In Chapter 1, Geoffrey Moore and Phillip Lay described two types of business networks, "coordinated" and "collaborative". Since a great deal of the "transformation" in business network transformation occurs when industries shift from a coordinated model to a collaborative model, we can use the well-known automotive industry as an example of how trust is built, managed, and often-times destroyed in the evolving relationships between the "concentrator" (e.g., automakers) and its suppliers as the industry shifts towards more collaborative relationships. By studying the role of trust in the relationships in the automotive business network, we can examine the costs of mistrust and provide strong evidence that trust lowers transaction costs throughout business networks. We also discuss the important role that trust plays in increasing information sharing between suppliers and automakers and examine the issue of how firms can develop trusting relationships within the business network.

Surprisingly, we find that the most trusted automakers do not develop trust with suppliers primarily based on personal relationships between their employees and their supplier's employees. Nor is it based primarily on the stock ownership it holds in its strategic suppliers. Rather, trust between large organizations is based largely on each firm's institutionalized processes for dealing with participants in its business network.

Defining Trust

Since trust is a concept with many potential meanings, it is first important to define what we mean by trust. For the purposes of this chapter, we will define trust as *one party's confidence that the other party in the exchange relationship will fulfill its commitments and will not exploit its vulnerabilities.*[3] This confidence (trust) would be expected to emerge in situations where the "trustworthy" party in the exchange relationship (1) makes "good faith" efforts to fulfill prior commitments, (2) makes adjustments (e.g., as market conditions change) in ways perceived as "fair" by the exchange partner, and (3) does not take advantage of an exchange partner even when the opportunity is available. Thus, trust exists when the other party is reliable, fair, and shows goodwill.

According to "The Collaboration Advantage," a 2008 survey of over 500 global C-level executives conducted by the Economist Intelligence Unit, over half of the respondents felt that building trust is the most critical challenge to effectively managing collaborative relationships. Over two-thirds of those same executives felt that the key to establishing, or breaking, trust lies in building personal relationships with their business partners. Conceptually, organizations are not able to trust each other; trust has its basis in individuals. Trust can only be placed by one individual in another individual or in a group of individuals, such as a partner organization. However, individuals in an organization may *share an orientation* toward individuals within another organization. From this perspective, *inter-firm trust* describes the extent to which there is a collectively-held "trust orientation" by organizational members toward another firm.[4]

It is also important to acknowledge that risk is requisite to trust. The need for trust only arises in a risky situation because without some vulnerability, there is no need to trust.[5] This is important to understand in the context of the automotive industry because supplier-automaker relationships are fraught with risk and vulnerabilities—which is why trust is particularly important in the automobile industry. The automobile is a complex product with thousands of components that must work together as a system with an extremely high degree of reliability and safety. Components are often tailored to specific models and as a result suppliers must make dedicated (automaker-specific) investments in people, plants, tools, and equipment. Since these investments are not easily re-deployable to other uses, suppliers are at risk if their customers behave opportunistically. For example, after a supplier has invested in a dedicated asset, the automaker may opportunistically try to renegotiate a contract, threatening to switch to another supplier if the price is not lowered. Furthermore, the auto industry is characterized by a high degree of market uncertainty (as witnessed by the 2008 auto industry bailout efforts),[6] which increases both the risks associated with transacting as well as the importance of information sharing. For example, the automaker may expect to sell 100,000 units of a particular model and request that the supplier make the necessary investments to produce parts for 100,000 units. But due to market uncertainty, the automaker may only be able to sell 50,000 or 75,000 units, thereby placing the supplier in the difficult situation of having invested in assets that are not needed. The supplier will lose money on this investment unless it can trust the automaker to help it recoup its investment (or, alternatively, the supplier must anticipate the potential problem and write provisions for it in a legal contract). Unfortunately, many potential problems are difficult to foresee and, therefore, write in a contract. Thus, an automaker's trustworthiness is of particular importance in the auto industry due to supplier investments in dedicated assets (combined with market uncertainty), which places suppliers in a vulnerable position.

Differences in Automaker Trustworthiness

Over the past several years, 236 suppliers were surveyed to find out how much they trusted the automakers that accounted for more than two-thirds of sales in the United States and Japan. The results were interesting, though perhaps not surprising given that numerous trade and popular journals have reported that suppliers are less likely to trust automakers that use "hardball" procurement strategies (see Table 9.1, "Automaker Differences in Trust, Transaction Costs, and Information Sharing"). The results reported in Table 9.1 show that Toyota is the automaker most trusted by suppliers, meaning that Toyota is most likely to follow through on commitments, most likely to treat the supplier in ways perceived as "fair," and least likely to take advantage of a supplier. Nissan was the next most trusted automaker, followed by Chrysler, Ford, and finally General Motors. Interestingly, the survey results also indicate that *Toyota had developed significantly higher levels of trust with U.S. suppliers than U.S. automakers*. Thus, trust *can* be developed relatively quickly with foreign suppliers in a new country. The question of how Toyota was able to quickly develop trusting relationships with U.S. suppliers is an important one that we will address shortly. First, it is important to point out that these differences in trustworthiness between Toyota and GM and Ford are (statistically) significant. However, the more important question is whether or not these differences are *substantive*, at least in the sense that they really make a difference in the economic performance of these firms.

Table 9.1 Automaker Differences in Trust, Transaction Costs, and Information Sharing

	Chrysler N = 135	Ford N = 135	GM N = 135	Nissan N = 101	Toyota N = 101
1. Supplier Trust in the Automaker*					
Extent to which automaker can be trusted to treat supplier fairly	5.4	5.0	3.2	6.1	6.4
If given the chance, extent to which automaker might try to take unfair advantage of supplier	2.9	3.6	5.4	1.8	1.4
Automaker has a reputation for fairness among supplier community	5.2	4.8	2.8	5.7	6.3
2. Transaction Costs					
Dollar value of goods procured per procurement employee	$5.7m	$5.3m	$1.6m	$9.6m	$12.6m
3. Information Sharing*					
Extent to which supplier shares confidential information	4.3	3.6	2.6	5.4	6.4

*Average supplier response on 1–7 Likert scale: 1 = Not at all
4 = To some extent
7 = To a very great extent

Trust Lowers Transaction Costs (or "The Costs of Mistrust")

Historically, a firm has been viewed by economists (and most executives) as a "production function." Consequently, the firm with the most efficient, or lowest cost, production function should win in the marketplace. The value chain reflected the combined production functions of all of the firms that engaged in exchanges, from "upstream" raw materials to "downstream" final assembly. Theoretically, the value chain comprised of firms with the combined "low cost" production functions would produce the final assembled product at the lowest total cost. However, in the past two decades work in economics has recognized that the productivity of a value chain or business network is a function of both production costs and transaction costs. *Transaction costs* involve all of the costs associated with conducting exchanges between firms. Transaction costs take many everyday forms—management meetings, conferences, phone conversations, sales calls, bidding rituals, reports, memos—but their underlying economic purpose is always to enable the exchange of goods, services, or ideas. The sales, marketing, distribution, procurement, logistics, and legal functions within most companies tend to represent a firm's investment in transacting with other parties.

Not only do we recognize that transaction costs exist, but we are now beginning to realize that in some industrial settings transaction costs are significant. Indeed, Nobel prize winner Douglas North estimates that transaction costs may represent as much as 35–40 percent of the costs associated with economic activity.[7] Similarly, a study by strategy consultant McKinsey & Company found that "Interactions—the searching, coordinating, and monitoring that people and firms do when they exchange goods services or ideas ... account for over a third of economic activity in the United States." The McKinsey study further found that "At an economy level, interactions [similar to transaction costs] represent as much as 51 percent of labor activity in the United States—the equivalent of over a third of GDP."[8] If true (or even if both Douglas North and

McKinsey & Company have overestimated transaction costs by a factor of two), then the business network that achieves the lowest transaction costs should win in the marketplace.

Transaction costs can be divided into three separate costs related to transacting: (1) search costs, (2) contracting costs, and (3) monitoring and enforcement costs. *Search costs* include the costs of gathering information to identify and evaluate potential trading partners—to find the "right" party with which to exchange. *Contracting costs* refer to the costs associated with negotiating and writing an agreement or legal contract. *Monitoring and enforcement costs* refer to the costs associated with monitoring the agreement to ensure that each party fulfills the predetermined set of obligations.

In general, trust is more effective than legal contracts (third-party enforcement mechanisms) at minimizing transaction costs. Trust lowers transaction costs for a number of reasons. First, search costs are lower for the buyer because the buyer does not need to comparison shop in order to be sure they are getting a "fair" deal. Assuming the supplier is relatively efficient, the buyer can trust that the price and quality offered by the supplier is fair. Second, negotiation and contracting costs are reduced because the exchange partners are more likely to openly share information and trust that payoffs will be divided fairly. Consequently, exchange partners do not have to bear the cost, or time, of specifying every detail of the agreement in a contract. Further, contracts are less effective than trust at controlling opportunism because they fail to anticipate all forms of "cheating" that may occur. Third, trust lowers monitoring costs because trust relies on *self-monitoring* rather than external or third-party monitoring. Exchange partners do not need to invest in costly monitoring mechanisms to ensure contract fulfillment and to document infractions to the satisfaction of a third party (e.g., court). Finally, trust is superior to contracts at minimizing transaction costs over the *long run* because trust is not subject to the time limitations of contracts. Contracts are typically written for a fixed duration and, in effect, *depreciate* because they only provide protection during the designated length of the agreement. At the end of the contract duration the alliance partners need to write a new contract. Trust allows suppliers and automakers to avoid the costs of "re-contracting." In fact, rather than depreciating, trust may *appreciate* over time in the sense that trust usually increases with increased familiarity and interaction. In summary, there are a number of ways that trust lowers transaction costs within the business network.

In my research on trust in business networks, two measures of transaction costs have been used to determine the costs of mistrust. First, suppliers were asked to estimate how much of their face-to-face communication time with automakers involved negotiating a price or contract (bargaining before the contract is signed) or assigning blame for problems in the course of transacting (haggling after the contract is signed). This percentage is shown in Figure 9.1 along with each automaker's average score for supplier trust on the three trust sub-measures (from Table 9.1).

The results show that when supplier trust is high, transaction costs are low. The higher the trust, the lower the transaction costs. More specifically, the most trusted automakers, Toyota and Chrysler,

Figure 9.1 Trustworthiness Lowers Transaction Costs

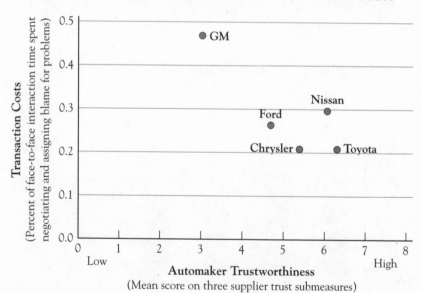

(Mean score on three supplier trust submeasures)

spent only about 21 percent of their face-to-face interaction time negotiating contracts/prices and assigning blame for problems. By comparison, General Motors spent 47 percent of its face-to-face interaction time on non-productive, transaction-oriented activities (see Figure 9.2). As a result, GM *and its suppliers need to invest in 50 percent more face-to-face contact time in order to get the same number of hours of productive work time.* As one supplier executive observed:

> We spend considerably more time with GM on non-productive activities. Because they bid more frequently, we have to spend a lot more time preparing bids and responding to requests for information. And if we win the bid, we are more likely to want to spell out the details of our agreement in a legal contract. It's costly but it helps protect us and also helps to make sure there are no misunderstandings down the road.[9]

While these differences in transaction costs may not be fully attributed to trusting relations between the firms, the fact that Toyota and Chrysler were twice as productive in their face-to-face interactions with suppliers when compared to General Motors is certainly significant.

Figure 9.2   Differences in Transactions Costs Among Automakers

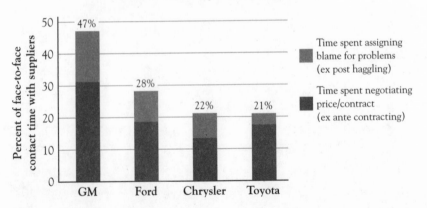

To further confirm that trust lowers transaction costs, another measure of each automaker's transaction costs based on more objective data was needed. The total number of employees in the procurement functions of each automaker (including management, purchasing agents/buyers, lawyers, and support staff), as well as the total value of goods purchased were also obtained. By dividing the number of procurement employees by the value of the goods purchased, a rough estimate of the efficiency of each automaker's purchasing function was estimated. This is expressed as the dollar value of goods (parts) purchased per procurement employee ($/emp). This measure is, in effect, the reverse of transaction costs. This is a reasonably accurate measure of the relative procurement (transaction) costs incurred by each automaker because the procurement staff is responsible for a) *searching* for new suppliers, b) *contracting* with suppliers, c) *monitoring* supplier performance (gathering information from the other operational units to create an overall evaluation), and d) *enforcing* performance. Thus, this measure is a reasonable proxy for the relative transaction costs incurred by automakers.

Not surprisingly, this measure is highly correlated with the previous measure of transaction costs.[10] When you plot this measure of procurement (transaction) costs for each automaker, along with the automaker's "trustworthiness" score, you find a very strong correlation between trust and procurement costs (see Figure 9.3).[11] So we see that the least trusted automaker, General Motors, incurred procurement (transaction) costs that were more than twice those of Chrysler and Ford, and almost six times higher than Toyota. When asked why GM had so many purchasing personnel and so many suppliers, one GM executive responded, "Our purchasing activities are huge and extensive. Most activities have been geared to making sure we don't get stung by an unscrupulous supplier out there." Although there are undoubtedly a number of factors that will influence an automaker's procurement efficiency, this research shows that trust is clearly an important factor.

In summary, supplier-automaker relationships with higher levels of trust had substantially lower transaction costs. Given the

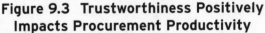

Figure 9.3 Trustworthiness Positively Impacts Procurement Productivity

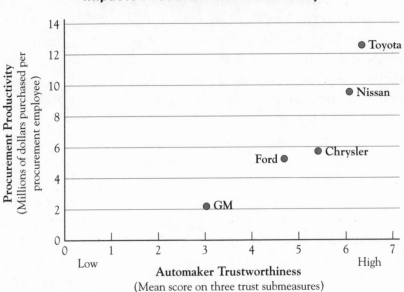

magnitude of the differences (and the fact that transaction costs are not trivial costs), the costs saved as a result of trusting relationships in the business network are large enough to be a real source of competitive advantage.

Trust Increases Knowledge Sharing

In addition to lowering transaction costs, trust has a profound influence on information sharing in supplier-buyer relationships. Not surprisingly, when suppliers trust their automaker customer they are more likely to share information with regard to product designs, technology, costs, manufacturing processes, etc. Suppliers were asked to report on the extent to which they shared confidential information with their automaker customer. The results, reported in Figure 9.4, show that suppliers are much more likely to share confidential information with automakers they trust, notably Toyota, Nissan, and Chrysler. This finding was echoed in interviews

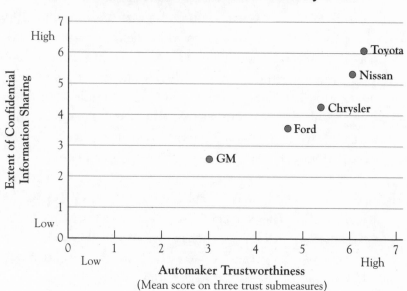

Figure 9.4 Trustworthiness Increases Confidential Information Sharing

with supplier executives, who claimed that they were much more likely to bring new product designs and proprietary technologies to "trustworthy" automakers. Stated one supplier executive:

> We are much more likely to bring a new product design to Chrysler than to General Motors. The reason is simple. General Motors has been known to take our proprietary blueprints and send them to our competitors to see if they can make the part at lower cost. They claim they are simply trying to maintain competitive bidding. But because we can't trust them to treat us fairly, we don't take our new designs to them. We take them to Chrysler because we have learned that we can trust Chrysler.[12]

In addition, suppliers are much more likely to openly share information about their problems and request assistance when necessary. Most Toyota suppliers claimed that they would be willing to open their factories to Toyota consultants—based upon the following reasoning. First, they believed that the Toyota consultants were experienced and possessed knowledge that could be truly valuable to their plants. However, just as important was the fact that they trusted Toyota to offer the assistance without demanding an immediate price cut in return for cost improvements. In contrast, many General Motors suppliers indicated that they would prefer *not* to have General Motors' consultants come to their plants. Indeed, GM has sent such consultants to suppliers to help them with their productivity. But they have had a very different reception—largely because suppliers do not trust GM. As described by one supplier executive:

> We don't want a GM team in our plant. I don't want them poking around our plant. They will just find the "low hanging" fruit—the stuff that's relatively easy to see and fix. We all have things in our plants that we know need to be fixed. They'll just come in, see it, and ask for a price decrease. We'd prefer to find it ourselves and keep all of the savings.

Thus, even though suppliers may be able to learn something from GM, they are reluctant to accept assistance or share any information because they do not trust GM or its motives. Consequently, GM may try to do the same things to help suppliers as Toyota does, but due to a lack of trust it is not interpreted in a positive light.

In summary, trust unleashes the awesome power of information and knowledge, particularly valuable knowledge that may be viewed as proprietary by the supplier. This is particularly important because the supplier's new designs and innovations may be critical in helping the buyer to differentiate its product in the marketplace.

Finally, we would expect a combination of lower transaction costs and greater information sharing to improve profit performance. In fact, when we plot each automaker's transaction costs and average trustworthiness score along with its average profitability (ROA or pre-tax profits divided by assets) from 1988–1998, the results indicate an inverse correlation between automaker transaction costs and profitability (the higher the transaction costs, the lower the profitability) (see Figure 9.5) and a significant positive correlation between automaker trustworthiness and profitability (see Figure 9.6). Although there are a number of factors that undoubtedly influence performance differences among automakers, these findings suggest that trustworthiness is a contributing factor

Figure 9.5 Lower Transaction Costs Increase Profitability

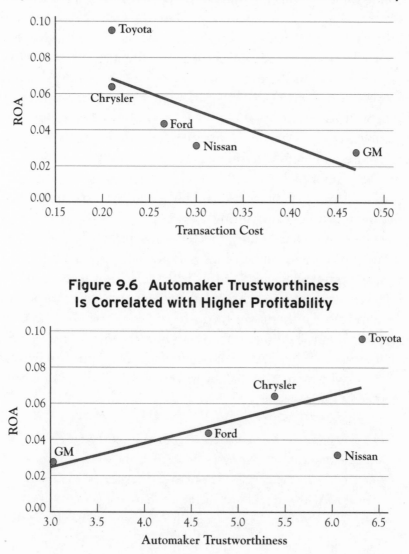

Figure 9.6 Automaker Trustworthiness Is Correlated with Higher Profitability

since it reduces the automaker's transaction costs, thereby improving automaker profitability.

The Determinants of Trust Within Business Networks

Now that we have established that trust can create significant economic value by lowering transaction costs and increasing knowledge sharing, let us turn our attention to the issue of how to build trust within the business network as a whole. It was previously argued that inter-firm trust refers to a trust orientation by a group of individuals in one organization towards a group of individuals in another organization. This is different from *interpersonal* trust, which is trust between two individuals in two organizations. It is possible to have instances of interpersonal trust between organizations without having inter-firm trust.

We previously learned that U.S. suppliers trust Toyota more than they trust U.S. automakers. The question of how Toyota was able to quickly develop trusting relationships with U.S. suppliers is an important one. Certainly, there was less time for U.S. suppliers to develop personal relationships with Toyota personnel compared to their long-standing relationships with U.S. automakers. And one would expect language and cultural differences to create barriers to building trust. Furthermore, Toyota has no stock ownership in U.S. suppliers like they do with many of their Japanese suppliers. So what is going on here? The comment of a U.S. supplier executive, when asked why he trusted Toyota more than U.S. automakers, sheds light on this issue:

> We cannot trust U.S. automakers as much as Toyota because whenever they bring in new management, we get a whole new set of procurement rules and policies. The rules of the game are constantly changing. With Toyota, we don't seem to have the same problems because their policies and personnel are consistent and stable.[13]

This executive reported, as did many supplier executives, that the rules and policies at U.S. automakers were unpredictable and inconsistent. The predictable consequence of frequent changes in purchasing management and policies is that suppliers realize that implicit, and even explicit, promises made by the automaker may be broken when new management arrives. In short, the suppliers do not trust that the U.S. automaker's *processes* for working with suppliers will be fair and consistent. Another supplier executive illustrated another dimension of the difference between interpersonal and inter-firm trust.

> It's not that I don't trust the person sitting across from me at General Motors. In fact, I may feel more comfortable with him than his Japanese counterpart at Toyota. I may trust him completely. But what I don't trust is that he will be sitting there a year from now. U.S. automakers are constantly rotating their people through purchasing. And even if he's there, he may have to play by a new set of rules.[14]

Thus, U.S. suppliers claimed that their trust in Toyota was not based on greater interpersonal trust, but rather greater trust in the fairness, stability, and predictability of Toyota's routines and processes. I refer to this as *process-based trust* and unfortunately this type of trust has been almost completely ignored in the literature on inter-firm trust. I have found that process-based trust is critical for creating a trust orientation between individuals in two large organizations. Process-based trust differs from interpersonal trust because the supplier's trust orientation towards the automaker is not based on personal relationships, but rather on a set of institutionalized processes and routines employed at the automaker. The "boundary-spanning" person at the automaker behaves in a trustworthy manner because the organizational culture and processes demand that someone in his particular boundary-spanning role behave in a "trustworthy" manner. Thus, the automaker is viewed as trustworthy when it has institutionalized a set of practices and routines for dealing with a partner organization that transcends the influence of the individual boundary spanner. Process-based trust recognizes that inter-firm trust may be built upon impersonal processes and routines that create a stable context for exchange. Individuals may come and go at the two organizations but the trust orientation will not be affected because trust is not based on individual relationships.

Assuming that trust is based more on processes than people, this begs the question of what processes are key to building trust. My research suggests that there are a number of practices that are important in developing trust within the business network.

Supplier-Selection Processes That Demonstrate Commitment

One of the key processes that can either foster, or destroy, supplier trust is the process used by the automaker to select a supplier for a new vehicle model. In some instances, buyers use a competitive bidding process whereby incumbents are not given any advantage in ensuing rounds, regardless of past performance. This is an arms-length competitive bidding process typically used by U.S. companies such as General Motors. In other instances, automakers may select suppliers based upon their track record for performance and give incumbents the first opportunity to garner new business. This is a selection process that favors incumbents and is often said to typify Japanese supplier-buyer relationships (though many U.S. firms, including Chrysler in the mid-1990s, use this approach). The research shows that the competitive bidding process fosters mistrust and that automakers that aggressively use competitive bidding are virtually *always* viewed as less trustworthy. According to suppliers, the competitive bidding system immediately creates an adversarial relationship with the automaker because the exchange relationship is set up as a zero-sum game. The automaker may further exacerbate the problem by using the price comparisons to back up threats to switch business away unless it gets a better deal. As a result, suppliers feel like the automaker views them as expendable and cares little for their profitability or survival. In short, the competitive bidding process does not make the supplier feel like they are an important member of the business network. Instead they are a temporary member of a value chain—and the supplier knows he had better make as much profit on the current piece of business as possible because there are no future guarantees. Of course, this may be perfectly appropriate when the supplier's product is purely a commodity and when the potential to create a customized input is low, but in the rapidly transforming technology and interdependence in automobiles, fewer and fewer pure commodities are utilized. Greater emphasis on integrated systems and value-added components has created an environment where suppliers play an even greater role in influencing the performance of the finished automobile.

In contrast, Toyota does not choose suppliers by competitive bid, but rather selects suppliers for new models based upon their track record for performance and previous history with Toyota. If a supplier has manufactured the braking system or air conditioner on the previous Toyota Camry or Corolla, then there is a better than 90 percent chance that it will "re-win" the business at the model change. Of course, the ability to re-win the business at the model change will depend on the supplier's performance (on cost, quality, delivery, etc.) on the previous model and the ability to meet the "target price" given by Toyota. But if the supplier performs well, it knows it can count on getting the business on the next model. Supplier trust emerges under these conditions because the supplier can count on a long-term relationship and it knows that there is a low probability that the automaker will switch (perhaps opportunistically) the business to a competitor. In the language of game theory, giving incumbents an advantage in the next round serves as a signal to the supplier that the automaker is playing a long-run "cooperative equilibrium" or a "repeated game." Repeated exchange is particularly important to the development of supplier trust in situations where suppliers have invested in dedicated assets. Under these conditions, an automaker's willingness to stay with the same supplier is interpreted by the supplier as a signal of commitment and trustworthiness.

To demonstrate the relationship between supplier selection processes and trust, suppliers were asked to provide their historical experience with regard to re-winning the contract when there was a model change. In the automotive industry, the model change is a natural time for buyers to re-evaluate suppliers and make a change if deemed appropriate. Automakers who use competitive bidding and frequently change suppliers will have a lower re-win rate than automakers who have selection processes that favor incumbents. Suppliers to GM reported that historically they only re-win the business 58 percent of the time at contract renewal (See Table 9.1). Thus, they have had almost a 50 percent chance of getting thrown out at the model change. These suppliers also report relatively low trust in General Motors. In contrast, Toyota suppliers report that they have experienced a 92 percent re-win rate. Suppliers to Toyota expect a long-term, continuous relationship and feel that they are an important member of Toyota's business network. Not surprisingly, they view Toyota as a more trustworthy customer.

"Free" Assistance to the Supplier

A second way that Toyota builds supplier trust is by providing assistance to help suppliers improve. Toyota has created a consulting group (called the Operations Management Consulting Division) and sends these consultants—free of charge—to transfer knowledge to suppliers to help them improve productivity and quality. In addition to improving supplier productivity and quality, this appears to be an important method of building trust. U.S. suppliers reported that they received significantly more assistance from Toyota than they did from their U.S. customers (See Table 9.1). Indeed, some U.S. suppliers claimed that they received more help from Toyota than they felt they deserved given their short-term relationship. As the vice president of planning for a supplier of plastic interior parts stated:

> I couldn't believe it but Toyota sent approximately 2–4 consultants *every day* for a period of 3–4 months as we attempted to implement Toyota Production System concepts in a new plant. They gave us a valuable gift [the Toyota Production System] ... Naturally we feel indebted towards Toyota and view them as a special customer; they sincerely want to help us improve.[15]

This type of "assistance-giving" behavior on the part of Toyota was a catalyst for creating a norm of reciprocal obligation and trust.

The importance of "gift exchange" in creating trust and reciprocity in exchange relationships has long been argued by a distinguished line of anthropologists and sociologists.[16] For example, in a seminal article sociologist Alvin Gouldner[17] argued that a "norm of reciprocity" between exchange partners begins with a "starting mechanism," which may take the form of a gift or other acts of assistance. Suppliers interpret Toyota's assistance-giving behavior as a signal of goodwill and commitment—an indication that Toyota is genuinely concerned with the well-being of the supplier. In effect, the assistance is viewed by the supplier as a signal that Toyota does not have opportunistic intent.

Stable, Long-Term Employment

Much has been written about the Japanese employment practice of long-term employment within one firm.[18] Its importance in developing trust between individuals across firms cannot be ignored. Although I have tried to highlight that trust between large organizations can be, and often is, based upon processes rather than personal relationships, stability of employment and relationships also results in stability of processes. Further, trust is greatest among companies when *both interpersonal and process-based trust exist*. In Japan, trust between Toyota and its suppliers is higher than in the United

States because process-based trust is combined with interpersonal trust. There are strong personal relations between the purchasing manager of Toyota and the manager or owner of a supplier. The importance of these personal relationships should not be underestimated. Naturally, you are more likely to trust someone with whom you've done business for a long period of time. It is much harder to build a trusting relationship with someone if you think they will be gone in six months, as happens in many U.S. companies. Hence, because Toyota's people can develop long-standing relationships with their counterparts at the supplier or buyer, it is not surprising that Toyota has been able to develop significantly greater trust within its business network.

Both U.S. and Japanese suppliers contend that Toyota is more trustworthy than U.S. automakers due to its lifetime employment and "promotion-from-within" policies, which foster stability in personnel and policies. To test these assertions about stability, employee tenure in two Japanese (Toyota and Nissan) and two U.S. (Ford and Chrysler) automakers was examined. A random sample of 100 U.S. and 100 Japanese purchasing and engineering employees was surveyed to determine the average tenure of employment (these employees were roughly the same age). It was learned that purchasing and engineering employees at Toyota and Nissan had been with their employer for an average of 16.2 years, while their counterparts at Ford and Chrysler had only been at their company for 8.8 years. Thus, there is almost twice the employment stability at Toyota relative to its U.S. counterparts. Furthermore, a study by Susan Helper and Mari Sako[19] also found greater stability of employment among supplier employees in Japan. In a sample of 472 executives of Japanese suppliers and 671 executives at U.S. suppliers, Helper and Sako found that Japanese supplier executives had been with their companies an average of 22 years, while U.S. executives had only been with their companies for 11 years. These data show that employment stability is much greater at both Toyota and its suppliers. This stability leads to greater trust within the business network because (1) suppliers have greater confidence that interorganizational processes will not change, and (2) personal ties and interpersonal trust develop between employees in the two organizations.

The previous three practices have been important in helping Toyota build trusting supplier relationships in both the U.S. and Japan. However, in addition to these practices, Toyota uses two other important practices to build trust that are unique to Japan.

Career Paths Between Firms

Toyota also builds trust by requiring career paths in which employees transfer from firm to firm (or are simply allowed to work at partner firm facilities). Employee transfers, both temporary (usually two years) and permanent, are common between Toyota and its suppliers. Thus, job rotations occur across firm boundaries within the business network. MIT professor Michael Cusumano has described how executive transfers were particularly important in the auto industry because they "usually preceded technical assistance, loans, or exclusive procurement contracts." It is important to note that Cusumano found that employee transfers *preceded* additional partner-specific investments on the part of the automakers.[20] The point is this: Toyota is more likely to make investments in suppliers when it trusts the individuals it is dealing with—and who better to trust than former employees or people with whom you've worked for years? In my study I found Toyota transfers roughly 120–130 employees per year to work in supplier companies. Moreover, 23 percent of the top managers at Toyota's "affiliated suppliers" (suppliers in whom Toyota owns some stock) were former Toyota employees. Almost one-fourth of the top executives at Toyota's partner suppliers are former Toyota employees. Clearly, this is an unusual practice that helps Toyota and its suppliers work cooperatively.

Moreover, in addition to permanent and temporary employee swaps, suppliers often send guest engineers to work at Toyota's technical center on an ongoing basis. We previously discussed how this is an important practice that facilitates information sharing and improves product quality and speed to market. In 1997 Toyota had roughly 700 guest engineers housed at its main technical center in Japan. These engineers are a part of the design team and are given desks in the same room with the Toyota engineers. Thus, supplier and automaker engineers jointly design the component for a new car model. Supplier engineers may work at Toyota's facility for as long as 2–3 years. Not only do these career-path practices help build trust within the business network, but also transferred and guest employees are better able to understand how to optimize the efficiency of the business network because they know both customer and supplier operations.

Minority Ownership

By now it is no secret that Japanese firms like Toyota, instead of vertically integrating, will often take significant minority ownership positions in key suppliers. This is an important practice for creating an attitude of "mutual destiny" and cooperation within the business network. For example, Toyota owns roughly 28 percent (on average) of the shares of its top ten major supplier partners. This is a significant enough ownership stake to build goal congruence—and trust between—Toyota and its supplier partners. Stock ownership among Japanese companies represents credible commitments that firms have made to each other and in many ways they are an arrangement that is akin to an "exchange of hostages." If I own a portion of my partner supplier then I am less willing to take advantage of him because I will be hurt financially. Thus, the practice of taking minority ownership positions in suppliers increases goal congruence and trust within the business network.

Conclusion

Evidence from the automotive industry and other studies shows that trust between organizations can lower transaction costs, increase information sharing, and improve performance. While there are undoubtedly situations where companies get burned by misplacing trust in another organization, the potential to create economic value from properly placed trust is real.

To determine whether or not building trust with suppliers/ alliance partners is critical to your company, you might consider the fact that trust in supplier-buyer relations is a particularly important asset in industrial settings in which (1) transaction costs are high due to conditions that create transactional difficulties (e.g., environmental uncertainty and a need for investments in dedicated assets), and (2) there is a high value associated with information sharing due to product complexity and industry uncertainty.

Regardless of the industry your company competes in, it is probably worth your time to explore areas where you can experiment with these trust-building concepts to increase trust with suppliers and alliance partners in hopes of reducing transaction costs and increasing information sharing. Try to identify one or two key business partners where your relationships aren't performing as well as you would like to see them and where you think it is in both companies' strategic interests to build more trust.

- **Step 1.** *Analyze* the relationship from the transaction cost and information-sharing perspectives discussed in this chapter to identify where you might find opportunities to proactively build trust with your partners. Identify what costs might be high due to lack of trust, and what information might not be shared due to a lack of trust.
- **Step 2.** *Assess* what knowledge your company possesses that would not only benefit your partner, but would benefit your company if your partner had access to that information.
- **Step 3.** *Communicate* with your partner away from the traditional "negotiation table" about how they view your relationship and what your companies could do jointly to make your relationship more profitable and successful. Avoid discussions about pricing and contracts and focus on lowering transaction costs for both companies.

Building trust in your business network will not be easy, especially if your business network has a history of fighting with each other over sharing the jointly created pie, as opposed to working together to expand the pie. But building trust within your business network can be a critical first step towards creating a higher-value ecosystem for all the participants and for extracting higher returns for your company and for the business network as a whole.

Chapter 10

The Role of IT in Business Network Transformation

Andrew McAfee

Associate Professor of Business Administration
Harvard Business School

I had the chance in December 2008 to join Leo Apotheker, CEO of SAP AG, for a conversation with Charlie Rose about the impact of IT. In response to one of Charlie's initial questions, Leo listed a number of capabilities provided by modern corporate IT. Included among these was the fact that information technology enables globalization.

Leo knew, of course, that globalization of trade started *long* before computers showed up, and that it's likely that many parts of the world were in fact settled by early traders. His point was that the modern style of globalization, with its massive, rapid, and precise flows of products and services, would simply not be possible without today's information and communications technologies. Unplug all the world's computers and the world's businesses and markets would simply cease to function, within days if not hours.

But what roles do all the different types of information technology play in the ongoing story of global business network transformation? In particular, where does the type of software made by Leo's company fit in? In most descriptions of globalization, IT assists by generating, processing, and storing required information, then sending it from one place to another. As the expense of doing all these things drops, more global possibilities open up.

In particular, as the cost of transmitting an additional bit of information has dropped essentially to zero in the era of high-bandwidth networks and Internet pricing, some truly novel business models become feasible.

In this description, IT facilitates business network transformation by lowering and removing cost and time constraints. This is an accurate story, but an incomplete one. A more complete account includes the critical fact that enterprise technology helps by *imposing* some types of constraint on the parties involved in a far-flung business network.

The Challenge of Building Network Relationships

To see this counterintuitive phenomenon at work, let's take a hypothetical but commonplace example of globalization and business network transformation. Snazzy, a U.S.-based designer and marketer of cutting-edge consumer electronics products, wants to make its latest product in China in order to take advantage of the low wages, manufacturing expertise, and large base of suppliers there. This product is highly customizable; consumers use Snazzy's web site to configure and order exactly the product that they want. Snazzy wants never to touch the product; it wants its subcontractor to ship the finished goods directly to consumers.

AbFab, a Chinese contract manufacturer, has deep experience assembling customized products, and is willing and able to take on the project. However, the product contains a chip that is very difficult to fabricate; many suppliers offer it, but only a couple can actually deliver high enough quality and reliability. And these suppliers, of course, are the most expensive ones. To complicate matters, this chip doesn't fail immediately when it's not made well, but instead stops working after a few months. Luckily, a testing machine is available that indicates whether each chip is "good" or not.

Snazzy's challenge here is assuring that only good chips wind up in its product. This would be easier to do if the factory were locally owned and operated; the company would simply deal only with the good suppliers and test all of their products. But when the factory is halfway around the world, and owned and managed by strangers, the challenge becomes vastly more difficult. In effect, Snazzy must ensure that its contractors and their subcontractors manage the manufacturing, quality assurance, and fulfillment processes exactly as Snazzy itself would.

If left entirely on its own, AbFab could attempt to cut costs by buying the chip from uncertified suppliers, or it could simply fail to be diligent enough in procurement, and inadvertently purchase poor chips instead of good ones. Snazzy could mandate that AbFab must test all chips before they go into the product and use only the ones that pass, but how would this mandate be enforced? In short, it's hard for Snazzy to ensure that its contractor is acting exactly as Snazzy itself would in these circumstances. Economists call these types of situations "agency problems." They arise whenever an agent (AbFab in this case) has an incentive to act in ways that are at odds with the wishes of the principal (Snazzy) that engages the agent.[1]

The classic way to resolve agency problems is to try to align the incentives of the two parties, usually via smartly written contracts. A contract clause could state, for example, that Snazzy would be entitled to withhold payments to AbFab if consumers' products started to fail at too high a rate. But in this example bad chips only start to fail after months of use, and there are plenty of other factors (drops, coffee spills, etc.) that could cause the product to stop working after that long. AbFab could reasonably object that this clause is unfair. Alternatively, Snazzy could employ an auditor to station itself in AbFab's factory and conduct testing. This solution, however, adds expense, leads to further complications (does the auditor have the right to shut down AbFab's assembly line depending on test results?) and brings up potential agency problems with the auditor itself. In many cases, agency problems can be so severe that they prevent some business arrangements that would be beneficial to both parties.

Information technology, in particular the kinds of enterprise applications that Apotheker's company builds and sells, offers hope for many types of agency problems. Enterprise software lets companies define business processes, then deploy them wherever desired. In the era of the Internet it's technically trivial for Snazzy to deploy its own enterprise applications as far as AbFab's factory and even into the chip supplier's business as well.

And what kinds of business processes would Snazzy define? To deal with the agency problem, it would define a process in which chip testing occurred early in the product assembly sequence and was immediately followed by installation of all the customized options. Furthermore, the software would not release the configuration information unless and until the chip had successfully passed the test.

With this business process in place, it would be very difficult for AbFab to make products that contained low-quality chips. The subcontractor could conceivably use good chips to pass the test, then swap them immediately afterward for low-quality ones and proceed with configuration, but it would probably be possible to design the assembly line itself so that this would be difficult to do. More fundamentally, though, this kind of subterfuge is difficult to maintain over time, and it might well be less trouble for AbFab simply to comply with the process as designed by Snazzy, and therefore to obtain chips from the official supplier. It's not the case, in other words, that enterprise systems always ensure 100 percent compliance with 100 percent confidence. What they can often do, though, is make the cost, time, and effort required for noncompliance so high that it's simply easier and more efficient to execute business processes as designed.

One final point from this example: if AbFab is a reputable subcontractor, it will actually *welcome* this new process and the enterprise software that supports it. It wants to provide all possible assurances to Snazzy that it is operating as agreed in order to become a trusted and valued partner for Snazzy as they grow. Enterprise IT can be an extremely powerful tool for ensuring that is the case. Enterprise systems, in summary, are often welcomed by honest agents because they overcome problems that could otherwise keep principals away.

This example shows the power and importance of business processes (also called *workflows*) that are managed with enterprise applications and deployed when the software itself is. The role that IT plays in modern business network transformation is not just to record, process, and transmit huge amounts of data; its function is also to reduce agency problems, and to assure principals that processes will be executed as designed, no matter where on the planet they occur or how many different people, locations, and companies they include.

Network-Enabled Business Processes

In my recent research I've come across many examples of companies using enterprise IT to transform themselves, to address actual or potential agency problems, and to put in place consistent business processes across a large organizational footprint. These examples include the following:

- **Pharmacy service improvement at CVS** In 2002 CVS formed a cross-functional team to investigate low customer satisfaction levels at the company's in-store pharmacies. The team concluded that delays, exceptions, and interruptions would be greatly reduced if two steps in the fulfillment process were switched so that the customer's insurance verification was completed before the automated drug safety check was performed. The team also advocated doing the insurance verification at the time that customers dropped off their prescriptions instead of waiting until later. Many pharmacists around the country did not agree that these process changes would be beneficial; they felt that delaying the drug safety check was an unnecessary risk. However, after the company's pharmacy support applications were reconfigured so that the insurance check always came first, it was simply not possible to continue to do prescription fulfillment the old way; pharmacists at the more than 4,000 locations around the country had very little choice except to go along with the new process. The new work-flow led to a nearly 15 percent improvement in customer satis-faction scores and savings of hundreds of millions of dollars.[2]

- **Los Grobo's network organization for agriculture in Latin America** In a part of the world not known for technology innovation, and in one of the most traditional of all industries, Argentina's Los Grobo has built a true network organization. The company employs relatively few people and owns only a small percentage of the land it farms. Yet all activities on each piece of land are tightly monitored and controlled, as are processes for transporting, storing, and selling harvests. Los Grobo has accomplished this by interconnecting all of the par-ticipants in its network—landowners, agronomists, branch office managers, employees at headquarters, etc.—via the Inter-net and requiring them to enter all of their activities into the company's enterprise systems. These activities are linked together into a set of business processes that are executed con-sistently across multiple countries. Los Grobo believes so strongly in standardized, repeatable processes that it has taken the step, unusual in its industry, of seeking and obtaining ISO 9000 certification. The Los Grobo network organization has grown by more than 30 percent in each of the last several years.[3]

- **Zara's processes to support "fast fashion"** The Spanish cloth-ing company Zara is well known in the apparel industry for its ability to sense and respond rapidly to consumer tastes: to fig-ure out what garments are desired by young, fashion-forward people around the world and to satisfy these desires by getting a steady stream of new clothes into its more than 1,500 stores. What's less well known is that Zara achieves this impressive feat by relying on a small number of processes that are exe-cuted week after week with complete consistency across all these stores. Twice a week, each store receives a digital order form listing all items available to order for each section of the store. The stores must complete this form and send it back within a specified time window. Headquarters then compares total demand to total supply, decides who gets what if there's not enough to go around, and sends the requested clothes to each location. This cycle of request and fulfill repeats itself like clockwork throughout the calendar and around the globe. Zara has achieved consistently excellent operational and financial performance, and in recent years has overtaken H&M and The Gap as the world's largest clothing retailer.[4]

In each of these examples, and in many others I've seen, headquarters (in other words, the center of the organization) is active in business network transformation in two ways. First, the processes that flow throughout the company and its business network are centrally defined, and the enterprise software that supports them is purchased and configured right at the middle of the business. Second, headquarters uses enterprise IT to monitor activities and events and ensure that processes are being executed as designed. There was a saying in imperial China that "The mountains are high, and the emperor is far away." In that environment, regional bureaucrats could operate with great autonomy because oversight was so difficult. An environment supported by enterprise IT is quite different; the emperor is always close by (in fact, he's looking over everyone's shoulder), making it much harder to ignore his ideas about how things should be run.

The capabilities that enterprise technologies give to "headquarters" bring up an intriguing and unsettling question: won't most businesses use this tool to transform their networks in the direction of more centralization? In other words, won't companies generally use enterprise applications to build more top-heavy networks, ones in which the most important decisions are made centrally while the rest of the organization becomes more peripheral (in every sense of the word)?

Given the power of enterprise IT this seems like a likely scenario, but I don't think it will actually come to pass in most well-managed companies. This is because some important decisions *should* be made far away from the center, and well-managed companies realize this.

They will use enterprise systems to provide global visibility into processes throughout their networks, but decisions within these processes will often be left at the local level. The emperor, in other words, might want to see the results of decisions made throughout his realm, but that doesn't mean he wants to make all the decisions himself.

Zara, for example, understands that it is extremely difficult (if not impossible) to accurately forecast what demand will be for high-fashion clothes by analyzing historical data. So they don't even try. Instead of trying to figure out at headquarters what clothes will sell in each store, the company relies on store managers to simply order the clothes they could immediately sell; headquarters then ships these clothes to them as quickly as possible. Zara has used enterprise IT not to centralize important decisions, but instead to build a network in which the company's most important decisions are totally *decentralized*. However, by centralizing the *information* from all of its operations, Zara can maintain global *visibility* to see bigger trends than any individual store manager could see.

Similar patterns are apparent in the other two examples given above. The Los Grobo network has a strong center that's deeply involved in many processes, but it's simultaneously highly decentralized. Agronomists make decisions about the best way to manage each plot of land in order to maximize crop yields; headquarters wants to be informed about these choices, but does not want to make all of them. And at CVS, the improvements to the pharmacy fulfillment process were devised at headquarters, but these changes did not leave the company more centralized than it was before. Store pharmacists had all the same rights and tasks in the new process as in the old one; they just exercised them in a different order.

The IT-Enabled Business Network Journey

The great power that modern IT supplies for business network transformation, then, is the power to design or redesign a set of processes, to embed them in technology, to deploy them as widely as necessary, and to ensure that they will be executed as designed over time and across great distances. One final but critical point about this work of IT-enabled business network transformation is that it's never finished; the design that makes sense at one point in time for one portion of a business is not necessarily going to be appropriate always and everywhere.

A pair of cases written by Prof. Warren McFarlan and his colleagues about the Otis Elevator company illustrates this fact. In the first, set in 1985, Otis executives led by George David realized that the company's highly decentralized field service organization was failing to provide uniformly excellent service to customers with problems, and also failing to provide the company with timely and accurate information about service calls. So the company built and implemented OTISLINE, a highly centralized mainframe enterprise system. After OTISLINE was in place, customers with service problems called a toll-free number and spoke to a customer service representative at headquarters in Connecticut. The representative recorded all relevant information about the problem, then dispatched a mechanic to make repairs. When the mechanic was finished, he called headquarters again to describe the repairs he made and their results. OTISLINE, it is fair to say, completely transformed the company's field service organization, making it more centralized, and also much more responsive, efficient, and analytical.

The second case, written in 2004, concerns Ari Bousbib's efforts to improve the process not of repairing elevators, but of installing them in the first place. As he said in a conversation with McFarlan, "When I came to Otis I realized that in our 26 factories around the world we had $150 million of inventory at most, and that inventory was turning at ten turns or more, which was pretty good. At the same time, we had more than $2.5 billion worth of inventory sitting on 35,000 job sites around the world. And that inventory was turning at one turn." Bousbib's solution, called e*Logistics, defined and used IT to deploy a number of new workflows for processes such as delivery of elevator assemblies to job sites. In contrast to OTISLINE, however, these new workflows were generally not more centralized than the ones they replaced. In fact, they often increased the responsibilities of front-line employees. Under e*Logistics, for example, field supervisors had to certify that job sites were ready for their elevators to be installed; previously, elevators were just delivered to sites as soon as Otis factories had finished manufacturing them.[5]

Otis's history reveals three important characteristics of IT-enabled business network transformation. First, there is no shortage of good ideas out there. Even after companies have spent much time and effort trying to improve themselves, insightful business leaders can still find substantial untapped opportunities. Second, these types of efforts can be strong contributors to overall corporate performance. Otis's parent company, United Technologies, has posted excellent results and kept investors happy over the years, and its leaders often discuss technology when discussing how they achieve their results. Third, these leaders themselves are often the originators and leaders of IT-based transformation efforts. Many companies treat enterprise IT deployments as large-scale but low-level efforts, or as IT projects. Otis, in contrast, treated OTISLINE and e*Logistics as broad and deep organizational transformations (which they were) and managed them accordingly. And success in these efforts paid off for the executive in charge. George David became the CEO of United Technologies, and Ari Bousbib is at present a vice president of the corporation, and the president of all of United's commercial companies.

Deploy, Innovate, and Propagate

In a July/August 2008 *Harvard Business Review* article, Erik Brynjolfsson and I proposed "deploy, innovate, propagate" as a mantra for IT-enabled business network transformation.[6] In addition to specifying activities for the leaders of these efforts, this mantra also helps put into context three of the most important current trends in corporate computing: the availability of commercial enterprise systems like those sold by SAP; Enterprise 2.0, or the use of Web 2.0 tools and philosophies by businesses; and the systems integration approach known as *service-oriented architecture*.

First is *deploy*, which in this case means installing, configuring, testing, and conducting training on the enterprise system(s) that support processes across a business network. Two points about this activity deserve special attention here. First, there are very few modern business activities that are not supported by IT. It is easy to overlook how pervasive corporate enterprise technology has become. It is important not to, however, because to ignore or down-play the role of IT is to miss opportunities for improvement, redesign, standardization, and the other types of business network transformation illustrated by the examples given earlier in this chapter and this book.

The second important point about deployment is that in most industries today it is largely a process of configuring commercial software rather than writing code from scratch. The "market share" of packaged enterprise systems has increased steadily since the first modern ones were introduced in the early 1990s, and they are now available for a huge range of tasks, processes, and business environments. Most large deployments still involve some amount of coding, of course, but today's business networks are being transformed with the support of systems that are bought, not built.

Even the most brilliant deployment is unlikely to keep delivering value and contributing to competitive differentiation over a long time period if left in its initial state. The second imperative, then, is to *innovate*—to consider business network transformation as something closer to an ongoing series of evolutionary steps rather than a one-time event. As I've worked with business students and management teams over the years I've noticed a consistent and largely unexamined assumption about innovation: that it is the responsibility of a small, pre-defined group of people. Their titles often contain terms like executive, strategic, consultant, etc., and it is their job to plan the next round of business network transformation (just as it's their job to execute the transformation by leading the work of deployment).

It's true that these people are often experienced and insightful, and so are effective business innovators. But it's also true that they're far from the only ones with good ideas. A very promising recent trend is the democratization of innovation within companies and across business networks. Several terms are used to describe this trend, including *open innovation* (as discussed in Henry Chesbrough's chapter in this book), *collective intelligence*, and *Enterprise 2.0*. I prefer Enterprise 2.0 because it alludes to the phenomenon of Web 2.0 and indicates the central importance of IT in enabling the new modes of innovation. Enterprise 2.0 involves enterprise-scale technologies that let communities form organically and interact and collaborate without specifying in advance who belongs in the community or how its members should interact with each other. Given the emergent nature of these collaborative innovation processes and the free-flowing nature of information and ideas between companies and individuals, the rigid process models of standard enterprise software aren't appropriate for them. The new processes of collaboration, however, are still enterprise processes and the concepts of central visibility, localized decision-making, and shared analytics still apply to them. A key challenge is the integration of these fast-moving, semi-structured collaborative Enterprise 2.0 processes with the highly structured and coordinated processes from Enterprise 1.0.

A few examples give an idea of the current wave of technology-facilitated innovations in business network transformation.

- Rite-Solutions, a small Rhode Island–based engineering firm and defense contractor, established a collaborative internal intranet workspace where employees can submit ideas, recruit colleagues to flesh them out and work on them, post project plans, and track progress against them. The company's leaders see this as a way to let its people self-organize and be helpful to each other in ways that were not previously possible.[7]

- Google maintains a less formal online forum, called the Idea-Board, where employees can post their ideas and receive feedback on them. As the company grows and opens labs and offices around the world, it becomes difficult for its people to find colleagues with the skills and motivation to work together on side projects. The IdeaBoard can act as a catalyst for these projects, which have been important to the company. They've yielded innovations such as Gmail, Google News, and AdSense.[8]

- InnoCentive, a spinoff from pharma giant Eli Lilly, collects unsolved problems from research labs, anonymizes them, and posts them to the Web along with a monetary reward offered for solving them. Anyone around the world can download the problem, work on it, and upload their solution. One study found that almost 30 percent of problems posted to InnoCentive were solved, and that the best predictor that a solution would be found, it turned out, was the diversity of scientific backgrounds among those who downloaded it. This fact underscores the serendipitous virtues of open innovation and Enterprise 2.0 and also shows the value of using analytics to accurately identify predictors of success based on data captured in Enterprise 2.0 systems.[9]

The final important third of our mantra is *propagate*—spread the transformed ways of working as widely as is appropriate throughout the business network. In my experience, most business innovations are not propagated as widely as they could or should be. This is due in part to local managers' preference for maintaining autonomy (as indicated by the Chinese saying about high mountains and distant emperors), and also due to fragmented legacy systems, which make process consistency and standardization exceedingly difficult.

As is the case with deployment and innovation, modern corporate technologies are helping leading companies propagate their good ideas. The tools of Enterprise 2.0, for example, can be effective in spreading one person's insights throughout an organization. The construction company IntraWest witnessed this after it gave all its employees the opportunity to blog internally. One manager used his blog to describe a new method of installing a radiant heated floor that saved $500,000 on a project with a baseline cost of $2,000,000.

This innovation thus became instantly and permanently visible to everyone at IntraWest, and it soon propagated; colleagues posted questions to the original blog post asking how they could put the new method into practice.[10]

Betting on the Next Wave

Service-oriented architecture (SOA) is a relatively novel approach for propagating more detailed and formal business innovations such as cross-functional business processes. It has historically been difficult to spread these past the boundaries of a single enterprise system because of the time and effort required to integrate disparate systems. SOA is essentially an approach to systems integration in which many of the ground rules for combining systems are specified in advance. These ground rules cover how involved systems will exchange data, and also the types of data and services that they are ready, willing, and able to exchange with each other.

It can be expensive for a large company to put in place an SOA but a growing number, including Aetna Insurance and British Telecom, are making the investment. They are doing so in hopes of reaping two broad types of benefits. The first is the ability to propagate processes more widely, including beyond the four walls of the company. The second is the ability to propagate them more quickly and cost effectively. With an SOA in place systems can be interconnected much more rapidly and cheaply than was the case previously. As the pace of competition heats up and the need to seize opportunities and respond to others' moves quickly become acute, this ability becomes highly valuable. Companies that invest in creating an SOA today are betting that they'll need the flexibility it offers tomorrow—that they'll have to widely and quickly propagate their business innovations. This seems like a safe bet.

Executives who are interested in expanding the role of IT in business network transformation don't need to become programmers, gadget freaks, or part-time CIOs. Instead, they need to think about how technology can better help their companies innovate, then propagate these innovations. To start this work, I encourage people to think about three simple questions, the answers to which go a long way toward defining appropriate IT initiatives for a company.

- Do we have in place an infrastructure that lets us deploy process and business network innovations widely and with high fidelity? If not, investment in consistent enterprise systems might well be worthwhile.

- What are our current sources of innovation? Are we giving all motivated and informed people opportunities to contribute their ideas and energy? If not, a company should start experimenting with Enterprise 2.0.

- How quickly can we propagate innovations and improvements throughout our business network? Would it take weeks, months, or years to accomplish a significant effort like a merger, acquisition, or major outsourcing deal? If propagation is slow, enterprise systems and SOA can help speed it up.

Modern information technologies do much more than simply enable or facilitate business network transformation. As this book and this chapter have hopefully made clear, technology extends and accelerates many of the changes now taking place in the world of business and makes them stick. Once modern enterprise systems are deployed they give companies new ways to innovate and to propagate their innovations. Insightful business leaders are taking advantage of these opportunities in many ways and are shaping the nature of competition in their industries. Businesses that are unaware or unconvinced of the power of IT, meanwhile, are likely to find themselves falling behind.

Chapter 11

Road Map to Transform Your Business Network

Philip Lay and Geoffrey Moore

Managing Directors, TCG Advisors

When we left off at the end of Chapter 1, we explained that we would revisit the strategic implications of BNT after you had the opportunity to explore the various angles of BNT in the remaining chapters of the book. Now that you have seen how BNT manifests itself in the different operational areas of your company, how leading firms have successfully used BNT to leverage the capabilities of their partners, suppliers, and customers, and how IT enables BNT, we will explain how firms travel through the evolutionary journey towards full BNT maturity. We have witnessed that companies evolve through a certain set of phases as they embrace BNT into more areas of their business. As BNT becomes more pervasive, different goals, skills, and IT capabilities are needed to advance towards higher value levels of BNT maturity.

Strategic Phases of Business Network Transformation

Turning to the goal of proactively engaging in business network transformation, there is an escalating series of motives for so doing. Each step on the Business Network Maturity Model (Figure 11.1) involves different strategic and tactical steps, and companies move up the "staircase" at different speeds, depending on the impact that BNT is having on their competitive situation.

Figure 11.1 Business Network Maturity Model

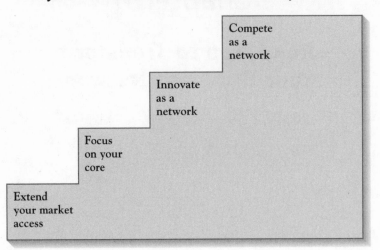

At the start, the goal for most companies is simply to leverage an existing business network to extend your company's market access. The focus is on *participation*. For example, a company might join a new network to gain access to a new set of customers or relationships.

Once part of a network, a company's further growth depends upon continued differentiation through an increasingly intense focus on "core" capabilities. This requires one to outsource non-core work, which in turn makes a market for other network partners. The bigger the market you make, the more you can influence the behavior of the network to support your overall strategic intent.

The next step in BNT is to leverage the resources of a trusted set of partners to create next-generation offerings that no one company by itself could field. This requires collaborating across enterprise boundaries, which in turn requires careful alignment of both short-term and long-term incentives.

Finally, the highest return on business networks comes from competing as a network, fielding a continuously improving set of offers that integrate the talents of each of the companies involved. This requires strong leadership for a core orchestrator or concentrator who, at key intervals, sponsors acts of "strategic generosity" to ensure the network as a whole prospers.

As companies move up the staircase and networks mature, new activities gain more importance. These new activities rely on trust and relationships that have been cultivated on lower steps, building higher value as the network evolves. These new activities increasingly focus on higher value interactions with network participants. That isn't to say that doing the day-to-day work of the business becomes less relevant. It is more a function of the increased value that can be extracted from the network to support "core" business activities.

In Figure 11.2, we explore some of the new activities that emerge as companies and their networks mature. We also identify key mechanisms that align networks at each stage, as well as the focus of IT systems to enable both the new activities and new alignment mechanisms.

- **Extend Market Access.** This is business as usual in a networked environment. Newcomers seek to become well-behaved citizens in this segment, and they focus on the nuts and bolts of

Figure 11.2 Primary Business Focus at Each Stair

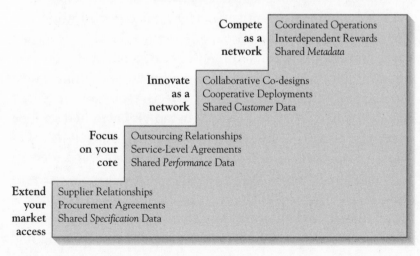

| Compete as a network | Coordinated Operations
Interdependent Rewards
Shared *Metadata* |

| Innovate as a network | Collaborative Co-designs
Cooperative Deployments
Shared *Customer* Data |

| Focus on your core | Outsourcing Relationships
Service-Level Agreements
Shared *Performance* Data |

| Extend your market access | Supplier Relationships
Procurement Agreements
Shared *Specification* Data |

commerce to do so. IT systems focus on RFPs, contracts, EDI, and the like.

- **Focus on Core.** This is the focus of established players who, in the need to differentiate, have committed more and more resources to specialization and thus must find more and more ways to offload non-core or "context" work. The good news is that, whatever is "context" for you is likely to be "core" for someone else, so there are partners who very much want to take over responsibility for your "context" business. When you give it to them, they become part of your business network. The issues develop around work that, while not core, is mission-critical. This puts a lot of pressure on service-level agreements, and IT must go beyond specification and acceptance data, and get into the world of real-time performance monitoring and issue escalation management.

- **Innovate as a Network**. Here the focus is on core, and the realization is that, all by ourselves, we cannot create a sufficiently differentiated offer to win. We need to combine our efforts with other specialists, including the customer. Whether during the design phase, the deployment phase, or even the optimization phase, we need IT systems that continually reflect the experience of the customer or the consumer, so that we can develop on-point, value-added responses to underserved needs.

- **Compete as a Network.** Here our differentiation is a function of maintaining an ongoing service-level relationship to the customer base, something that is dependent not only on our own behavior but also on our ability to synchronize with partners and allies. For this to work effectively over time, either one company must be so powerful it can unilaterally discipline everyone else (and even then it may encounter passive-aggressive resistance) or rewards must be shared or interdependent in some win/win model. In either case, the key to synchronization is to anticipate the need of the customer before it is articulated, and the only way that is possible is to infer it from the history of the customer's past actions. Sharing and sifting through such metadata is the critical IT enabler for this step in the staircase.

The following are some more examples to further explain how these new capabilities manifest themselves in different industries:

- **Extend Market Access.** New entrants to a network make great strides when they can leverage the network to qualify as a vendor for a heretofore-restricted supply chain, get their products sold into markets in emerging geographies, or when they can get additional products from network partners to sell through their own distribution channel. All three of these motives warrant making the Business Process Reeingineering and IT investments necessary to put one's house in order so that one can participate as a "good citizen" in a global business network.
- **Focus on Core.** Established global enterprises must continually fund next-generation innovation investments by extracting resources out of non-core or "context" processes. These processes may be mission-critical—that is, failure is not an option—but they no longer differentiate the company's offers, and thus they no longer can create the Return On Invested Capital (ROIC) that a more innovative investment can. At this stage the business network consists of trusted third parties to whom the company can offload these mission-critical processes, whether these be the manufacturing of their flagship products, the management of whatever processes are non-core for their business—accounts payable, IT data center hosting, or customer support—or the management and maintenance of older (but still actively used) product lines nearing end of life.
- **Innovate as a Network**. As global competition intensifies, next-generation innovations require more and more expertise, and this in turn has led to partnering on efforts that are beyond the scope of any one enterprise. Open source software is a flagship example of the kind of collaboration that can outperform even the most stellar of enterprises operating on their own.

In the financial markets, next-generation innovations in financial instruments, admittedly, are currently in the doghouse. That said, few would deny they have revolutionized the underwriting of risk, enabling capital to deploy to much-needed developing economies, and for the most part created superior returns. Finally, in new drug discovery, academic researchers, venture-backed start-ups, clinical trial outsourcers, regulatory officials, research hospitals, insurance companies, health care delivery organizations, and major pharmaceutical companies must all choreograph their activities tightly to bring next-generation therapies to market.

• **Compete as a Network.** As networks become the basis for delivering goods and services globally, inevitably they will begin to compete among themselves. We are already seeing this in a few industries. Online advertising requires agencies, publishers, and ad-server networks to interoperate continuously and seamlessly in order to compete for audience attention on the Internet. Providing mobile video on demand requires the carrier, the device manufacturer, the video content owner, and the video broadcast streamer to all coordinate perfectly in order to provide

Business Examples at Each Stair

Compete as a network	Online Advertising Mobile Video on Demand Silicon Valley Venture Capital
Innovate as a network	Open Source Software Stacks Derivatives and Collateralized Securities New Drug Development
Focus on your core	Contract Manufacturing Business Process Outsourcing Life Cycle Management (mature products)
Extend your market access	Qualifying for New Supply Chains Entering New Geographies Leveraging (or serving as) Indirect Distribution Channels

the right "video snack" to the consumer in line at Starbucks. Finally, consider the example of Silicon Valley's sustained success in incubating next-generation technology sectors by aligning angel investors, venture capital, university research, executive recruiting, outsourced services providers, and investment banks to create a continuous flow of new businesses into the economy.

Developing Your BNT Strategy

Many companies have opportunities on multiple stairs. The key question here is, given present realities, where would it benefit your company the most to focus? The table shown on the following page provides some hints for diagnosing which stairs your company is investing in today—and the answer may well be more than one and as many as three, as well as which single stair would make most sense for you to prioritize today.

The Role of IT in Enabling Business Network Transformation

Following is a generic framework for defining the investments required for each stage of network maturity. In order to make this template applicable to your specific industry or your company, it is a relatively simple matter for a management team and/or company board to identify the equivalent investments that make most sense in your industry and with your business network partners in mind.

IT Investments Required for Different Stages of BNT

• **Extending Market Access.** The basic IT requirement for participating in a global business network is an ERP system that interfaces directly with one or both of the two global leaders in enterprise application software. Follow-on investments include Customer Relationship Management (CRM) to keep ahead of

Which Stair Makes Most Sense for You?

Access Adjacent Markets	Focus on Your Core	Innovate as a Network	Compete as a Network
You lack critical mass to enter this market alone.	Competition is pressuring margins.	Market problem requires diverse disciplines to solve.	Market rewards rapid adaptation to changing conditions at scale.
You have modest assets to bring to this table.	There are non-core processes to divest.	Collaborating cross-functional teams offer the best approach.	Life cycles must be managed end-to-end flawlessly.
You complement an incumbent's offer beautifully.	Your context could be someone else's core.	Your problem domain expertise empowers you to orchestrate collaborative behavior.	Your marketplace power enables you to drive coordinated behavior.

Use the *Stairway to Heaven* to organize a board-level discussion of your Business Network Transformation strategy.

one's customers, and Supply Chain Management (SCM) and Supplier Relationship Management (SRM) to keep track of one's suppliers. There is no competitive advantage to be gained by these systems; companies simply must have them to compete at this level. Thus, the more integrated they are, the lower the total cost of ownership and the more IT resources one can deploy further up this stairway.

• **Focusing on Core.** The first requirement for enabling the migration of non-core work to another enterprise is the ability to detach its governance from the underlying enterprise systems. This requires an abstraction layer that modularizes every process relative to the underlying infrastructure. The enabling architecture is called Services-Oriented Architecture (SOA), and the result is a Business Process Platform. Once transferred, the next requirement is to maintain ongoing visibility and control over the outputs, something that is enabled by running operational analytics focused on monitoring service-level agreements, whether at the outsourcer's site or your own. Finally, as outsourced processes continue to scale, a new layer of inter-enterprise process management is required, and this is enabled through composite applications that build on top of the business process platform.

• **Innovating as a Network.** Collaborating across a business network, even within one's own enterprise, is more of a communications problem than a data processing issue. It begins with laying down a fabric of collaborative utilities from the Web 2.0 world, including chat, instant messaging, shared video à la YouTube, shared workspaces à la Facebook, wikis, search, buddy list tracking, and the like. These sessions, in turn, imply a network of advanced communications facilities, including high-bandwidth networks, unified communications, and next-generation video conferencing. The final step involves using existing data-centric transactional interfaces with user-centric applications that allow "on-demand" access to information during live problem-solving sessions in order to "close the loop" from strategy to execution.

Using IT to Climb Each Stair

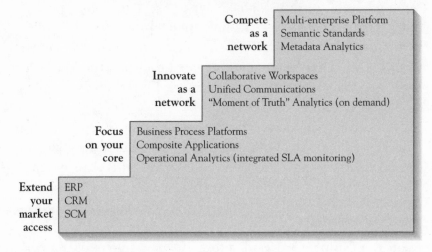

Compete as a network
- Multi-enterprise Platform
- Semantic Standards
- Metadata Analytics

Innovate as a network
- Collaborative Workspaces
- Unified Communications
- "Moment of Truth" Analytics (on demand)

Focus on your core
- Business Process Platforms
- Composite Applications
- Operational Analytics (integrated SLA monitoring)

Extend your market access
- ERP
- CRM
- SCM

• **Competing as a Network.** If companies are to genuinely compete as a network, then they must transform their relationship into a "virtual enterprise" and operate accordingly. This means their individual systems of record must appear to be integrated into a single virtual system of record, their unique master data sets into a standardized network "lingua franca," and their point-to-point commercial transactions into a multiparticipant commerce network. Whether or not these relationships are formalized as "hubs" or "exchanges," they are orchestrated through common commitment to multi-enterprise platform standards, semantic standards, and business network performance metrics and alerts, orchestrated either by a dominant player in the network or a trusted third party. Increasingly a candidate for serving as the trusted third party is being identified as the incumbent enterprise application system of record vendor serving the major players in the network already.

Getting Started

Here are some questions that can help management teams determine where to start their BNT journey. Companies must establish what type of business network they are in, whether or not they have an opportunity or obligation to develop a BNT strategy, and make some initial choices about which BNT strategy to adopt:

- Which type of business network predominates in your market—collaborative or coordinated?
- Is your business network undergoing a transformation? If so, can you describe it in terms of who, what, where, when, why, and how?
- In your primary business network, is there an orchestrator or concentrator, and if so who is it?
- Either way, how are the dynamics of your business network playing out, and what impact are they having on your business strategy?
- In the context of the Business Network Maturity Model, is there a stair that best represents your current status? If so, is there another stair that best reflects your strategic intent?
- In terms of BNT-enabling IT investments, is there a stair that best represents your current status? If so, is there another stair that best reflects your strategic intent?
- Overall, where do you see opportunities for the business network to…
  - Feed more business into your core?
  - Offload non-core opportunities/tasks to help you focus more on your core?

Hopefully, the exercise of discussing these questions with the frameworks presented in this chapter and throughout the rest of this book will give your company the ability to effectively map out a winning BNT strategy. Remember: business network transformation is a journey, not an end state. In order to embark on this journey, you need a good map, sufficient resources, and strong leadership. We're certain that with the tools found in this book, you'll soon be guiding your organization through a successful business network transformation.

References and Notes

Chapter 1

Notes

1. G.A. Moore. *Dealing with Darwin: How Great Companies Innovate at Every Phase of Their Evolution*, New York: Portfolio, 2005.
2. M. Porter. *Competitive Advantage*, New York: Free Press, 1985.
3. Joseph A. Schumpeter. *Capitalism, Socialism and Democracy*, New York: Harper, 1975.

Chapter 3

Notes

1. See http://www.motorola.com/secondnature for the destination site for the Motorola "Technology That's Second Nature" campaign.
2. Arik Hesseldahl. "Unpeeling Apple's Nano," *BusinessWeek Online*, September 22, 2005.

References

Afuah, A. *Innovation Management: Strategies, Implication, and Profit*, Oxford: Oxford University Press, 2003.

Andal-Ancion, A., P.A. Cartwright, and G.S. Yip. "The Digital Transformation," *MIT Sloan Management Review*, 2003.

Bagozzi, R. "Marketing as Exchange," *Journal of Marketing*, 1975.

Blackshaw, Pete. *Satisfied Customers Tell Three Friends, Angry Customers Tell 3,000: Running a Business in Today's Consumer-Driven World*, New York: Doubleday Business, 2008.

Evans, P.B. and T. S. Wurster. "Strategy and the New Economics of Information," *Harvard Business Review*, 1999.

Gulati, R. "Does Familiarity Breed Trust? The Implications of Repeated Ties on Contractual Choice in Alliances," *Academy of Management Journal*, vol. 38, 1995, pp 85–112.

———. *Managing Network Resources: Alliances, Affiliations, and Other Relational Assets*, Oxford: Oxford University Press, 2007.

——— and M. Gargiulo. "Where Do Interorganizational Networks Come From?" *American Journal of Sociology*, 1999.

——— and D. Kletter. "Shrinking Core, Expanding Periphery: The Relational Architecture of High-Performing Organizations," *California Management Review*, 2005.

———, D. Lavie, and H. Singh. "The Nature of Partnering Experience and the Gains from Alliances," *Strategic Management Journal*, Forthcoming 2009.

———, and L. Wang. "Size of the Pie and Share of the Pie: Implications of Structural Embeddedness for Value Creation and Value Appropriation in Joint Ventures," *Research in the Sociology of Organizations*, 2003, 20: 209–242.

Kale P., J.H. Dyer, and H. Singh. "Alliance Capability, Stock Market Response, and Long-Term Alliance Success: The Role of the Alliance Function," *Strategic Management Journal*, 2002, 23(8): 747–767.

Lafley, A.G. and R. Charan. *The Game-Changer: How You Can Drive Revenue and Profit Growth with Innovation*, New York: Crown Business, 2008.

Nambisan, S. "Designing Virtual Customer Environments for New Product Development: Toward a Theory," *The Academy of Management Review*, 2002.

——— and M. Sawhney. *The Global Brain: Your Roadmap for Innovating Smarter and Faster in a Networked World*, Wharton School Publishing, 2007.

Prahalad, C.K. and V. Ramaswamy. *The Future of Competition: Co-Creating Unique Value with Customers*, Boston: Harvard Business School Press, 2004.

Reichheld, F. F. and P. Shefter. "E-loyalty: Your Secret Weapon on the Web," *Harvard Business Review*, 2000, 78(4): 105–114.

Sawhney, M. "Don't Just Relate: Collaborate," *MIT Sloan Management Review*, 2002.

——— and P. Kotler. "Marketing in the Age of Information Democracy," in *Kellogg on Marketing*, John Wiley and Sons, 1999.

——— and E. Prandelli. "Communities of Creation: Managing Distributed Knowledge in Turbulent Markets," *California Management Review*, 2000.

Seybold, P.B. *Outside Innovation: How Your Customers Will Co-design Your Company's Future*, New York: Collins Business, 2006.

Chapter 4

Notes

1. Researchers have described related ideas as "network resources" to refer to those resources that become available to firms through their interorganizational relationships. While the focus of such prior research has primarily been on the benefits that accrue to firms through their alliances, our usage of the term relational capital is broader and encompasses connections with suppliers, customers, and between internal business units as well. For a more detailed account of network resources, see R. Gulati, "Network Location and Learning: The Influence of Network Resources and Firm Capabilities on Alliance Formation," *Strategic Management Journal*, May 1999, 20/5: 397–420.

2. Based on five-year total return to investors from 1995–2000 and 1997–2002 of Fortune 1000 companies; includes both price appreciation and dividend yield on stock.

3. Details of the methodology used for the survey and interviews along with a list of select questions that were asked in the survey are available from the authors upon request. All survey questions were asked on a scale of one to seven.

4. For a detailed account of how Starbucks manages its relationships, see R. Gulati, S. Huffman, and G. Neilson, "The Barista Principle: Starbucks and the Rise of Relational Capital," *strategy+business*, Third Quarter 2002, pp. 1–12.

5. A number of scholars have directed attention to the growing customer demands in the last decade, and these include G.S. Day, *The Market Driven Organizations: Understanding, Attracting and Keeping Valuable Customers*, New York: Free Press, 1999; N. Kumar, *Marketing as Strategy*, Boston: Harvard Business School Press, 2003; M. Hammer, *The Agenda: What Every Business Must Do to Dominate the Decade*, New York: Crown Business, 2001.

6. For a complete account of the growing challenges of commoditization and growth, see R. Gulati, "How CEOs Manage Growth

Agendas: A Commentary," *Harvard Business Review*, July/August 2004, 82/7–8: 124–126.

7. Some recent articles that elaborate on the theme of customer solutions include N. Foote, J. Galbraith, Q. Hope, and D. Miller, "Making Solutions the Answer," *McKinsey Quarterly*, 2001, 3: 84–93; D. Sharma, C. Lucier, and R. Molloy, "From Solutions to Symbiosis: Blending with Your Customers," *strategy+business*, Second Quarter 2002.

8. The theme of customer relationships and how to create, maintain, and sustain them remains an important one for both marketing and strategy. A recent study of some of the challenges associated with such efforts and a description of that journey can be found in R. Gulati and J.B. Oldroyd, "The Quest for Customer Focus," *Harvard Business Review*, April 2005.

9. For a recent book that describes such a co-creation of products in collaboration with customers, see C.K. Prahalad and V. Ramaswamy, *The Future of Competition: Co-Creating Unique Value with Customers*, Boston: Harvard Business School Press, 2004.

10. Some researchers have suggested the importance of relationships on another vertical dimension: channel partners. One instance of this rich body of research is N. Kumar, L.K. Scheer, and J.-B.E.M. Steenkamp, "The Effects of Perceived Interdependence on Dealer Attitudes," *Journal of Marketing Research*, August 1995, 32/3: 348–356.

11. For a detailed account of one such instance of close collaborations that Toyota has set up with its suppliers, see J.H. Dyer, *Collaborative Advantage: Winning Through Extended Enterprise Supplier Networks*, Oxford: Oxford University Press, 2000.

12. In a comprehensive empirical study, Zaheer et al. showed that interorganizational trust mitigates the frequency of interorganizational conflict and enhances performance of buyer-supplier relationships. See A. Zaheer, B. McKevily, and V. Perrone, "Does Trust Matter? Exploring the Effects of Interorganizational Trust on Performance," *Organization Science*, March/April 1998,

9/2, 123–141. In another paper, Gulati and Sytch have highlighted the multiple mechanisms through which interorganizational trust emerges from the history of interaction between firms and from the history of interaction between their boundary spanning agents. See R. Gulati and M. Sytch, "Does Familiarity Breed Trust? Revisiting the Antecedents of Trust," *Managerial and Decision Economics*, 2008. For a recent account of the factors that can engender such positive interaction between suppliers and buyers, see R. Gulati and M. Sytch, "Exploring the Effects of Organizational Interdependence on Performance: The Role of Power and Embeddedness," working paper, 2005.

13. Gulati and Sytch show that joint dependence of business partners in a relationship (the sum of firms' dependencies on each other in a business relationship) greatly enhanced the performance of the relationship by fostering higher levels of joint action, trust, and accurate information exchange. Gulati and Sytch, working paper, 2005.

14. Some of the following studies have provided a vivid account of the growth of such constellations of firms: N. Nohria and C. Garcia-Pont, "Global Strategic Linkages and Industry Structure," *Strategic Management Journal*, Summer 1991, 12/4: 105–124; R. Gulati, "Alliances and Networks," *Strategic Management Journal*, April 1998, 19: 293–317; B. Gomes-Casseres, *The Alliance Revolution: The New Shape of Business Rivalry*, Cambridge, MA: Harvard University Press, 1996.

15. Jack Welch uses this term to describe his goals to open GE up to similar external constituents. J. Welch and J.A. Byrne, *Jack: Straight From the Gut*, New York: Warner Books, 2001.

16. For a recent account of how firms may develop capabilities to enhance their alliance management skills, see J.H. Dyer, P. Kale, and H. Singh, "How to Make Strategic Alliances Work," *Sloan Management Review*, Summer 2001, 42/4: 37–43. For a discussion of governance and coordination challenges, see R. Gulati, P. Lawrence, and P. Puranam, "Adaptation in

Vertical Relationships: Beyond Incentive Conflict," *Strategic Management Journal*, vol. 26, 2005, pp. 415–440.

17. For a more detailed account of how firms can deepen their connection with key alliance partners, see Y. Doz and G. Hamel, *Alliance Advantage: The Art of Creating Value Through Partnering*, Boston: Harvard Business School Press, 1998; J.H. Dyer and H. Singh, "The Relational View: Cooperative Strategy and Sources of Interorganizational Competitive Advantage," *Academy of Management Review*, 1998, 23/4: 660–680.

18. Some recent accounts of the coordination challenges posed by internal units are described in M.T. Hansen and B.V. Oetinger, "Introducing T-Shaped Managers: Knowledge Management's Next Generation," *Harvard Business Review*, March 2001, 79/3: 106–116. See also M.T. Hansen and N. Nohria, "How to Build Collaborative Advantage," *Sloan Management Review*, Fall 2004, 46/1: 22–30.

19. For a more elaborate discussion of the distinction between cooperation and coordination, see R. Gulati and H. Singh, "The Architecture of Cooperation: Managing Coordination Costs and Appropriation Concerns in Strategic Alliances," *Administrative ScienceQuarterly*, 1998, 43: 781–814; R. Gulati, P. Lawrence, and P. Puranam "Adaptation in Vertical Relationships: Beyond Incentive Conflict," *Strategic Management Journal*, vol. 26, 2005, pp. 415–440.

Chapter 5

Notes

1. http://www.wired.com/wired/archive/7.11/sony_pr.html.
2. http://www.dellremoteaccess.com/.
3. http://gizmodo.com/341052/whirlpool-plug+and+play-refrigerator-has-docks-for-ipod-photo-frames-and-tablet-computers.
4. For a good overview of architecture, see Carliss Baldwin and Kim Clark, *Design Rules*, Cambridge, MA: MIT Press, 2000.

5. For a framework on business model innovations, see my chapter with John C. Henderson titled "Four Vectors of Business Model Innovation: Value Capture in a Network Era" in Daniel Pantaleo and Nirmal Pal (eds), *From Strategy to Execution: Turning Accelerated Global Change into Opportunity*, New York: Springer, 2008, pp. 259–280.

Chapter 6
Notes

1. "Flattening world" is a metaphor derived from Thomas Friedman's book, *The World Is Flat* (Farrar, Straus, and Giroux, 2005), describing the world as a level playing field in terms of commerce, where all competitors have an equal opportunity.
2. The data and information for the cases used in this study come from interviews conducted with executives in these firms.
3. For more information on Li & Fung, see John Hagel and John Seely Brown, *The Only Sustainable Edge*, Boston: Harvard Business School Press, 2005.
4. John Hagel, "Leveraged Growth: Expanding Sales Without Sacrificing Profits," *Harvard Business Review*, October 2002. Detailed interviews over the past year with Li & Fung executives and business partners supplemented our understanding of their approach and practices.
5. Maxtra Racing news, http://www.maxtra-racing.com. Last accessed January 1, 2009.
6. China Business Daily, http://china-business-daily.blogspot.com/2008/11/chongqing-motorcycle-production-up-to.html: Last accessed January 1, 2009.
7. Myelin is the substance that coats our nerves and helps to accelerate the passage of electrical signals through our nerves. In multiple sclerosis, the myelin coating on our nerves begins to degrade, resulting in a host of symptoms, including fatigue,

blindness, loss of balance, slurred speech, and problems with cognition, ultimately leading to paralysis and death. MRF is known to undertake the research process end-to-end from recruiting researchers, setting the research agenda, coordinating the problem solving, and finally commercializing the drug.

Chapter 7

Notes

1. R. Walter Kiechel, "Corporate Strategists Under Fire," *Fortune*, December 27, 1982; R. Charan and G. Colvin, "Why CEOs Fail," *Fortune*, June 21, 1999.
2. Study described in Chris Zook and James Allen, *Profit from the Core*, Boston: Harvard Business School Press, 2001.
3. Thomas G. Donlan, "Delusions of Adequacy," *Barron's*, March 6, 2006.
4. A 2006 Palladium survey of the Balanced Scorecard Online community; cited in Robert S. Kaplan and David P. Norton, *The Execution Premium: Linking Strategy to Operations for Competitive Advantage*, Boston: Harvard Business Press, 2008, p. 4.
5. Ibid., p. 1.
6. For more on this subject, see R. S. Kaplan and D. P. Norton, "Integrating Strategy Planning and Operational Execution: A Six-Stage System," Balanced Scorecard Report, May–June 2008; Kaplan and Norton, "Mastering the Management System," *Harvard Business Review*, January 2008; and Kaplan and Norton, *The Execution Premium*, Boston: Harvard Business Press, 2008.
7. Michael Porter, *Competitive Advantage: Creating and Sustaining Superior Performance*, New York: Free Press, 1985.
8. Aaron D. Crabtree and Gerald K. DeBusk, "The Effects of Adopting the Balanced Scorecard Returns," *Advances in Accounting, Incorporating Advances in International Accounting*, 2008, 24: 8–15. This study provides an independent confirmation of the

relationship between Balanced Scorecard usage and the achievement of improved shareholder returns.

Chapter 8
Notes

1. http://www.kpcb.com/initiatives/ifund/index.html.
2. The UCB study, headed by Prof. Robert Leachman, showed that the starting defect rate in mass production per wafer was higher, and the end point to where defects were reduced after three years in production was also higher, as line widths narrowed from .5 micron, to .35, and to .25. IBM's Bernie Meyerson claims that as you get below .13 micron, you are no longer guaranteed faster performance, because of nano-scale interactions that arise in the materials in the circuit (Meyerson interview on Dan Hutcheson's VLSI web site).
3. BusinessWire, August 19, 2008, http://findarticles.com/p/articles/mi_m0EIN/is_2008_August_19/ai_n28010922. Last visited October 15, 2008.
4. http://www.eetasia.com/ART_880520035_480100_NT_2flc5bcb.htm. Posted April 30, 2008 by Mark LaPedus, last visited October 15, 2008.

References

Hu interview, 2004. Interview with Professor Chen Ming Hu at his Berkeley campus office, October 11, 2004.

Leachman, R.C., J. Kang, and V. Lin. "SLIM: Short Cycle Time and Low Inventory in Manufacturing at Samsung Electronics," *Interfaces*, January–February 2002, pp. 61–77.

Macher, Jeffrey. "Vertical Disintegration and Process Innovation in Semiconductor Manufacturing," Presentation to strategy mini-conference, Wharton School of Business, 2001.

———— and David Mowery. "Managing Learning by Doing: An Empirical Study of the Semiconductor Industry," *Journal of Product Innovation Management*, 2003, vol. 20 (5): 391–410.

Monteverde, Kirk. "Technical Dialog as an Incentive for Vertical Integration in the Semiconductor Industry," *Management Science*, October 1995, 41: 1624–1638.

Moore, Gordon. "Some Personal Perspectives on Research in the Semiconductor Industry," In *Engines of Innovation: Industrial Research at the End of an Era*, by Richard Rosenbloom and William Spencer. Boston: Harvard Business School Press, 1996.

Pugh, Emerson. *Building IBM: Shaping an Industry and Its Technology*, Cambridge, MA: MIT Press, 1995.

Saxenian, Annalee. *The New Argonauts*, Berkeley, CA: University of California Press, 2005.

Strojwas, Marcin. "An Empirical Study of Vertical Integration in the Semiconductor Industry," Unpublished dissertation, Harvard University, 2005.

Chapter 9

Notes

1. P.T. Butler et al. (1997). "A Revolution in Interaction." *McKinsey Quarterly*, No. 1, p. 5.
2. M. Casson. *The Economics of Business Culture*, (Oxford: Clarendon Press, 1991); "Trust in Me," *The Economist*, December, 16, 1996, p. 61; Francis Fukuyama, *Trust: The Social Virtues and the Creation of Prosperity*, New York: The Free Press, 1995.
3. Ronald Dore. "Goodwill and the Spirit of Market Capitalism," *British Journal of Sociology*, 1983, vol. XXXIV, No. 4; Peter S. Ring and Andrew H. Van de Ven, "Structuring Cooperative Relationships Between Organization," *Strategic Management Journal*, 1992, No. 13, 483–498; Charles Sabel, "Studied Trust: Building a New Form of Cooperation in a Volatile Economy," *Human Relations*, 1993, 46, 9, 1133–1170; Barney, Jay B. and Michael H. Hansen, "Trustworthiness as a Source of Competitive Advantage," *Strategic Management Journal*, 1994, vol. 15, 175–190.
4. A. Zaheer, B. McEvily, and V. Perrone. "Does Trust Matter? Exploring the Effects of Interorganizational and Interpersonal Trust on Performance," Organization Science, 1998, vol. 9, No. 2, pp. 141–159.

5. M. Deutsch. "Trust and Suspicion," *Journal of Conflict Resolution*, 1958, 2:265–279; R.C. Mayer, J. H. Davis and F. D. Schoorman, "An Integrative Model of Organizational Trust," Academy of Management Review, 1995, vol. 20, No. 3, 709–734.

6. B.J. Pine II. *Mass Customization*, Cambridge: Harvard University Press, 1993.

7. See Douglass C. North, *Institutions, Institutional Change and Economic Performance*. Cambridge: Cambridge University Press, 1990.

8. Ibid, p. 7.

9. Author interview, September 25, 1994.

10. The Pearson correlation between the automaker's procurement costs and the percentage of time spent on bargaining and assigning blame for problems was very high at r=.60.

11. The Pearson correlation between the automaker's trustworthiness score and its procurement costs was very high at r=.66.

12. Author interview, September 25, 1994.

13. Interview, September 12, 1992.

14. Interview, September 11, 1992.

15. Interview, November 19, 1996.

16. B. Malinowski. *Argonauts of the Western Pacific*, London: Routledge & Kegan Paul, 1932; Marcel Mauss, *The Gift: Forms and Functions of Exchange in Archaic Societies*, New York: Norton, 1967; Alvin W. Gouldner, Alvin W., "The Norm of Reciprocity: A Preliminary Statement," *American Sociological Review*, 1960, vol. 25, No. 1, 161–178.

17. Alvin W. Gouldner. "The Norm of Reciprocity: A Preliminary Statement," *American Sociological Review*, 1960, vol. 25, No. 1, 161–178.

18. See William Ouchi. *Theory Z*, Reading: Addison-Wesley Publishing Company, 1981; W. Mark Fruin, *The Japanese Enterprise System*, New York: Oxford University Press, 1992.

19. Susan Helper and Mari Sako. "Supplier Relations in Japan and the United States: Are They Converging?" *Sloan Management Review*, Spring 1995, pp. 77–84.

20. M. Cusumano. *The Japanese Automobile Industry: Technology and Management at Nissan and Toyota*, Cambridge, MA: The Council on East Asian Studies, Harvard University, 1985.

References

Fukuyama, Francis. *Trust: The Social Virtues and the Creation of Prosperity*, New York: Free Press, 1995.

Chapter 10
Notes

1. K.J. Arrow, J.W. Pratt, R.J. Zeckhauser. *Principals and Agents: The Structure of Business*, Boston: Harvard Business School Press, 1985; K.M. Eisenhardt, "Agency Theory: An Assessment and Review," *Academy of Management Review*, 1989.
2. A. McAfee. "Pharmacy Service Improvement at CVS (a)," Case study 606-015, Boston: Harvard Business School, 2005; A. McAfee, "Pharmacy Service Improvement at CVS (b)," Case study 606-029, Boston: Harvard Business School, 2005.
3. A. McAfee and A. de Royere. "Los Grobo," Case study 606-014, Boston: Harvard Business School, 2005.
4. A. McAfee, V. Dessain, and A. Sjoman. "Zara: IT for Fast Fashion," Case study 604-081, Boston: Harvard Business School, 2004. Also, G. Keeley and A. Clark, "Zara Overtakes Gap to Become World's Largest Clothing Retailer," *The Guardian* (U.K.). Retrieved January 6, 2009, from http://www.guardian.co.uk/business/2008/aug/11/zara.gap.fashion?gusrc=rss&feed=networkfront.
5. F.W. McFarlan and D. B. Stoddard. "Otisline (a)," Case study 186-304, Boston: Harvard Business School, 1990; F.W. McFarlan and B.J. Delacey, "Otis Elevator: Accelerating Business Transformation with IT," Case study 9-305-048, Boston: Harvard Business School, 2004; F.W. McFarlan and B.J. Delacey, "Otis Elevator: An Interview with Ari Bousbib," Video (DVD), Boston, Harvard Business School, 2005.

6. A. McAfee and E. Brynjolfsson. "Investing in the IT That Makes a Competitive Difference," *Harvard Business Review*, 2008, 86: 98–107.

7. W.C. Taylor. "Here's an Idea: Let Everyone Have Ideas," *The New York Times*, 2006.

8. P. Coles, K. Kalhani, and A. P. McAfee. "Prediction Markets at Google," Case study 607-088, Boston: Harvard Business School, 2007.

9. K.R. Lakhani, L. B. Jeppesen, P. A. Lohse, and J. A. Panetta. "The Value of Openness in Scientific Problem Solving," Working paper, Boston: Harvard Business School, 2007.

10. http://www.socialtext.net/cases2/index.cgi?intrawest_wiki_intranet. Accessed January 6, 2009.

About the Authors

Henry Chesbrough is the executive director of the Center for Open Innovation at the Haas School of Business at UC Berkeley. He is the author of *Open Business Models: How to Thrive in the New Innovation Landscape*. Professor Chesbrough is an authority on open innovation, open business models, and open approaches to intellectual property management.

Jeffrey H. Dyer is the chair of the Organizational Leadership & Strategy Department and Horace Beesley Professor of Strategy at the Marriott School, Brigham Young University. He is the author of *Collaborative Advantage: Winning Through Extended Enterprise Supplier Networks*, which was awarded the Shingo Prize research award. Professor Dyer is an expert on supplier relationships, trust, and team building.

Ranjay Gulati is the Jaime and Josefina Chua Tiampo Professor of Business Administration at Harvard Business School. He is the author of *Managing Network Resources: Alliances, Affiliations, and Other Relational Assets*. His next book is titled *From Inside-Out to Outside-In: Reconfiguring Silos to Build Customer Centric Organizations in Turbulent Markets*. Professor Gulati is an expert on strategic and organizational issues related to organizational growth.

John Hagel III is the co-chairman of Deloitte Center for Edge Innovation. He has nearly thirty years' experience as a management consultant, author, speaker, and entrepreneur. John has helped companies improve their performance by effectively applying information technology to reshape business strategies. He is the coauthor of *The Only Sustainable Edge: Why Business Strategy Depends* on *Productive Friction and Dynamic Specialization* and several other bestselling business books, including *Net Gain*, *Net Worth*, and *Out of the Box*.

Marco Iansiti is the David Sarnoff Professor of Business Administration at Harvard Business School. He is the coauthor of *The Keystone Advantage: What the New Dynamics of Business Ecosystems Mean for Strategy, Innovation, and Sustainability*. Professor Iansiti is an expert on technology and operations strategy and the management of innovation. His latest research studies innovation and operations in networks of organizations, examining the strategy and innovation processes of key organizations.

Gautam Kasthurirangan is a research fellow at the Deloitte Center for Edge Innovation. His research interests are in the area of managing innovation in inter-organizational networks, investment valuation models using real-option methodologies, and corporate venturing activities of large firms. His industry and consulting experience also span a number of industries including automotive, aerospace, and pharmaceutical sectors.

David Kletter is a vice president at Booz Allen Hamilton based in New York City. His work focuses on strategy and organization, which he has applied to create lasting improvements in a wide variety of organizations. He has advised executives of Fortune 500 companies, as well as senior leaders in government agencies, in areas such as international growth, competitive strategy, organizational design, and change.

Philip Lay is a co-founder and managing director at TCG Advisors. With over twenty-five years' experience in the IT industry, mostly in executive-level operating roles and since 1995 in his advisory role, Philip works with executive teams and boards of enterprise software and systems companies to address strategic problems affecting their success in the marketplace.

Andrew McAfee is an associate professor in the Technology and Operations Management area at Harvard Business School, and a visiting associate professor at the Center for Digital Business in the MIT Sloan School of Management. His research investigates how IT changes the way companies perform, organize themselves, and compete. His book on Enterprise 2.0 will be published in 2009.

Geoffrey Moore is a bestselling author and a managing director at TCG Advisors. His most recent book is *Dealing with Darwin: How Great Companies Innovate at Every Phase of Their Evolution*. Geoffrey has made the understanding and exploitation of disruptive technologies the core of his life's work. His other books, *Crossing the Chasm*, *Inside the Tornado*, *The Gorilla Game*, and *Living on the Fault Line* are best-sellers and required reading at leading business schools.

Randall Russell is a vice president and the director of research at the Palladium Group. He is also executive editor of "Balanced Scorecard Report," published by Harvard Business School Publishing. During the past ten years he has worked closely with Drs. Kaplan and Norton to advance the state of the art in strategy management science. He has led numerous research efforts including action learning communities, quantitative research studies, and case studies. His work with executives from around the world has led to the development of successful new approaches to strategy management.

Mohanbir Sawhney is a globally recognized scholar, teacher, consultant, and speaker in strategic marketing, innovation, and new media. His research and teaching interests include marketing and media in the digital world, process-centric marketing, collaborative marketing, organic growth, and network-centric innovation. Professor Sawhney is the coauthor of *Collaborating with Customers to Create* and *The Global Brain: Your Roadmap for Innovating Smarter and Faster in the Networked World*.

John Seely Brown is a prolific writer, speaker, and educator. He serves as the independent co-chairman of the Silicon Valley–based Deloitte Center for Edge Innovation, which conducts original research and develops substantive points of view for new corporate growth. In addition, he is a visiting scholar and advisor to the provost at USC. He is the former chief scientist of Xerox Corporation and served as director of the Xerox Palo Alto Research Center for twelve years. He is the coauthor of *The Only Sustainable Edge: Why Business Strategy Depends on Productive Friction and Dynamic Specialization* and *The Social Life of Information.*

Ross Sullivan is a partner with Keystone Strategy and leads Keystone's Boston office, where he specializes in business strategy, product development, and portfolio management. Ross has twenty years of management consulting, product development, and operations leadership experience with technology firms.

N. Venkatraman is the David J. McGrath Jr. Professor of Management at Boston University and chairman of the Department of Information Systems. He has previously served on the faculties at the MIT Sloan School of Management and London Business School. Professor Venkatraman specializes in applying a network-centric view to business strategy, IT strategy, and IT sourcing. He has been recently recognized as one of the top-cited researchers in the field of management over the last twenty-five years. He is working on a book on competing in the network era.

Subject Index

Company Index